# The
# LORD *Is*
# MY SHEPHERD

# The
# LORD *Is*
# MY SHEPHERD

## The Theology of a Caring God

## MICHAEL SAMUEL

**JASON ARONSON INC.**
*Northvale, New Jersey*
*London*

This book was set in 10pt. Times Roman by Alabama Book Composition of Deatsville, Alabama, and printed and bound by Book-mart Press of North Bergen, New Jersey.

Copyright © 1996 by Michael Samuel

10  9  8  7  6  5  4  3  2  1

**Library of Congress Cataloging-in-Publication Data**

Samuel, Michael.
    The Lord is my shepherd : the theology of a caring God / Michael Samuel.
        p.  cm.
    Includes bibliographical references and index.
    ISBN 1-56821-912-1 (alk. paper)
    1. God (Judaism)—History of doctrines.  2. Bible.  O.T.  Psalms XXIII—
Criticism, interpretation, etc.  3. Shepherds in the Bible.  4. Caring—Religious
aspects—Judaism.  5. Judaism—20th century.
    I. Title.
    BM610.S26   1996
    296.3'11—dc20                                                    96-12052
                                                                          CIP

Manufactured in the United States of America. Jason Aronson Inc. offers books and cassettes. For information and catalog write to Jason Aronson Inc., 230 Livingston Street, Northvale, New Jersey 07647.

This book is dedicated to the righteous memory of my beloved father, Leo Israel
Samuel (1924–1996) זצ"ל who died on the night of Purim, 5756 (1996).

Despite his pain and loss,
my father affirmed that Adonai was his Shepherd
But like his Father in Heaven, he too was a shepherd
Calm and peaceful was his spirit
His heart was full of thanksgiving—he lived without want.

When it came to hospitality, My father's spirit
helped the stranger feel at ease
My father was a humble man,
genuine and sincere, a man of peace

Though he lost much of his family in the Auschwitz and
Maidanek concentration camps,
My father never allowed his soul to be tainted
with insensitivity, coldness, or hate.

My father was *my* shepherd and teacher
On my father's table stood the Bread of Presence.
When he lit our Chanuka menorah, he affirmed
the triumph of light over darkness and life over death.

He guided us along paths of righteousness and justice—
By example he taught kindness
With patience he disciplined
His love was ever supporting

Like Isaac before him, my father continued to laugh
Despair could not defeat him, his cup was always full
Wherever he went, goodness and mercy followed
Him each day of his radiant life,
May he dwell in the house of the Lord forever.

# CONTENTS

# PREFACE

This book is largely based on my doctoral dissertation, which I wrote while at the San Francisco Theological Seminary. I am indebted to a number of outstanding professors who had a dramatic impact on the substance of this book. Without their vision, understanding, and knowledge, this work would never have gotten off the ground. The great second-century theologian, Tertulian, once said: "Most importantly, their support taught me that there is much each respective religious community can teach the other, if only we are willing to break through the language barrier of faith."

I would like to thank my advisor, Dr. Gene Allen, head of the Pastoral Care Department at the San Antonio Baptist Medical Center. Gene spent countless hours helping me develop my dissertation. His patience and wisdom guided me in all stages of the development of this book. Every doctoral student should be so fortunate as to study under such a great and magnanimous advisor. Special thanks goes to Dr. Lou Rambo, for teaching me about the spiritual and psychological processes of religious conversions. Special thanks goes to Dr. Walt Davis, Dr. Warren Lee, and Dr. Morton Kelsey, who taught me much about the pervasive power of the spiritual world. Each of these outstanding teachers has made this dissertation project an exciting adventure.

I would also like to thank my dear friends, Father Michael Abraham, Rev. Aaron Fleigspelt, Rev. Bill Eckhart, for their guidance and interest in the project. A special show of gratitude goes to my good friend and poet Paul Pines, my mother-in-law Dr. Dorothy Chary, Sindy Weiner, Paul Buchman, Marcus Webb, Steven Palme, Rona Miller and Rachel Solomon, and Phil and Charlotte Lefton, who always offered help freely whenever I needed feedback from a non-theological perspective. I would like to thank my congregation here in Glens Falls, New York, for giving numerous hours in workshops and classes dealing with this vital image of faith. Last but certainly not least, I would like to thank my wonderful wife Mina for letting me work late hours on this project. She is a true *eshet hayil*, a woman of valor. I would also like to thank my son Moshe, for his interest and support. It is my hope and prayer that this book will strike a healing chord in the hearts of many Jewish young people who are searching for their God.

Michael Samuel
August 25, 1995

# Psalm 23

*The Lord is my shepherd,*
  *I shall not want.*
*He makes me lie down in*
  *green pastures;*
*He leads me beside still waters;*
  *He restores my soul.*
*He leads me in right paths*
  *for His name's sake.*
*Even though I walk through the*
  *valley of the shadow of death,*
  *I fear no evil; for You are with me;*
  *Your rod and Your staff—*
  *they comfort me.*
*You prepare a table before me*
  *in the presence of my*
  *enemies;*
*You anoint my head with oil;*
  *my cup overflows.*
*Surely goodness and mercy*
  *shall follow me*
  *all the days of my life,*
*and I will dwell in the house of the*
  *Lord forever.*

# 1

# THE DISAPPEARANCE

# OF A PRIMORDIAL SYMBOL

*When man is reduced to his empirical self and confined within its limits, he is, so to speak, excluded from himself, cut off from his roots, condemned to a spiritual death by thirst and starvation in a wilderness of externals. In this wilderness there can be no living symbols, only dead symbols of dryness and destruction which bear witness to man's own inner ruin. But he cannot "see" these symbols, since he is incapable of interior response.[1]*

Thomas Merton

My interest in the shepherd imagery began twenty-four years ago when my best friend in the Lubavitch Rabbinical Seminary shared with me the following story:

At a Jewish wedding, the *Hazan* (cantor) sang a special rendition of the Twenty-third Psalm to the bride and groom. Everybody was thrilled with the melodic voice of the *Hazan*. The audience asked him for an encore so they might hear him sing again. Afterward, a pious *melamud* (schoolteacher) came up to the platform and asked the young married couple whether he also could sing the Twenty-third Psalm. The couple nodded their heads yes, as the *melamud* began.

Although the *melamud's* voice was not as melodic as the *Hazan's*, his old feeble voice repeated the Psalm—"The Lord is my Shepherd." After he finished, there was a respectful silence, and then the festivities continued. One friend of the groom asked the *Hazan* why the people's reaction to Psalm 23 differed so significantly

---

1. Thomas Merton, *Love and Living* (Orlando, FL: Harcourt, Brace, Jovanovich, 1979), p. 69.

when the *melamud* chanted the melody. The cantor replied, *"You see, I know the tune of 'The Lord is my Shepherd,' but the* melamud *knows the Shepherd!"*

For many years however, I forgot this anecdote. I never gave much thought to this tale's deeper meaning. I never thought that the shepherd metaphor would become an important part of my own personal spiritual journey. Four years ago, I decided to work on my Doctorate of Ministry at the San Francisco Theological Seminary. Professor Lou Rambo asked me to write a term paper about my personal theology of ministry, which utilized images drawn from the *Tenach* (Scriptures) and the *midrash*. It was then that the story about the old *melamud* came back to me. With the help of a Hebrew concordance, I decided to do a word study of the shepherd metaphor as it was developed in the *Tenach*. Each Biblical passage I came across was like a part of a large jigsaw puzzle waiting to be assembled. It was then that I realized a fascinating theological portrait of the shepherd metaphor could produce an original, organic Jewish theology with a living message for the twenty-first century.

I then proceeded to examine the etymological data of the Hebrew word for shepherd (*ro'eh*) and soon discovered its rich nuances. Later I went to the biblical commentaries to see if any early sources (for example, Rashi, Seforno, Ibn Ezra, and so on) attempted to weave together the shepherd metaphor's various nuances and connotations. With the exceptions of the twelfth-century grammarians David Kimchi[2] and Ibn Yanach, none of the other medieval Judaic sources explicitly stated what I was looking for. The next step involved piecing together all the biblical passages dealing with the shepherd imagery.

Many of my rabbinic colleagues did not share my enthusiasm and did not think the shepherd metaphor was a worthy Jewish topic for study. Nearly all of them were oblivious to its earthy but spiritual implications. One elderly colleague to whom I showed a copy of my preliminary outline politely responded, "Michael, what you are working on is pre-nineteenth-century-ish. Nobody thinks of God as a Shepherd any more." Most rabbinical colleagues I later surveyed concurred. Most of them thought that the shepherd metaphor reflected a certain naiveté that modern people could no longer accept. They felt the shepherd image was theologically spurious, false, and ultimately dissatisfying for the modern Jew. It seemed as if the words of the *Hazan* were more true than I realized. Many have heard that God is a Shepherd, but few *know or experience Him as a Shepherd.* I began wondering: Why was the shepherd metaphor so irrelevant to several rabbis and their followers? I was convinced that there was a deeper

---

2. A complete list of nuances may be found in David Kimchi's *Sefer Hashorasheem—Radicum Liber Hebraeum Bibliorum Lexicon* ed. Jo. H. R. Biesenthal and F. Lebrecht (Jerusalem: reprinted 1967), considerable detail is given to the *ro'eh* (shepherd) metaphor and its various cognate forms. Gensenius follows Kimchi's examples while adding several of his own.

nonverbal, unconscious message my colleagues were giving me. Here are several reasons that may explain how and why the shepherd imagery became outdated.

## Objections to the Shepherd Metaphor

1. Many Jews do not consider the shepherd metaphor as particularly Jewish. One Orthodox rabbinical colleague of mine perceived the shepherd as a distinctly Christian metaphor. Christianity co-opted the shepherd image as a personification of Jesus, the "Good Shepherd." In a desire to differentiate Christianity from Judaism, most Jews conceded the shepherd to Christianity. The artistic renditions of Jesus carrying a lost lamb over his shoulder had an effect on the way Jews came to look at the shepherd metaphor. Understandably, many uninformed Jews believe that Psalm 23 is a Christian prayer.

2. Most Jews no longer live in an agrarian society. The rustic image of the shepherd disappeared long ago, shortly after the original Israelites arrived in ancient Canaan.[3] Wittgenstein is correct in asserting that a poem or story is shaped by the culture that has produced it. Today's urbanized society makes it nearly impossible to know what the pastoral world of the shepherd was like. Consequently, the modern urbanite has no inkling of the historical, cultural, and spiritual milieu that inspired Psalm 23.

3. To acknowledge God as "Shepherd" is to imply that we are His "sheep." The semantical use of the word *sheep* often carries a pejorative association. It has been argued that educated people do not like to be compared to "dumb sheep." Sheep are passive and timid creatures that are easily manipulated and easily led to their slaughter.[4] Dictators all over the world have maintained their hold on power by reducing their people to the status of sheep. Sheep are also compelled by a mob instinct. If one sheep panics, the rest of the flock will panic also. The objections moderns have toward the shepherd metaphor is not a new phenomenon. Many of the ancient philosophers and poets alike felt a cynicism toward the shepherd metaphor.[5]

---

3. For an excellent overview of how the pastoral world of the Bible was eventually displaced by urbanization, see Etan Levine's article "The Land Flowing with Milk and Honey," in his anthology *Diaspora: Exile and the Contemporary Jewish Condition* (New York: Steimatzsky and Shapolsky, 1986), pp. 43–54.

4. See Psalms 44:11, 44:22, 74:1; all depict the sheep metaphor in a negative way.

5. In Plato's *Republic* in the debate between Socrates and Thrasymachus:

. . . you did not observe a like exactness when speaking of the shepherd; *you thought that the shepherd as a shepherd tends the sheep not with a view to their own good, but like a mere*

4. The most common objections raised against the imagery of Psalm 23 come from those who experienced the horrors of the Holocaust. Holocaust theologian Richard Rubenstein contends that the Holocaust represents the final chapter in the terrible story of the God of History. Rubenstein contends that "the world will forever remain a place of pain . . . and ultimate defeat." The Holocaust represents a complete contradiction of the fundamental premises of Psalm 23, which speaks of a God who guides, nourishes, and protects His "flock" from evil. The almost total destruction of the European Jewish community exemplified "Divine abandonment." Indeed, many thoughtful people have wondered how a Jew can even recite this Psalm in light of the Holocaust. Arthur Green, a leading exponent of Jewish Reconstructionism, echoes a similar objection:

> It is time to admit that *parental, royal, and pastoral metaphors* we have inherited, beloved as they are, are not adequate for describing the relationship between God and world as we experience and understand it. Providence, the sense of an *all-powerful* God *"out there"* who watches over us and keeps us from harm is not, in its simple sense, the center of faith as we know it. The terrible course of Jewish history in our century has made this most conventional of Western understandings of religion impossible, even blasphemous, for us. If there is a God of history, an independent being who shapes the historic process, such a God's indifference to human—and Jewish—suffering might lead us to cynicism or despair, but not to worship.[6]

There are times when a person's (or people's) primal images of faith are deeply challenged. In moments of calamity and loss, many have found that their ideas of faith have withered and died. The very legitimacy of Psalm 23 is challenged by the horrors of the Holocaust. Where was God while the six million perished? If God is all-powerful, why didn't He intervene for His people? Are we to acquiesce in the assertion that the God of history perished with the rest of the six million?

Earlier generations have asked similiar tough questions. When Jerusalem was

---

*diner or banqueter with a view to the pleasures of the table; or, again, as a trader for sale in the market, and not as a shepherd* (Plato, *The Republic*, trans. Benjamin Jowett, Great Books of the Western World [Chicago: Encyclopedia Britannica, 1952], Book I, paragraph 325; emphasis added).

Socrates reasoned that just as the true physician is concerned with the welfare of the patient and aims to be a healer to the sick, the same is true of the true leader; a genuine leader is concerned with the welfare of the flock, much as a shepherd is with his sheep. Thrasymachus disagreed and argued that the metaphor of the shepherd represents an exploitation of the governed, as we see is often the case.

6. Arthur Green, *Seek My Face, Speak My Name* (Northvale, NJ: Jason Aronson, 1992), p. 15; emphasis added.

destroyed, our ancestors had to make sense of the meaning of their collective suffering. Each traumatic event of our people's tortured history made our ancestors wonder about the nature and mystery of God's presence. Like Jacob, we too have had our share of nocturnal battles with the angel of darkness. Like Jacob, seldom have we walked away whole. Thus, in Psalm 80 we find:

> Give ear, O Shepherd of Israel,
>> you who lead Joseph like a flock!
> You who are enthroned upon the cherubim,
>
> Shine forth before Ephraim and
> Benjamin and Manasseh.
> Stir up your might,
>> and come to save us!
>
>> O God; let your face shine,
>> that we may be saved.
> O Lord God of hosts,
>> how long will you be angry
>> with your people's prayers?
>
> You have fed them
>> with the bread of tears,
>> and given them tears
>> to drink in full measure.
>
> You make us the scorn
>> of our neighbors;
>> our enemies laugh among themselves.
> Restore us, O God of hosts;
>> let your face shine,
>> that we may be saved.
>
> Psalms 80:1–7

The imagery of Psalm 23 and Psalm 80 conflict with one another. For the composer of Psalm 80, the Shepherd of Israel seems to be deaf to the cries of His people. For the psalmist of Psalm 23, God sets before him a table in front of his enemies; his cup overflows with blessing, but for the Psalmist of Psalm 80, the only cup that overflows is the cup of tears. Defeated and vanquished, the Jewish community became a laughingstock before their enemies. The composer of Psalm 23 experiences God's restoration; in contrast, the writer of Psalm 80 yearns for restoration of God's Presence. If anything, Jewish history for the greater part has reflected more the bitter experiences of Psalm 80 than the pastoral imagery of Psalm 23.

Are we to admit that the words of Psalm 23 are what Nietzsche once described as "illusions of which one has forgotten that they are illusions; worn-out metaphors that have become powerless to affect the senses"? Is it any wonder that the psalm's message has been discarded and condemned to a liturgical phantom zone? The pastoral implications raised by the Holocaust (or any traumatic experience) cannot be understated. What kind of meaning might the sufferer derive from Psalm 23? How can the psalm's message be articulated to those who have experienced trauma and evil? Can we awaken the imagination that inspired Psalm 23?

What do the words "The Lord is my Shepherd" *actually signify?* What kind of imaginative thought or picture enters our consciousness when we say these words? What are we saying? What are we affirming? Or are the words "The Lord is my Shepherd" nostalgic yearning for an age that humanity has long forgotten? If God is compared to a Shepherd, what are its practical implications for the community of faith?

Psalm 23 assumes that a personal and intimate relationship is possible with God. Is this proclamation of faith still possible in a postmodern era? If the shepherd metaphor is passé, how ought we to talk about God? How should the Jewish faith act if it is no longer able to think of a personal God and thus no longer understands itself as previous generations once did?

Beyond that, we may ask: Does God even have a place in our language? If God does, then what is the nature of our relationship with God? The validity of the entire religious enterprise rests upon the answer to these questions.

The answers to these questions cannot be merely intellectual. We must find a spiritual language of faith that is pastoral with our spirits. This book argues that the shepherd metaphor is a spiritual response to the acute anguish, pain, and despondency that makes our hearts ache and withers our capacity to experience the Sacred.

A thorough examination of how this ancient metaphor was used will reveal that there is more to this misunderstood archetype than is commonly assumed. Traditional biblical language contains numerous hidden nuances that are spiritually profound and vital. The shepherd is one of the most important primal archetypal symbols and metaphors our ancient forebears bequeathed to future generations. Encoded in the shepherd symbolism is a wise and elaborate metaphysical schema for how relationships, society, politics, ethics, and global consciousness are to be envisioned. The shepherd metaphor offers a down-to-earth plan of how the power of faith can conquer the problems of moral indifference and psychic numbing so emblematic of Western culture and society, especially in the twentieth century.

Whenever a sacred text is studied, religious reflection must always begin with what human beings have experienced. It is critical to see the psalm through the eyes of generations that have been affected by its imagery. If a mythic image, metaphor or symbol is to be properly understood, we must be empathetic to the message it is conveying. We cannot stand on the outside like voyeurs peering into the personal world of the psalmists. We must participate in the spiritual reality they attested to. To grasp the deeper meaning of the Twenty-third Psalm, a theological sensitivity prompts us to imagine a world where God's presence is tangibly, visibly, and sensuously present.

As with any classical text in literature, interacting, questioning, listening, encountering, and experiencing the psalm will present new possibilities of meaning. Engaging the text in this manner is, in the classical sense, *midrashic*. Through the course of the book, the reader will be encouraged to enter into a dialogue and wrestle with the psalm's imagery. It is my hope that each person will come to see the Twenty-third Psalm as a personal *midrash* of his or her spiritual life. I am convinced that a careful analysis of the shepherd metaphor will reveal a faith that is practical and theologically challenging. The shepherd imagery offers a spiritually searching generation a new (but ancient) imaginative paradigm of faith.

In the opinion of this author, the key to reawakening our sense of the spiritual life lies in our ability to grasp the primal images, charged with latent content, that inspired our ancestors. Timeless and inspiring, the shepherd image addresses the fundamental relationship between God and man, with respect to an earthly journey that includes suffering and despair. If the image of the shepherd seems archaic to some, it speaks directly to questions raised by a century of Holocausts and their profound resonance in the Book of Job. What is the nature of suffering in a just universe? How does suffering alter our perception of God and our experience of faith?

Throughout this book, attempts will be made to wed some of the modern insights of depth/archetypal psychology with the primordial wisdom of biblical imagery and Jewish spirituality. We hope this interdisciplinary approach will help make the shepherd imagery of Twenty-third Psalm more relevant in helping each person come to see and experience his/her life as part of a never-ending spiritual journey.

# 2

# RECOVERING OUR PRIMAL IMAGES

# OF FAITH AND SPIRITUALITY

*Authentic spiritual language about God does not confuse the map with the territory, the symbol with the thing. Literalism concentrates on the letter and misses the spirit; it gets the words but never the music, creates a spiritual tone-deafness. You can starve to death trying to eat a cookbook.*[1]

Sam Keen

The image of God as Shepherd contains a far deeper message than is commonly assumed. Critics of the shepherd metaphor have neglected to consider how the shepherd is a *root metaphor.* Root metaphors reflect the basic primal and mythic questions every people and civilization has asked since the beginning of time dealing with the nature and mystery of human existence—for example, "Why are we alive?" "What is the nature of good and evil?" "Why do we suffer?" "What happens to us after we die?" "What is God like?" "Is the universe a friendly or chaotic place?" *Root metaphors expresses humanity's deepest existential concerns and touch upon issues that matter most in a people's lives. They shape the way we view and experience the world. Root metaphors stir our consciousness and challenge our awareness.*

Root metaphors embrace many different areas of life; they provide us with familiar and dependable patterns for living. Our emotions, our thoughts, our dreams, and our behavior are influenced and defined by the root metaphor.

---

1. Sam Keen, *Hymns to an Unknown God* (New York: Bantam, 1994), p. 54.

Norms, ethics, and standards by which we measure ourselves as a society are all affected by its various hues. The strata of cultural, ethical, theological, and psychological connotations lying beneath the root metaphor need to be carefully explored and examined. The root metaphor opens our eyes to how the world might be.

What is true about the root metaphor in general is true about the shepherd metaphor in particular. For the followers of Judaism and Christianity, the shepherd is one of the most important primal symbols. Reflecting a timeless religious intuition, the shepherd metaphor provides an important prism through which we see the world. It conveys what is essential about the God/human/world relationship. Every sphere of human relationship is re-visioned and refracted by the shepherd archetype.

The shepherd imagery has always shaped the inner pattern of our thinking in incalculable ways, even for those who openly reject it. This ancient archetype contains a social ethos that permeates every aspect of our tradition, our history, our holidays (for example, Pesach and Succot), our rituals (shofar and *tefillin*), our way of relating to the world. From the personal to the interpersonal, from the communal to the political, from the transpersonal to the cosmic, the shepherd image served to shape and fashion all segments of Judaic community into a compassionate and just society. Lastly, the shepherd imagery offers a visionary monistic theology of hope and redemption for the individual, community, and world.

It is no linguistic accident that the Hebrew word for shepherd, *ro'eh,* is a cognate cousin of the Hebrew word for neighbor and friend, *re'ah,* which signifies *love, belovedness and companionship.*[2] In addition, the Hebrew word for shepherd, *ro'eh, implies nurturing and feeding.* The Latin word "pastor" (shepherd) also has the same meaning, for to pastor is to feed or nurture.[3] This would suggest that a friend is defined as one who nurtures, loves, and shepherds. If this observation is correct, then the great biblical precept, "You shall love your neighbor (*re'echa'*) as yourself" (Leviticus 19:18), must be understood in terms of shepherding. The unconscious verbal association is unmistakably clear: if we

---

2. For an example, the *Midrash Socher Tov* explains the shepherding metaphor in a way that suggests that there is a linguistic relationship between the Hebrew word *ro'eh* (shepherd) and that for love (*re'ut*) in the Twenty-third Psalm (cf. Genesis 38:12, Psalms 45:15, Proverbs 3:28). Rashi also noticed this linguistic connection. See *Shabbat* s.v. *Daalachah sanai,* and his commentary on Proverbs 27:10: *Do not forsake your friend* (raiacha) *or your father's friend* (viraia avecha); "The Holy One, blessed be He is called a friend to Israel; and your father's friend, for He endeared your forefathers." A similar observation has been made by the eminent Christian scholar Samuel Terrien, who observed: "After all, the Hebrew word for 'neighbor' and 'friend' is derived from the term 'grazer,' 'fellow sheep.'" (Samuel Terrien, *The Psalms and Their Meaning for Today* [New York: Bobbs-Merrill, 1952], p. 235.) See also David Kimchi's *Sefer Hasorasheem* s.v. *Ro'eh.*

3. Cf. Hosea 9:2, Isaiah 5:17, 11:7.

want to understand what constitutes a loving relationship, be it marital love or the love of a friend, we need only observe the life of the good shepherd (*ro'eh*). Lastly, the *ro'eh* metaphor denotes *leadership and power*, for the ancient kings and leaders were often compared to shepherds in cultures throughout the world. The human intuitions about nature and humanity may be reflected in the verbal roots that underlie our language.

Nuance, syntax, and symbolic language all combine to offer important tools in redefining the deeper meanings embedded in the shepherd metaphor. The historical and narrative context in which this word is used will reveal much about its meaning, and it will also reveal how the shepherd symbol affected the spiritual consciousness of ancient Israel.

The philosopher Paul Ricoeur has correctly observed that symbols occur when language is used to convey more than just the obvious. The true meaning of symbolic language lies in its power to reveal a hidden and mysterious relationship that we would normally overlook in the object that we are symbolizing. *Symbolic language is enigmatic;* its purpose is not to conceal understanding but to provoke and arouse understanding.[4]

*The Lord is my Shepherd*—Biblical metaphors purposely challenge the reader to unearth their hidden message. The shepherd metaphor must be stripped of the semantic dross and impurities that conceal its genuine value. Only then will we rediscover and realize the purity and possibilities of the shepherd metaphor and its vital meaning for today. Root metaphors, like all metaphors, require a special philosophical discourse that is capable of recognizing the distinctive content of the metaphor at hand. We need to see how the root metaphor is used in order to have an imaginative picture of what its message truly is.

*The Lord is my Shepherd*—As a paradigm of faith the shepherd metaphor offers a window through which we can glimpse the Divine presence that stands at the center of all reality. This idea occurs repeatedly throughout the Scriptures. In the creation stories of Genesis, Adam stood as the steward of creation (Genesis 2:15–17). Although he was given dominion (*rada*) over creation, Adam's power was never a license to abuse or destroy. Adam's "dominion" must be understood in the context of caregiving, mindfulness, and nurturing. Humanity must emulate God's caring and concern toward nature as God, in turn, relates toward creation. Destruction to the natural world occurs when humanity violates and misuses its directive "to guard and protect," as evidenced in the story concerning the Tree of Knowledge. When human beings claim to be the "master" of creation, the earth

---

4. Ricoeur states, "Enigma does not block understanding but provokes it; there is something to unfold, to "dis-implicate" in symbols. That which arouses understanding is precisely the double meaning, the intending of the second meaning in and through the first." (Paul Ricoeur, *Freud and Philosophy*, trans. D. Savage [New Haven, CT: Yale University Press, 1970], p. 18.)

is encumbered by "a heavy burden" or "pain" (*itsabon*). Similarly, the Torah regards the murderer as one who *"pollutes the land"* (see Numbers 35:33, Ezekiel 36:18). *Political power according to the Bible is always conceived and practiced in terms of stewardship and shepherding.*[5] The Noah narrative teaches us the importance of biocentric love, for Noah was beckoned to rescue and care for all God's creatures.

The entire ethos of the Bible is aimed at creating a society that looks after the welfare of all its people. The same principle is also extended to the animal, plant, and mineral kingdoms. For instance, the biblical legislation dealing with the Sabbath and the Sabbatical and Jubilee years reminds us that human beings are responsible for providing rest for the earth to renew itself. Both of these institutions address social injustices and remind the wealthy that every person has an inalienable right to the land. The prophets repeatedly stress that he who oppresses the earth and its creatures will most likely oppress human beings.

The precepts dealing with *ts'ar balley hayim* (preventing cruelty to animals) also underscore the importance of shepherding and stewardship. In the Book of Proverbs we find, "The righteous know the soul of their animals, but the mercy of the wicked is cruel" (Proverbs 12:10). The Hebrew word for "know," *yada,* also denotes love and consideration. The Hebrew word for soul, *nefesh,* denotes the life principle by which something lives. The righteous are considerate of the needs of animals, in contrast to the wicked, who have no regard or reverence for life. The Bible would have scorned the Cartesian view that animals are nothing but machines and that the suffering of animals means nothing more than "the creaking of a wheel." The righteous are thoughtful not to cause any animal needless suffering or discomfort.[6] Only the wicked treat life as something cheap.

For instance, when Cain was asked where his brother was (Genesis 4:1–16), he replied, "Am I my brother's keeper?" The Hebrew word for "keeper," *shomer,* clearly implies shepherd.[7] Cain's question to God might be rephrased as, "Am I the shepherd of my brother?" In the spirit of midrashic exegesis, Rashi, the great medieval biblical commentator (1040–1105), notes that Cain's question implied sarcasm:

---

5. I will elaborate on this later in chapter 10.

6. *Yehuda HaHasid* of Regensburg notes: "The cruel person is he who gives his animal a great amount of straw to eat and on the morrow requires that it climb up high mountains. Should the animal, however, be unable to run quickly enough in accordance with its master's desires, his master beats it mercilessly. Mercy and kindness have in this instance evolved into cruelty." Quoted in Noah Cohen's pioneering work *Ts'ar Ba'ale Hayim—The Prevention of Cruelty to Animals* (New York: Feldheim, 1959), pp. 45–46.

7. See for an example Exodus 22:6, 9; and I Samuel 17:20.

[If] You call yourself the Keeper (that is, Shepherd of all beings), then You should have looked after him while we were quarreling with each other. Now that he is dead, You want to look for him?[8]

Cain's argument was simple: If God is the Keeper (Shepherd) of all beings, then it is His duty to shepherd His creation. In Cain's worldview, human beings are under no responsibility to emulate their Creator. Cain lacked reverence for life and did not hesitate to destroy it. To Cain, the world was to be possessed and manipulated instead of honored and respected. Moral indifference, hardness of heart, and deafness to human suffering are all moral attitudes intimated by Cain's famous question, "Am I my brother's keeper?" Moral indifference is the failure to see, acknowledge, respond and act on behalf of the person who is in need. It is precisely this attitude the shepherd metaphor comes to correct.

As God's own creatures, we find the image and likeness of God within our own nature and personality. Being created in the divine image suggests a worldview in which, as human beings, we share, relate to, and participate in God's wholeness and holiness. Since shepherding is inherently a part of God's nature, the same must also apply to human beings. Thus, to emulate God is to treat life with dignity and sentience. The misery and ecological havoc that exists in the world today stems from a Cain-like attitude that continues to ravage the earth. The shepherd archetype offers a life-affirming paradigm for restoring the ecological balance in the world.

The Noah narratives teach us that destruction occurs whenever humanity fails to act as a shepherd and steward toward creation. Noah and his wife thus became the new Adam and Eve, and were entrusted like Adam to oversee and minister to all creation.

All the patriarchs were shepherds whose desert tents provided food and respite for the hungry and wandering stranger (Genesis 18:1–9). In the Joseph narratives, the young shepherd lad became a provider and shepherd for a world that was starving for food and sustenance. Other theological aspects of shepherding to which the Joseph narratives allude will be examined later.

The narratives about the Exodus contain a panorama of pastoral imagery in which God rescues, redeems, and saves Israel (symbolized by the lamb) from the

---

8. Quoted in the *Musafe Rashi* (Addendum to Rashi's Commentary). In the *Midrash Rabbah* 22:9, the entire dialogue is seen in a pastoral light.

It was as if a man entered a pasture ground, seized a goat, and slung it behind him. The owner of the pasture pursued him, demanding, "What have you got in your hand?"—"Nothing."—"But the goat you have stolen is bleating behind you!" exclaimed the owner. In the same way the Holy One, Blessed be He, confronted Cain: *Listen; Your brother's blood cries out to Me from the ground.* (Genesis 4:10).

Egyptians. As the exemplar of shepherding, Moses led the Israelites in the wilderness, much as he led his father-in-law Jethro's sheep. Moses and David were the prototypes of the "good shepherd" who later inspired Jesus (John 10). In the Exodus narratives, God and human leadership acted as shepherds redeeming the flock (Israel) out of the land of Egypt. As is true with the Joseph narratives, God shepherds through human shepherds. Much of the Mosaic legislation codified in the books of Exodus, Leviticus, and Deuteronomy deal with how the weakest members of society are to be protected, cared for, provided for, and ultimately restored to wholeness (see Deuteronomy 15:14 for a prime example). The ancient prophets intuited that the social salvation of any society depended upon how government and people embodied the shepherd image in their public and private lives. They reminded Jewish leadership on every level that their first and foremost duty was to look after the welfare of the people like the shepherd who cared for the sheep. Moreover, the shepherd imagery inspired the first practical response to the problems raised by human suffering and evil.

Finally, the shepherd symbol provides a locus by which the spiritual harmonies of God and the soul converge into one another. Shepherding brings a person to the recognition that there are transcendental processes reason can never grasp, manipulate, or control. These processes emanate both within the human spirit and also beyond it. As a symbol, the shepherd provides us with a practical model by which we can establish communion with God and bring sanctity to our interpersonal relationships.

### Sublime Words, Sublime Secrets

While the shepherd imagery is central to the biblical narratives concerning stewardship and liberation, its conspicuous absence from current Jewish theology raises questions as to why this vital imagery became so powerless. Aside from some of the answers considered so far, there is one more reason that is often overlooked. Part of the answer lies in the reductionist way many present-day Jews and their rabbis approach the Holy Scriptures. Modern twentieth-century Bible criticism has for the most part seldom considered the spiritual message behind the document it was examining. The study of Scriptures is often treated as if they were nothing but the archives of a long-extinct people whose records and institutions perpetuate obsolete structures of an antiquated age. The spiritual imagination of the individual has been kept out of the text, and it is largely for this reason that the Bible does not inspire people as it did in earlier times. We would do well to consider the Zohar's admonition concerning how a sacred text ought to be approached:

Rabbi Shimon said:

Woe to the person who says
that Torah presents mere stories and *ordinary words!* . . .
Ah, but *all the words of Torah are sublime words, sublime secrets!*

So this story of Torah is the garment of Torah.
Whosoever thinks that the garment is the real Torah and not something else—
may his spirit deflate! He will have no portion in the world that is coming. . . .

Fools of the world look only at [the garment],
the story of Torah and nothing more.
They do not look at what is under the garment. . . .

As wine must sit in a jar
so Torah must sit in this garment
*So look only at what is under the garment!*[9] (emphasis added)

The writers of the Bible, for the most part, are seldom considered to be thinkers who have bequeathed any enduring theology or philosophy. Modern man finds it hard, if not impossible, to believe that his ancient ancestors were capable of highly abstract and spiritual thought centuries before the Greeks introduced rational philosophy. Yet many scholars[10] have demonstrated that even archaic man was capable of highly sophisticated metaphysical thought, expressed through myth and symbolism. The existence of a primal spirituality has always been basic to human civilization, and only recently has its existence come into question. The greater part of world history has always been mindful of a spiritual center where heaven and earth met and still meet. It is arrogant and naïve to assume that the biblical poets and writers were imprisoned by ignorance and superstition.[11]

This ancient psalm has been treasured by over twenty-five centuries of people for good reason. Psalm 23 contains a timeless message that deals with the problems of our fragmented present. Mircea Eliade (and others) have argued that the spiritual life of the so-called primitive peoples may hold a valuable key in

---

9. Daniel Matt, *Zohar, The Book of Enlightenment* (Philadelphia: Paulist Press, 1983), pp. 43–44.

10. Mircea Eliade, William D. Stahlman, Ernst Cassirer, and Claude Lévi-Strauss are only a few examples.

11. During the Neolithic period, our ancient ancestors were scientifically ingenious and learned how to weave, plant, and domesticate animals. Our ancestors were also aware of the movements of the heavenly bodies and were able to predict the occurrence of equinoxes. One of the greatest edifices of ancient man is the stones of Stonehenge, England. See Claude Lévi-Strauss's *The Savage Mind* for more examples.

helping the postmodern world recover a sense of the sacred. In the words of
Eliade:

> All that essential and indescribable part of man that is called imagination dwells in
> realms of symbolism and still lives upon archaic myths and theologies. It depends,
> as we said, upon modern man—to "reawaken" the inestimable treasures of images
> that he bears within him and to reawaken the images so as to contemplate them in
> their pristine purity and assimilate their message. Popular wisdom has many a time
> given expression to the importance of the imagination for the very health of the
> individual and for the balance and richness of his inner life.
>
> In some modern languages the man who "lacks imagination" is still pitied as a
> limited, second-rate and unhappy being. . . . To have imagination is to be able to
> see the world in its totality, for the power and the mission of the Images is to show
> all that remains refractory to the concept; hence the disfavor and failure of the man
> "without imagination"; he is cut off from the deeper reality of life and from his own
> soul.[12]

### The Closing of the Jewish Imagination

Here lies the problem: many rabbis and laypersons do not know how to discern
the message of biblical imagery or its symbolism. Our approach to the biblical
narratives is guided by historical-critical methods, etymological data, and the
process of demythologization. Higher Jewish schools of learning emphasize the
historicity and the factual nature of the Bible rather than its spiritual content and
message.

The phenomenon of religious experience is seldom explored as a reality in its
own right. Many are ambivalent about its dynamic unfolding; orthodoxies are
often skeptical of its present-day manifestations, whereas others view the
religious experience as the product of a superstitious world.[13] Rabbinical seminaries and universities alike examine a biblical text much as a medical student

---

12. Mircea Eliade, *Images and Symbols—Studies in Religious Symbolism* (Princeton: Princeton
University Press, 1952, 1991), pp. 19–20.

13. This problem is not unique to Judaism. Nearly every faith originated with a religious
experience that created in the person (or persons) undergoing it a new understanding of the self, the
world, and the meaning of life. For converts to the new faith, the testimonies of the founders were
set forth in a book such as the Torah, the New Testament, the Koran, the Vedas, or the Book of
Mormon. As time elapsed, the followers did not base their faith on experience but on the contents of
"the Book." Religious organizations and hierarchies were created to safeguard the purity of the
religion, and eventually any deviation from the orthodoxy was treated as an act of heresy. Heresy was
not just a religious crime; it was a political crime, since it threatened the political infrastructure.

examines a cadaver. Just as the cadaver lacks a pulse, so too does the text.[14] The Orthodox are not exempt from this analysis, for the primary area in which young rabbinic students concentrate their studies is the Talmud and *not* the *Tenach* (Bible).[15] The study of *Aggadic* portions (the moral and symbolic teachings) of the Talmud are often ignored out of deference to the *pilpil* (analytic) approach to Talmudic study.

When Allan Bloom wrote about the *Closing of the American Mind*, he described how young people lack an understanding of the past and a vision of the future. Instead, they live in the immediacy of the present. Students in universities around the country are not as well acquainted with the classical literary and philosophical traditions of the past as the students of earlier generations were. Higher education did not nurture a self-knowledge of how one fits in the world and universe.

In the Jewish community, the same malaise can be seen. I would prefer to describe it as the "Closing of the Jewish Imagination." Most Jewish young people grow up oblivious to the traditions, the stories, the symbols, and the values of their faith. If the children know anything about the Bible, it is often because they have watched the biblical stories portrayed in movies. One cannot ignore the effects video has had in contemporary times. The bombardment of predigested images has diminished the individual's capacity to imagine. Television images do not go through the same complex symbolic transformation as those that come from reading a good book. The child psychologist Bruno Bettelheim once noted, "Television captures the imagination but does not liberate it. A good book at once stimulates and frees the mind." Children, especially, have difficulty developing their visualization skills if they watch too much television, as many educators well know.

Another reason many Jews do not take the Bible seriously is the reemergence of religious fundamentalism in our society. It also should be noted that the trivialization of God in politics has also had a corrosive effect on the way the

---

14. For a modern critique of Bible criticism, see Jon D. Levenson, *The Hebrew Bible, The Old Testament and Historical Criticism* (Louisville, KY: Westminster/John Knox Press, 1993), chapter 1. Levenson argues that modern criticism has neglected the overall message of the biblical texts in favor of deconstruction.

15. This analysis is in keeping with that of the thirteenth-century talmudist *Rabbanu Tam*, who stated, "Nowadays, the study of the Babylonian Talmud has become the dominant focus of study, whereas the early generations of talmudists dedicated a third of studying to the Scriptures." (Cf. *Sanhedrin* 34a, *Tosfot* s.v. *"Belulah,"* and the *Tur* in *Yoreh Deah* 246: *Darchei Moshe*, and finally the *Aruch HaShulchan* 246:14.) According to the nineteenth-century talmudist Rabbi Yichiel Epstein, the above ruling of *Rabbanu Tam* applies only *if* the student is *already thoroughly conversant with the Tenach*. Nowadays however, most rabbinic students are not familiar with the *Tenach*. Interestingly, the average modern Orthodox woman is far more educated in the study of *Tenach* than is her male counterpart.

Bible has been perceived as a spiritual document.[16] The Bible has also been used by many literalists to suppress the civil rights of minorities and women,[17] while championing hostility toward nonbelievers. As an unfortunate consequence, many people (Jews and Christians alike) have consciously and unconsciously abandoned the Bible as a spiritual guide, never probing deeply into the more subtle and spiritual layers of the sacred text.

There is a well-known story about a youngster dealing with the crossing of the sea by the Israelites when they fled Egypt. Seven-year-old David returned home to his old religious *zeyde* (grandpa) to tell him the following story he learned in *heder* (school):

> As the Jews were running away from Egypt, Pharaoh and his army decided to bring them back, and so he began to chase after them. When the Jews came to the sea, Moses called in the engineers, who laid down pontoon bridges for his people to cross over. As soon as they reached the other side, Moses called in the air force, who bombed the Egyptians and wiped them out.

The *Zeyde* could scarcely believe his ears, "Is this what they taught you in *heder?*" he asked in amazement. "Grandpa," said David, "if I told you the story as my teacher told it, you would never believe it."[18]

The modern Jew has rejected the wooden-headed literalism advocated by the Orthodox and refuses to interpret the biblical stories at face value. People who might be seriously interested in the Bible's message are turned off by those "religious" individuals who insist that the creation took place in six days or that the world is 5756 years old.

Existing Jewish institutions, from the synagogue Sunday school to the advanced rabbinic seminaries, have not succeeded in transmitting the ancient wisdom of Judaic imagery to the searching souls of a young generation. Once the children reach Bar/Bat Mitzvah, they seldom go beyond the stories they learned as children. For many, God is a storybook character who lives only in the pages of the Bible. Etched in their memories, the Bible stories were treated like fairy-tales, myths, and other half-truths learned in elementary school. As they

---

16. For an excellent study dealing with this problem read Stephen L. Carter's *The Culture of Disbelief* (New York: Anchor Books, 1993). For another excellent work dealing with how the biblical message has been distorted, see John Shelby Spong, *Rescuing the Bible from Fundamentalism* (San Francisco: HarperCollins, 1991).

17. For centuries, women were not allowed to have a say regarding any matter pertaining to government. Even as late as the twentieth century, the Bible was used to justify excluding women from the right to vote. During the days of slavery, the Bible was used by preachers to justify the institution of slavery. For an excellent overview of this subject, see Riggins Earl, *Dark Symbols, Obscure Signs—God, Self, and Community in the Slave Mind* (Maryknoll, NY: Orbis, 1993).

18. Sidney Greenberg, *Lessons for Living* (Bridgeport, CT: Hartmore House, 1985), p. 52.

reach adulthood, the Bible becomes a widely misunderstood book and is seldom read for pleasure or spiritual guidance.

In addition, the modern Jew has forgotten how to read the *Tenach* in the original Hebrew and is similarly ignorant of the rich talmudic and midrashic texts. Faced with a translation of the Bible as with a landscape that has no horizon, the modern Jew does not know how to experience the Torah as a living spiritual guide. This is no less true of the Orthodox Jew than it is of the Reform. To the traditional Jew, the halachic system provides a framework and impetus for encountering God's Presence, yet even the *Halachah* per se can provide a body for a functional faith, but not its soul. True worship of the Divine must take us further on an interior journey into and through the heart. Genuine worship comes out of soul-searching questions; it is difficult work that requires effort, and for this reason it is termed *avodah*—the Hebrew word for both worship and arduous work. The teachers of *Mussar* (Jewish ethics), *Hasidut* and *Kabbalah* have long recognized the need for a living spirituality that would ignite the soul of the worshiper in all areas of life.

# 3

# THE CHALLENGE OF MODERNITY

*If we are honest, we will admit that most modern Jews in the period before Hitler cared little about God and expected almost nothing of God in history. . . . relying on God was old-fashioned and medieval. We relied on ourselves, on humanity, to a messianic extent.*[1]

Eugene Borowitz

*What does contemporary Jewish theology have to offer people like me? . . . the state of mind of a large section of the American rabbinate and much of the American Jewish community in general is a perversion of the Jewish religion into a shallow, if sincere humanitarianism, plus a thorough-going insensitivity to present-day spiritual problems.*[2]

Irving Kristol

Even if the Holocaust had never occurred, present-day Jewry would still struggle to define its spiritual character in a modern society. Many secular Jews and their rabbinic leaders feel ambivalent and confused when dealing with the reality of God as a personal Presence. This is partly due to the role religion has come to play in an open society. Modernity brought about a complete change in how we see and experience our historical consciousness.

---

1. Eugene Borowitz, *Reform Judaism Today*, book 1: *Reform in the Process of Change* (New York: Behrman House, 1978), p. 65.
2. Cf. Irving Kristol's critical review of Milton Steinberg's *Basic Judaism*—"How Basic Is 'Basic Judaism'?" *Commentary* 5 (January 1948), p. 28.

## *The Loss of Soul*

Psychologist Carl Jung once observed that when a primitive tribe's spiritual values are exposed to the impact of modern civilization, its people will lose the meaning of their lives; the social order disintegrates; the people themselves morally decay. This is what Jung describes as "loss of soul."[3] In this condition, man is out of touch with himself, and can no longer make sense and meaning out of his life. To the person who experiences "loss of soul" society's myths, rituals, symbols, images, and traditions cease to have any meaning. Such an individual has no sense of the past, nor any sense of future. Ultimate questions are intimidating, and life seems to have little meaning beyond mere existence and consumerism. When a person experiences soul loss, life seems to have no purpose or consequence. The loss of soul is the primary cause of the social discord and spiritual chaos of our times.

The Industrial Age produced rippling changes throughout the world. Before that time, people everywhere from Europe to Africa experienced the meaning of their lives in the context of the tribal and religious customs of the community. With industrialization, however, whole tribes were completely displaced from their ancestral roots. The old standards were severely shaken and irrevocably changed by technology.

As families scattered to the cities looking for work, the bonds that had integrated families and communities started to disintegrate. The social order began to unravel. Without faith, the individual was left unprotected. Isolated and cut off from their spiritual roots, the modern technological man and woman were left to fend for themselves in their attempt to make life meaningful.

Modernity produced what sociologist Peter Berger describes as the "heretical imperative." The English word *heresy* comes from the Greek verb *hairein*, which means "to choose."[4] Premodern society was a world of religious certainty; deviation was the exception rather than the norm. By contrast, the modern situation is a world of religious uncertainty; the boundaries differentiating the religious world are hazily defined. Religious affirmation must be consciously affirmed rather than assumed. Once the choice for self-definition was made, premodern societies began to unravel and disperse. Modernity helped fragment the historical consciousness of traditional religious societies.[5]

---

3. Carl Jung, *Man and His Symbols* (Garden City, NY: Doubleday, 1964), p. 94.

4. Peter Berger, *The Heretical Imperative* (New York: Anchor, Doubleday, 1979), pp. 26–31.

5. Robert Jay Lifton, in *The Protean Self* (New York: Basic Books, 1993), describes the modern age as "protean," a word derived from the name Proteus, a Greek sea-god of many forms. The protean age is one of great historical changes and is characterized by many social upheavals that have dramatically affected community and individual life alike. The social institutions that have traditionally anchored human lives have become ineffectual. Lifton sees modern men and women as

This would describe what happened in the post-emancipated Jewish world. Modernity and all its trappings, including the belief in individualism, have contributed to the break-up of the old communal *shtetel* (community). All this has produced loss of soul for many Jews who no longer feel compelled to identify with their ancestral traditions. There is an old story in Jewish folklore about a small *shtetel* in Eastern Europe that was captured by Napoleon in his conquest of Europe. At a school the children were yelling:

> "Rebbe! Napoleon has come to liberate us!" The rebbe cynically questioned, "Liberate us from what? From studying the Torah? Liberation from Talmud and *Mishnah*? Liberate us from *Mitzvot*? You call this liberation?"

Despite the daily pogroms, persecutions, and misery of the old European *shtetel*, the premodern Jew had an inner faith in a personal God who was always close to his heart. The Eastern European Jew resembled Shalom Aleichem's character Tevye, the old pious Jew who addressed God as freely and intimately as one would speak with a friend or neighbor. His spiritual language included metaphors that were shamelessly personal, passionately rich, and intensely anthropomorphic. It was a culture of intense intimacy, spirit, song, dance, and tears. The Eastern European Jew could still address God as *Tatte* (Yiddish for Daddy). God was perceived as a *Bore Olam*—Creator of all the world. God-talk contained many terms of endearment and signified how God's living Presence could be discerned in the world.

The political, social, and scientific events that shaped the seventeenth, eighteenth, nineteenth, and twentieth centuries exploded the naïveté and innocence that characterized the premodern Jewish world. An early twentieth-century Jewish existentialist, Franz Rosenzweig, tells about a conversation Hermann Cohen, a famous Jewish neo-Kantian philosopher, once had with an old pious Jew. This conversation typified the dilemma Jewish intellectuals in the post-Emancipation era experienced when the ghetto walls finally crumbled:

> He once expounded the God-idea of his *Ethics* to an old Jew of that city. The Jew listened with reverent attention, but when Cohen was through, he asked, "And where is the *Bore olam* (Creator)?" Cohen had no answer to this, and tears arose in his eyes.[6]

---

historically fragmented creatures who have adopted change (proteanism) as a way of overcoming homelessness.

6. Nachum N. Glatzer, *Franz Rosenzweig: His Life and Thought* (Philadelphia: Jewish Publication Society, 1953), p. 282.

Rosenzweig added:

> Here the term *Bore olam* does not mean something remote, as the content of the
> words seem to indicate. On the contrary: in popular speech the words are fraught
> with emotion, they are something near, and in the case of the God of the heart, the
> heart never for a moment forgets that He is the one—who is. So here the spark does
> not merely oscillate between the two poles of nearness and remoteness, but each
> pole has a positive and a negative charge, only in a different pattern. The Creator
> who is above the world takes up his "habitation," and the abstract God of
> philosophy has his "being in the crushed heart."[7]

Hermann Cohen's concept of "ethical monotheism" utilized the idea of God as
the organizing principal and nexus of ethical behavior. The God *idea* was a
necessary postulate in order to have a just and ethical world. However, Cohen's
reduction of God to an *idea* meant that Jews would not have to relate to God on
a personal level. Cohen was convinced that any "personalization" of God was
nothing more than a Christian aberration. Yet, despite Cohen's secularity, he still
felt a sense of homelessness when it came to his relationship with God. It did
touch his heart. In many ways this feeling is emblematic of the way many Jews
today feel about their faith in God. The current sensation of "homelessness"
stems from a fragmentation and "loss of soul" that have become commonplace
in today's postmodern Judaic community.

As if the changes initiated by the new historical consciousness were not
enough, the trauma of the Holocaust shattered the old pious worldview of the Jew
into a million pieces. As in the old nursery rhyme, "All the king's horses and all
the king's men, couldn't put Humpty Dumpty together again."

---

7. Ibid., p. 282.

# 4

# THE CONSPIRACY OF SILENCE

*The emperor marched in the procession under the beautiful canopy, and all who saw him in the street and out of the windows exclaimed: "Indeed, the emperor's new suit is incomparable! What a long train he has! How well it fits him!" Nobody wished to let others know he saw nothing, for then he would have been unfit for his office or too stupid. Never before were the emperor's clothes more admired. But there was a child who said, "But he has nothing on at all." "Good heavens! listen to the voice of an innocent child," said the father, and one whispered to the other what the child had said. "But he has nothing on at all," cried at last the whole people. That made a deep impression upon the emperor, for it seemed to him that they were right; but he thought to himself, "Now I must bear up to the end." And the chamberlains walked with still greater dignity, as if they carried the train which did not exist.[1]*

Hans Christian Andersen

*The numerous pre- and proscriptions of orthodox Judaism are likely to appear as so many absurdities, unless they remain linked to a world view that includes the supernatural. Lacking this, despite all sorts of traditional loyalties and nostalgias, the whole edifice of traditional piety takes on the character of a museum of religious history. People may like museums, but they are reluctant to live in them.[2]*

Peter Berger

The flock looks to the faithful shepherd for guidance, healing, nurturing, and support, and the same is true of the rabbi–congregant relationship. People look

---

1. Adapted from *The Library of the Future* (Garden Grove, CA: World Library, 1992).
2. Peter Berger, *The Rumour of Angels* (New York: Anchor, 1990), p. 16.

to their rabbinic leaders, and their lay-religious leaders, for *spiritual* guidance, support and nurturing. If the spiritual leaders of a synagogue see God as an uninvolved, apathetic parent figure, this view will have a mirroring effect on the kind of God-image the congregation will develop. More often than not, the spiritual leadership has become a part of the problem. The congregants' own spiritual ambivalence will in turn be reflected in the way they as parents engage their own offspring. The kind of God-image that a person has is to a large extent formulated at a very young age. Child psychologist David Heller illustrates how, in children's representation, God is often depicted as geographically and emotionally remote from them. *These children lament that they feel that God is distant and inaccessible.*[3]

### Three Tales of Estrangement

The sociologist James Hopewell observed that the myths and individual stories of a religious community often illustrate the parish's relationship with God and the universe.[4] These narratives can serve to measure the religious ideation of a community. Many of today's narratives of Jewish estrangement point to a spiritual hunger that has not been effectively met by many of the more traditional Jewish communities (Orthodox, Conservative, and Reform). Here are three examples:

### Story 1

For decades, there has been in the Jewish Theological Seminary what Neal Gillman, professor of rabbinics at the Jewish Theological Seminary, once described as "the conspiracy of silence"[5] when dealing with the reality of God.[6] Here is a good illustration of this common attitude:

> Joe Price was a professional cantor who became a "Jew for Jesus." Joe Price grew up in a Conservative Jewish home. It was Conservative not because of religious ideation but, rather, because of affiliation. While attending the Jewish Theological Seminary Cantorial School, Joe discov-

---

3. David Heller, *The Children's God* (Chicago: University of Chicago Press, 1986), pp. 61–63.

4. James Hopewell, *Congregation: Stories and Structures* (Philadelphia: Fortress Press, 1987). See pp. 29–33 for a more detailed exposition.

5. I heard this at a lecture he gave at Skidmore College, summer 1992.

6. Within the Conservative Movement, there are theologies ranging from the traditional to the atheistic. For a summary of all the various strands of theology within the Conservative Movement, see Elliot Dorf, "The Concept of God in the Conservative Movement," *Judaism* (Fall 1991), 431–432.

ered that, though he enjoyed studying to become a cantor, he had just one problem—*he did not believe in a personal God.* In Joe's words:

> I don't mean I didn't believe that God existed; I was sure He did. I believed some spiritual force we call God must exist; I couldn't make sense of creation as anything other than designed by Him. The problem was, I didn't know what to believe about God. *I didn't know who He was or how to relate to Him. I didn't have a sense of communion with Him.* I was basically offering prayers to a God I didn't know, and I felt like a hypocrite.[7] (Emphasis added.)

Joe went on to point out that he was not the only one at the Seminary who had a vague and undefined faith in God. He felt, even after he graduated, that he was offering prayers to a God that he simply did not know. Joe writes:

> One of my colleagues confided in me that he struggled with the issue of who is God for ten years. After ten years, he concluded that God is an energy force, and prayer a natural bodily function that had to be satisfied. This colleague was not alone in his views. Judaism is often looked upon as a body of traditions to be carried on from one generation to the next. *There is not necessarily a connection made between the handing down of our traditions and the idea that is at the root of those traditions, there is a God who wants a personal relationship with us.*[8] (Emphasis added.)

Joe served as cantor with some very prominent Conservative rabbis, and when he asked them what God personally meant to them, he sensed their spiritual ambivalence. Like any person who begins a new spiritual quest, he started to look for a new religious context to find some answers to his own spiritual questioning.

Through a series of events, he met with some Jews who had converted to Christianity. Price was impressed by the sincerity and clarity of their faith. God was portrayed in personal and endearing terms. They saw God as a God that is concerned.

> I thought, how could this guy who never went beyond bar mitzvah answer my questions so well, when the rabbis and the professors at the Jewish Theological Seminary couldn't even touch some of the answers he was giving me? . . .[9]

---

7. Ruth Rosen, *Jesus for Jews* (New York: Inquirer's Edition), pp. 90–91.
8. Ibid., p. 90.
9. Ibid., p. 90.

Joe and his wife Sue (whose father was an Orthodox-ordained rabbi) eventually converted to Christianity.

This story is not unusual. There are similar stories of spiritual-searching Jews who have embraced Sufism, Buddhism, Hinduism, and so on. Some outstanding young Jews are currently writing books on Christianity, Buddhism, or other faiths![10] When young Jews attempt to discover their own spiritual heritage, they often find the door shut in their faces. Jewish spirituality is often portrayed in solely exoteric rather than esoteric terms.

Jews are encouraged to see their faith within the broader framework of the community. The individual relationship with a personal God is portrayed as a Christian teaching and is considered foreign to the Jewish ethos, or at the very least is viewed with suspicion. Many of today's rabbis are either oblivious or indifferent to the experiential dimension of faith. Though there are many books about God, most of these books are anthologies of what famous rabbis have said about God at one time or another. Very few of these books urge people to see their own lives as part of the spiritual journey toward God. Faith continues to be portrayed in Apollonian, scientific terms designed to win the mind (but seldom the heart) of the skeptic. Science and rationalism are seen as the only true purveyors of reality. The vast majority of synagogues and rabbinic seminaries have forgotten the dynamic, pulsating forces that have created Judaism as a faith.

Abraham Maslow's adage "All pathologies dichotomize and all dichotomies pathologize" describes the spiritual polarity of Jews today. In much of contemporary Jewish theology, ultimate questions concerning the metaphysical and mystical aspects of faith are suppressed. The emphasis on interiority and experience in the Eastern faiths and its apparent absence in Judaism has caused many Jews to come to the erroneous conclusion that Judaism lacks a deep spiritual core. Many young, spiritually hungry Jews have rejected teachings that have stressed God's "otherness" from the world and sought answers outside the faith.

## Story 2

Esther was a young woman who grew up in an Orthodox Jewish home. While she was enrolled in a college, she took a course in comparative

---

10. Jacob Needleman has written a book on esoteric Christianity entitled *Lost Christianity*; Joseph Goldstein, Jack Kornfield, Ram Dass (Richard Alpert), and Stephen Levine have each written extensively on Buddhism and Hinduism. When I once asked Dr. Needleman why he didn't write a book on *Lost Judaism*, he replied that he already did — *Money and the Meaning of Life* (*sic*). Though he certainly spoke in jest, nonetheless, I couldn't help thinking he was partly serious.

religion. She was introduced to theosophy, which is a mystical philosophy that incorporates various esoteric religious systems. Esther was fascinated by her new discovery. She knew her parents would be horrified, if they knew she was studying it. One day Esther's mother noticed her daughter's interest in theosophy:

"What kind of *meshugas* (craziness) have you gotten yourself into?" her mother asked.

"It's not a *meshugas*, mother. I feel more at peace with the theosophical God than the vague one you've got in your religion."

Her mother looked at her with a mixture of anger and disbelief. "What do you mean, 'your' religion?" she snapped. "Remember, as long as you are a member of this family, our religion is your religion. And don't you forget it. The Jewish God has been with us for five thousand years, and you're not going to throw Him away for some fad like Theofoshy, or whatever you call it. It's nothing compared to the wisdom of Judaism!"

"I'm not against Judaism, mother, I want a more plausible meaning of God than the primitive one of Abraham, Isaac, and Jacob. There's been a lot of new thinking since the Jews discovered God. I want to keep abreast. That's not irreligious; it's being more religious."

"Look, I see you're pretty deep in whatever you're in, so before you get over your head, let's discuss it with your father and brothers. They'll pound some sense into you."[11]

The family met to discuss Esther's new interest in theosophy. Esther explained that she was fascinated with the common esoteric truths of all religions. She had a special interest in karma, evolution, and reincarnation. Ultimately she was given the choice to either conform or leave her family. Esther opted for the latter. When she was asked whether she had any regrets, she replied:

Some . . . I miss the warmth of my family. Even though I understand why they're shunning me, and I forgive them, it still hurts. And I feel badly because I know it hurts them too. But that's spiritual evolution at work. There's bound to be turbulence when the old gives way to the new. I lost familial love, but I found a wider window on eternity.[12]

This story underscores that even the Orthodox community is not invulnerable to the sincere spiritual yearnings of its own young people. The appeal to tradition and family nostalgia are not compelling reasons to identify Jewishly in today's

---

11. George Bockl, *God Beyond Religion: Personal Journeyings from Religiosity to Spirituality* (Marina Del Rey, CA: Devorss, 1988), pp. 13–18.

12. Ibid., p. 18.

times. Though Esther found refuge in the spiritual teachings of theosophy, she became a spiritually homeless person to her own family and faith. Neither Esther nor her observant family knew that spirituality and religiosity do not have to be in conflict. The inability to articulate a compelling *Jewish* spirituality poses a serious dilemma for all various denominations of Jewry.

*Story 3*

Psychologists Mary Ellen Donovan and William Ryan describe a Jewish woman named Sharon who, in her thirties, had some difficulties in receiving and giving human love. Her problems stemmed from her personal world spiritual view. Sharon relates:

> My parents were passionately involved with ethical and political issues, and we kids were raised with a lot of emphasis on examining questions of right and wrong, good and evil . . . we even formally studied comparative religions. As far as the moral component of religion, and the history of religion goes, my upbringing was great. What was lacking was the spiritual component. We never as a family shared any religious rituals, and there was never a sense of mystery or mysticism. Believing in God or some higher universal plan or cosmic force was considered insanity. I remember when I was ten saying I believe in God, and my parents were horrified. "How can you believe in God?" they said. In their view, only people with low levels of intelligence or without the courage to be independent thinkers believe in God.[13]

This typical story illustrates the way many sophisticated and educated Jews approach faith. Children have a natural affinity with God, yet, as they get older, their natural love can dwindle and fade away unless the child is encouraged to grow in his/her faith. As role models, parents can greatly affect their children's capacity to relate spiritually to God. Shame is often used to suppress the children's spiritual yearnings.

Donovan and Ryan pointed out that Sharon used to think of the universe as a cold and loveless place, a place of nothingness. She wanted to connect with God, not just with her mind but with her heart and soul, but she did not know how. While believing that love was in the cards for her, she was less convinced that God's love was available for her. On a deep level, Sharon could not feel satisfied with the rationalistic thinking of her folks. She hoped that human beings could fill all of her spiritual needs. She wanted to feel God's Presence, though her parents did not. Eventually, with the help of a nun (the synagogue she had gone to was of no help), she was able to validate her feelings in a God that loved her

---

13. Mary Ellen Donovan and William Ryan, *Love Blocks* (New York: Viking, 1989), pp. 149–150.

despite herself. Sharon wanted to know how God relates to her and how she could better relate to God; she wanted to put her own being within a spiritual context of ultimacy and intimacy. Overcoming her parent's secular bias against faith was not easy, but she eventually did.

The inability to relate meaningfully to God has dire consequences. Within each human being exists a profound and deep need to overcome one's sense of separateness and aloneness. Gradually the individual discovers that the world cannot fill the God-space each human being has inside. Without a cultivated spiritual life, the individual wanders and looks for the one relationship that will endow life with meaning. If a person does not find it in a spiritual relatedness with God, s/he may attempt to find a substitute such as power, sex, alcohol, or drugs.

Sharon's story is no isolated example; it is a common story that is pervasive in all spheres of Jewish life. Jewish estrangement is an issue that needs to be spiritually addressed. By painfully examining many of the stories of Jewish estrangement, Jewish leaders will be more adept in diagnosing the problems associated with spiritual myopia, which produces alienation.

Two recent surveys reflect the ambivalence among Jews when they are asked whether they believe in God. According to one poll, 38 percent of the Jewish population are convinced that God really exists. This study suggests that the majority of Jews are agnostic. Another study in 1986 indicated that Jews are convinced, by a two-to-one margin, that to be a good Jew, one did not have to believe in God. Some secular-minded Jews have gone out of their way to help eliminate God from any public activity or happening, arguing passionately for the separation of church and state.

Hershel Shanks, editor of the popular *Moment* magazine, in response to the question "Why be Jewish?" writes:

> One is because we Jews somehow have a divine attachment (through our books or beliefs) that others don't have or, two, because there is some reason why it is important that there be Jews (and Judaism) in two hundred or three hundred or five hundred years. Yet I really can't answer the question in these terms. I don't believe we've solved the problem of God—God's existence and relationship to what goes on down here. He, She, It remains a terrible and terrifying issue. I know that our answers, our Jewish answers, are inadequate. . . .[14]

There really is not much point to faith in God if God is not an active, participating Presence and reality in our lives. For today's modern Jews, there is a growing dissatisfaction with the lack of spiritual content and interiority that exists in present-day Jewish life. Though spiritually hungry, they have grown up

---

14. Hershel Shanks, "Why Be Jewish?" *Moment* (December 1992), 48.

with the message that we live only in the material world and that God is a human projection who has no reality other than what we assign to Him. To others, religion is identical with ethics—and nothing more. Young Jews are looking more and more outside the faith for some meaningful spiritual answers. Recently the Jewish Federations across the nation put together a new population study[15] that has concerned Jewish leaders everywhere. One of the details they discovered was that over 625,000 people born Jewish are now living another religion, while two million claim to have no religion at all. Some studies indicate that by the year 2000, intermarriage will make up 70% of all Jewish marriages and only 5–10% of the offspring will continue to raise their children as Jews.[16]

### *Religious Behaviorism*

Just how serious is the spiritual and personal alienation rabbis and laymen feel alike? One leading Reform Jewish scholar made the observation:

> Sizable segments of the lay and rabbinic populations do not believe in God. Some mouth the correct theological terminology. Some focus on the liturgy. Some avoid using the word God, saying that God-talk is for Christians, that it is not a Jewish activity. . . . God is not a four-letter word. Rabbis avoid talking about God because either they do not believe in God or they fear they will be considered to be hopelessly naïve and intellectually unsophisticated.[17]

The great Jewish theologian Abraham Joshua Heschel, in his classic *God in Search of Man*, poignantly described the phenomenon of spiritless religion as "religious behaviorism." It is rampant in all major Jewish denominations. In the world of religious behaviorism, one can function devoutly but live without faith. Advocates of this ideology enjoy emphasizing that Judaism attaches more importance to deeds than to creeds.[18] Emphasis is placed for the most part on the

---

15. Cf. Irving Greenberg, "For Whom the Shofar Blows," *The Jerusalem Report*, (September 12, 1991).

16. Barbara Skolnick Hoenig, *Jewish Environment Scan: Toward the Year 2000* (New York: Council of Jewish Federations, 1992), p. 3. Cited in Michael Goldberg, *Why Should Jews Survive?* (New York: Oxford University Press, 1995), p. 114.

17. Paul Meintoff in *Reform Judaism* (Spring 1985), 23–28.

18. See Abraham Joshua Heschel, *God in Search of Man: A Philosophy of Judaism* (New York: Farr, Straus, and Giroux, 1986), pp. 320–321. Religious behaviorism does have some support in the well-known teaching of *Rabbi Hiyya ben Abbahas*, who taught: *They have forsaken me and have not kept my law* (Jeremiah 16:11)—that is, God says: Would that they have forsaken Me and kept My Law, *for if they had occupied themselves with the Law, the light which is contained within it would have brought them back to the right path.* According to the Israeli scholar David Hartman, Mordecai Kaplan exemplified this midrashic teaching by placing "the primacy of practice above theology"

external aspects of religious life, while the subjective, experiential dimension of faith is neglected. This approach emphasizes that tradition ought to be observed for tradition's sake. Religious behaviorists believe that the tradition needs to be maintained; it is for them, as Heschel so clearly described, "the supreme article of faith."[19]

Rabbi Sherwin Wein, the founder of Humanistic Judaism, has argued in his controversial book that Judaism needs to emancipate itself from the belief in the existence of God.[20] Wein's Humanistic Judaism bears a familiar likness to the nineteenth-century French philosopher Auguste Comte's ill-fated "Religion of Humanity." Though an avowed atheist, Comte believed in "the solidarity of the human race." Comte's Religion of Humanity was complete with priests, prayers, a calendar of saints, and resembled a secularized version of Catholicism! Similarly, too, Humanistic Judaism is replete with the ritual accoutrements one would find in a theistic synagogue. Unlike Comte, Wein shows a profound disdain for the prophetic teachings of Jeremiah, Isaiah, Ezekiel, Amos. Wein's new denomination "Humanistic Judaism" is on the rise. More and more synagogues are now labeling themselves "Humanistic."

Martin Segal, a rabbi of a large synagogue in Lawrence, New York, pointed out in his autobiography:

> A young man in the confirmation class told me today he doubts whether he wants to be Jewish because he doesn't believe in God. "I don't believe in God, either," I told him. "But that has nothing to do with being Jewish."[21]

The story of the rabbi is no anomaly, for many of today's Jews see themselves in the same way Italian-Americans see themselves. There is a profound ethnic dimension to being Jewish. This can be seen in the foods, music, art, culture, and liberal politics. "Being Jewish," when looked at from this perspective, does not have to have anything to do with the faith per se. For a great number of American Jews, the commitment to American democracy, and the liberal Democratic platform in particular, has become a secular form of religion. Mordecai Kaplan, the founder of the Reconstructionism, was certainly not alone when he identified democracy as a "religion worthy of such commitment because it helps individu-

(David Hartman, *Conflicting Visions* [New York: Schoken Books Inc., 1990], pp. 184–206). For a sympathetic view of Kaplan's view of faith, see Elliot Dorf, *Knowing God* (Northvale, NJ: Jason Aronson, 1992), pp. 44–46.

19. Abraham Joshua Heschel, *Man's Quest for God* (New York: Scribners, 1954), pp. 53–54.

20. Sherwin Wein, *"Judaism beyond God" a Radical New Way to Be Jewish* (Buffalo, NY: Prometheus Books, 1985).

21. Martin Segal, *Amen: The Diary of Rabbi Martin Segal*, ed. Mel Zeigler (New York: World, 1971), pp. 52–53.

als and people achieve *self-realization"* —Kaplan's favorite pseudonym for "salvation." Americanism and Judaism are thus, for many American Jews, one and the same. Democracy has, for many Jews, become their own form of secular religion.

For a great number of Jews, their only point of contact with Judaism is when they are hatched (at the *bris*), matched (under the *huppa*), and dispatched (when they die). Many Jews attend synagogue because they are not Christians or Muslims. Jews are encouraged to think in the interest of the synagogue or the Jewish federation though many really do not know why. Jewish leaders often appeal to their audience's sense of nostalgia and tradition. The modern synagogue often functions as a place for social support than as a crucible of spiritual change and transformation.

Too many synagogues (across all denominations) have become bureaucracies that are more concerned with the problems of building maintenance and number-crunching than they are in fostering a healthy spiritual ambiance. Petty synagogue politics anesthetize the community from sensing God's Presence. There are a growing number of synagogues that are utilizing collection agencies to collect unpaid dues congregants owe to the synagogue. There are some synagogues that have even gone to Visa and Mastercard!

Many self-defined cultural Jews remain Jewish for nonreligious reasons. To some, leaving the faith would be an embarrassment for the family; these Jews would gladly renounce their faith completely if the non-Jewish world would let them assimilate in peace. For others, leaving the faith would be an act of treason against the victims and memory of the Holocaust.

According to one prominent Holocaust thinker, Emil Fackenheim, the Jewish people must continue to exist to frustrate Hitler's dream of having a Jew-free world. Survival for survival's sake has become "the 614th Commandment." Without minimizing Fackenheim's brilliant insight, the sad fact remains that for many Jews the Holocaust has become the primary *master story* (to borrow a phrase from theologian Michael Goldberg), replacing the traditional master stories of the Exodus and Sinai. While this is very understandable from the viewpoint of survivors and their children, a great number of Jews do not find this a compelling spiritual reason to remain Jewish.

This predicament has resulted in disillusionment for the spiritually sensitive, while causing agnosticism and skepticism for the more scientific-minded. It is a problem that affects all Jews, from the very Orthodox to the Reform or agnostic. In the past, anti-Semitism has been a cohesive force in maintaining Jewish identity. In America, for the most part, this is no longer the case. For the first time in recent history, the postmodern Jewish community is challenged to affirm and redefine its spiritual identity in a society that is pluralistic and tolerant.

## The Death of God

*"You are my witnesses, . . . and I am God."* (Isaiah 43:12)
*"If you are not my witnesses, then I am, as it were, not God."* (Pesikta D'Rav
Kahana, 102b.)

In the sixties, there was considerable debate in both Christian and Jewish circles
whether it was pertinent to believe in God any longer. In the Christian
community, a number of theologians argued that it is impossible to speak of God
in a secular age that can no longer discern the meaning or value of biblical
language. Gabriel Vahanian, the theologian who popularized the phrase "death of
God" back in the 1960s,[22] maintained that "it is easier to understand oneself
without God than with God." Harvey Cox, in his celebrated book *The Secular
City,* argues that the different biblical designations of God reflected a cultural and
political climate. To call God "King" could have meaning only in an age in which
monarchs reigned. To identify God as "Shepherd" could have meaning only in a
pastoral society. Using such archaic symbolizations of God may actually subvert
the message of faith instead of fostering it. The "death of God" movement is thus
a crisis in meaning—the modern era does not know how to make theological
sense out of its traditional metaphors of God. According to Cox:

> To insist on calling God the "shepherd" in an industrial society may seem pious but
> it really marks the height of unbelief. It suggests that God will somehow slip out
> of existence if men alter the names they use for Him.[23]

The "death of God theology" means different things to various modern Jewish
thinkers. Some argue that, because of the horrors of Auschwitz and Hiroshima,
it seemed as though God had gone on vacation. Leading the "Death of God"
crusade from the Jewish perspective is Richard Rubenstein. For Rubenstein,
Auschwitz demonstrated that human life could have no essential value because
no transcendental purpose or process seemed to be in control of the human
condition. Since the God model no longer seemed to provide ultimate meaning,
human beings would have to derive their sense of purpose from themselves. In
effect, community had to take the place of God. Religious precepts and rituals
could still be maintained, but only as sociological and psychological props. Jews,

---

22. Gabriel Vahanian, *The Death of God: The Culture of Our Post-Christian Era* (New York:
George Braziller, 1961), p. 147; cf. pp. 144–145. The actual phrase "death of God" can be traced to
Hegel's lecture *Philosophy of Religion* (Part 3, ed. Peter Hodgson [Berkeley, CA: University of
California Press, 1985], p. 212, and cf. p. 218). Hegel believed that the "death of God" characterized
the absence of God's Presence in the modern era. Hegel was convinced that this was a temporary
phase that humanity would eventually pass through.

23. Harvey Cox, *The Secular City* (New York: Collier, 1968), p. 229.

as a result of the Holocaust, must continue as a community, *but without* the God of Judaism. Rubenstein's view represents a broad segment of the secular Jewish intelligentsia. Many present-day Jews identify as Jews out of a desire to associate with other Jews—and not out of a desire to connect spiritually with God.

Other Jewish scholars view the "death of God theology" differently from Rubenstein and affirm that the "death of God theology" points to a loss or absence of the Divine in our contemporary age. Responding to the question "Is God dead?" Jacob Neusner, the distinguished Judaic scholar, writes:

> I do not understand the question what the "God is dead" theologians are saying. It seems to me they may be saying two things. First, the experience of the sacred, or God, is no longer widely available; second, that experience is no longer available in classical ways. Both of these statements describe Jewish existence, and have for some time, though we prefer to phrase them differently. I think it is clear that God is hiding His face from the world. . . . We are no longer able to approach the gates of heaven, surely not open them with the keys that used to work. God is "dead" for many Jews. In the Jewish community, even the flame of the yahrzeit candle long ago flickered out. In the synagogue, however, Jewry still keeps up the *graveyard*. I do not despair. We Jews have passed this way before. . . .[24] (Emphasis added.)

Neusner's evocative image of the "graveyard" is suggestive of numbness, death, and detachment. This metaphor would certainly describe the spiritual life of many modern Jews. Neusner's insightful words are revealing and may have antecedents in several rabbinic teachings that suggest that God has taken a leave of absence of the world. Some sages of the Talmud argued that the Divine Presence (*Shechinah*) has retreated to Heaven. In the words of the Midrash:

> When the Temple was burned,
> the Holy One (blessed be He) cried and said:
> I no longer have a seat upon earth.
> I shall remove my *Shechinah* from there
> and ascend to my first habitation.[25]

Emil Fackenheim, one of the leading post-Holocaust theologians of our time, noted that each denomination of Judaism seemed to want to keep God out of its modern religious lives.

> It [modern Jewish thought] allowed no room for a God dwelling beyond the world, yet entering into it to seek out man. He was an irrational incursion into a rational

---

24. *The Condition of Jewish Belief: A Symposium Compiled by the Editors of* Commentary *Magazine*, ed. Milton Himmelfarb (Northvale, NJ: Jason Aronson, 1988), pp. 156–157.
25. *Lamentations Rabbah* 24.

universe. At the same time, in its more congenial moods, modern thought gave substitute offerings to a deist First Cause or Cosmic Process outside man and unrelated to him, or an idealistic God-idea within him. Faced with this basic challenge, and these substitute offerings, orthodox and liberal Jewish theology both compromised. Orthodoxy held fast to the Jewish God, but confined His essential activity to a conveniently remote Biblical and Talmudic past, acting as though the sacred documents of the past could be exempted from modern criticism. Liberalism, for its part, wishing a present God, compromised the Jewish God Himself, now using the terms of Deism, then those of idealism, and in its still surviving forms the terms of a cosmic evolutionism.[26]

According to Eliade, the "death of God theology" has its roots in the religious life of primitive tribes. It was believed that the primitive High God would "retire" to the highest heaven and would become detached and indifferent to the affairs of this world. Once this happened:

Ultimately he is forgotten. In other words, *he dies*—not that there are myths relating his death, but he completely vanishes from the religious life and subsequently even from the myths.[27]

In Jungian terms, "the death of God" is a metaphor that describes a faith that is weak and no longer inspires. Ira Progoff, the distinguished exponent of Jungian psychology explains:

To speak of the death of God, then, refers to a psychological occupance which has actually taken place in modern times. It involves not only the weakening of the theological beliefs in God, but also the loss of feeling and fervor for the whole pattern of social values. The death of a god is always a historically important phenomenon because the God-symbol is the core in every society of the systems by which the society functions. *When a god dies, the structure of value loses its support; its vitality is gone, it loses its meaningfulness, its authority, and its ability to inspire. . . .* [28] (Emphasis added.)

Our images of God exert a dynamic effect on the human psyche and society. When Nietzsche spoke of "the death of God," he was referring to the demise of real, passionate faith that was conspicuously absent in the pre-Holocaust lives of German (and European) people. In Jungian terms, "the death of God" is a

26. Emil Fackenheim, *The Quest for Past and Future: Essays in Jewish Theology* (Boston: Beacon, 1968), p. 5.

27. Mircea Eliade, *The Quest—History and Meaning in Religion* (Chicago: University of Chicago Press, 1969), pp. 47–50.

28. Ira Progoff, *Jung's Psychology and Its Social Meaning* (New York: Dialogue House Library, 1953, 1981), pp. 216–217.

metaphor that describes a faith that is weak and no longer inspires. When people are cut off from the experience of transcendence, they risk being psychologically and socially destroyed. The death of God is always accompanied by the loss of soul; once we lose sight of our spiritual self, our perception of God immediately diminishes. The hasidic rebbes often refer to this loss of God's Presence in somewhat different but similiar terms. God is sometimes referred to as *Ayin—Nothing*. When a person gives no attention to God, and fails to live in accordance with His values and His will, then for all practical purposes, God is functionally "nothing." God has become a virtual non-Being in the devotional life of the so-called believer.

What are the implications of a faith that no longer facilities a close encounter with the spiritual? What are Jews to do when the "keys" of faith no longer work as they used to? To whom can they turn when their own spiritual leaders become ambivalent to the spiritual reality that is the heart of Judaism? How can we formulate a language that will faciliate and not inhibit our shared experiences of the Divine? If the current keys will not work, then we need to find keys that will. Clearly, the models of faith offered by many modern Jewish philosophers and thinkers have not opened doorways leading to inner integration and spiritual transformation. In the next chapter we shall attempt to explain why our faith has become so impotent.

# 5

# OVERCOMING OUR FRAGMENTED
# IMAGES OF GOD/WORLD/SOUL

*This life's five windows of the soul*
*Distort the heavens from pole to pole*
*And teach us to believe a lie*
*When we see with, not through, the eye.*
William Blake

*The compassion of man is*
*for his neighbor,*
*but the compassion of the Lord*
*is for all living beings.*
*He rebukes and trains*
*and teaches them,*
*and turns them back,*
*as a shepherd his flock.*
Ben Sira (18:13)

The stories about Joe Price, Esther, and Sharon are not unusual. They illustrate
how widespread the depersonalization of God is in Jewish life today. Many Jews
find that belief in a personal God is (1) not essential for religion, (2) childish and
mere superstition (Freud),[1] (3) incompatible with science, (4) a mere "projection

---

1. According to Freud, religious ideas are teachings and assertions about facts and conditions of
external (or internal) reality that tell something one has not discovered for oneself and which lay
claim to one's belief. And what is the basis of this claim? According to Freud, there are three answers

of humanity's most eminent qualities" (Feuerbach),[2] (5) impossible because of the Holocaust. Each of the above anecdotes reflects the spiritual homelessness that is becoming typical of contemporary Jewry.

## God-Talk and the Postmodern Jew

How common is the spiritual homelessness of today's Jewry? Leonard Fein, a well-known Jewish sociologist and social activist, once observed candidly:

> I had best say something about God-talk in general. Talk of God makes many people feel distinctly uncomfortable. Most of us learn what we know about God when we are small children, and although we come to know, as we grow older, that the God of our childhood is not quite the same God the theologians discuss and describe, we are stuck with our prepubescent notions. We do not want to discuss such notions, lest our childishness be exposed.
>
> We have neither the vocabulary nor the categories for serious conversation, and besides, we vaguely fear that our expression of interest in such conversation would be taken as evidence that we lack sophistication, that we are not fully at home in our definitely secular world. So we avoid the subject, which is not hard since our friends and neighbors, for the most part, also prefer to avoid it; they are no less intimidated than we by the thought of it.[3]

Later, Fein points out that many Jews hold that the notion of God is attributed to a prescientific mind as

> . . . a widely used way of explaining phenomena we otherwise do not understand. But as science, in its precise and powerful way, explains more and more of that

---

that mutually contradict one another: (1) We should believe without demanding proofs. Freud points out that such a demand reveals that on some unconscious level we really are not certain about the validity of our belief. (2) We should believe because our ancestors believed. Freud points out that our ancestors were far more ignorant and gullible than we; people today are less naïve and will not accept uncritically what their ancestors believed to be true. (3) We should believe because we possess proofs handed down to us from primeval times. Freud critiques this belief by stating that many of the ancient writings are full of inconsistencies, were frequently revised, and contain lies. Freud also attacks the spiritualists as people incapable of demonstrating that there is such a thing as a spiritual reality.

According to Freud, early human beings attempted to associate themselves with the great forces of nature by creating gods that enabled them magically to influence nature—that is, nature-gods. Freud was convinced that it was culture that produced religious ideas in the life of an individual and that *religion was like a security blanket that helped an impotent person face an intimidating world.* (Sigmund Freud, *The Future of an Illusion* [London: Hogarth Press, 1934]).

2. Ludwig Feuerbach, *The Essence of Christianity*, trans. George Eliot (New York: Harper and Row, 1957).

3. Leonard Fein, *Where Are We? The Inner Life of America's Jews* (New York: Harper and Row, 1988), p. 25.

which yesterday we did not understand, the value of God-as-explanation diminishes, the scope of religion shrinks. Indeed insofar as science and religion compete head to head, whether in explaining the origin of the species or why drought happens or the roots of evil, religion comes out the loser every time; and compared to the precision of the laboratory, it appears as murky superstition.[4]

Today's Jew suffers from a world view that is mundane, materialistic, and devoid of a spiritual vocabulary. The modern Jew resembles the sequestered people portrayed in Plato's famous allegory of the cave. It is as if all the words about the soul and consciousness did not exist. When they educated their children, the parents, the teachers, and the rabbis alike all used materialistic terms in describing themselves and the world as a collection of things in a mechanistic universe. Human existence is portrayed as tragic, humanity as but a solitary epiphenomenon, a homeless figure that lives in a soulless universe. Richard Rubenstein poignantly writes:

> Even as a child . . . I believed that when I died the whole world of my existence would disappear with me. My world would last only as long as I did. I was convinced that I had arisen out of nothingness and was destined to return to nothingness. All human beings were locked in the same fatality. In the final analysis, omnipotent nothingness was lord of creation. Nothing in the bleak cold, unfeeling universe was remotely concerned with human aspiration and longing. Even as a rabbi, I have never really departed from my earlier primordial feelings about my place in the cosmos.[5]

Rubenstein is not alone. Many leading Jewish thinkers of the Orthodox, Conservative, and Reform movements wrote off the spiritual and metaphysical dimension of the soul and the universe. Many leading Jewish theologians have redefined the Judaic belief in the immortality of the soul as "living through one's children or deeds." These Jews view the belief in the afterlife as a metaphysical escape from reality. The belief in personal immortality was (and still is) disparaged by many Jewish intellectuals as a "Christian doctrine," much as the belief in a personal God is also considered a "Christian" doctrine.[6] Because of their desire to distinguish Judaism from Christianity, they threw out the baby with

---

4. Ibid.

5. Richard Rubenstein, "The Making of a Rabbi," *Varieties of Jewish Belief*, ed. I. Eisenstein (New York: Reconstructionist Press, 1966), p. 179.

6. Christianity has traditionally been more concerned than Judaism with the salvation of the individual soul and its standing in the Hereafter. The great fifteenth-century commentator Don Isaac Abravanel notes in his commentary to Leviticus 26:1, "Why does the Torah confine its goals and rewards to material things, as mentioned in his comment, and omit the spiritual perfection and the reward of the soul after death—the true and ultimate goal of man? *Our enemies exploit this text and charge Israel with denying the principle of the soul's judgment in the Hereafter.*"

the bath water. These thinkers argued that the belief in an afterlife is not an important belief among modern Jews. According to Harold Schulweis:

> In this connection, modern Judaism favors a more symbolic and poetic interpretation of the hereafter. Heaven and hell are not geographic places, but states of mind, ways of living rather than spaces beyond the earth. . . .[7]

Some might even seriously consider that, if the spiritual realm existed, it certainly did not shape the real world, nor was any encounter with the world of spirit even considered a feasible possibility. The modern Jew was never taught that the spiritual realm represents a higher frequency of reality and does not occupy space in the physical sense. The biblical writers and their rabbinic heirs have long maintained *that behind the ordinary world of human strivings exists a more real realm that is the true home of the human spirit.* The soul is deathless, eternal, and positively real. Maimonides once wrote that knowledge of the spiritual world is comparable to that of the world of color. We cannot explain the phenomenon of color to a person who is congenitally blind. Without a personal experience of color, any explanation about color would be useless. Once the blind person has his vision restored to him, only then will s/he understand what color is. The same is true of the spiritual realm: once we have experienced it, only then will we have an inkling of what the spiritual realm actually is. There exists within our souls a longing for that experience of connectedness that links us to a reality that is larger than ourselves. Without spirit, we feel in our lives an emptiness and void that cannot be filled with mundane values; our perception of homelessness comes from our collective memories that we are creatures of eternity; our roots go deeper than this earthly world.

This idea is profoundly conveyed in the metaphors of the Twenty-third Psalm: "He restores my soul," (Psalms 23:3). What we yearn for is more than just physical food and material sustenance—our souls are hungry and thirsty. The ancient philosopher-King once observed: "He has also put eternity in their hearts," (Ecclesiastes 3:11). Within the heart of our spiritual being is a hunger that will not find contentment in the material world per se. There is nothing else that can sate the inner emptiness we as human beings feel. When we proclaim that the "Lord is my Shepherd," we are acknowledging that it is only God who can provide our souls with the sustenance they hunger for.

Despite the religious naturalism that pervades modern rabbinical seminaries, the liturgy is full of passages that speak of God as our Eternal Source and Home. When the Psalmist stated in Psalm 23, "And I shall dwell in the House of the Lord forever," was he not alluding to a transcendental realm beyond the bounds

---

7. Quoted in Rifat Sonsiono and Daniel Syme, *What Happens after I Die?—Jewish Views of Life after Death* (New York: UAHC Press, 1990), p. 100.

of earthly existence? Are these rabbis suggesting, as one congregant of mine perceptively said to me, "God lives forever, *but you are a temporary phenomenon*"? This is certainly the message that is being distilled in American synagogues today: "Dead is dead, and all that remains are our good deeds and nothing else." For the sick and the dying, this dangerous teaching has been a gospel of hopelessness and despair. An anonymous person once wrote the following note before committing suicide:

> I have no shepherd.
> I want and am in need.
> I have no one to feed me
>   in green pastures.
> I have no rest.
> I have no one to lead me
>   to quiet waters.
> I am thirsty.
> I have no one to restore
>   my anxious and despairing soul.
> I find no one to
>   guide me in right ways.
> I don't know where to turn.
> As I walk through the valley of the
>   shadow of death, evil surrounds me.
> I am terribly afraid, for no one is with
>   me to comfort me.
>
> I have no feast prepared for me.
> I am overwhelmed by my enemies.
> There is no one who will anoint my wounds
>   or fill my cup.
>
> My cup is empty.
> All the days of my life are filled
>   with disappointments and deceit.
> I have no home for eternity.
> Will I dwell in the house [of] evil forever?[8]

The message young and old Jews are receiving is unmistakably clear—as the pop-star Madonna once put it, "We are living in a material world and I am a material girl." Many rabbis and theologians *implied* in Freudian terms (though many of them were too embarrassed to admit it candidly)—that the belief in a

---

8. Parsons Technology, *Bible Illustrator for Windows*, version 1.0 (Hiawatha, IA: Parsons Technology, 1990–1992).

future life is simply "an illusion": In reality, death is total annihilation of the self as well as death of the soul. Freudian psychology has argued that the belief in an afterlife emanated from our primitive sense of despair and mortality. The loss of the spiritual dimension of faith (which we termed *soul*) has produced serious consequences. Thomas Moore, in his recent popular book *Care of the Soul*, remarks:

> The great malady of the twentieth century, implicated in all of our troubles and affecting us individually and socially, is "loss of soul." When soul is neglected, it doesn't just go away; it appears symptomatically in obsessions, addictions, violence, and loss of meaning. Our temptation is to isolate these symptoms or to try to eradicate them one by one; but the root problem is that we have lost our wisdom about the soul, even our interest in it.[9]

Moore's observation certainly applies to the postmodern Jewish community. The issue of soul needs to be recovered by present-day Jewish theologians and teachers alike. As a faith, Judaism cannot flourish without a transcendental and transpersonal language of soul that embraces the world in its totality. The phenomenon of despiritualization is a far greater, more pervasive threat to Judaism than is anti-Semitism. In the next section we shall examine some of its underlying metaphysical and historical reasons.

### The Cartesian Jewish Consciousness

Scientific interpretations are based on specific models or paradigms the scientist has of reality. Credible theological models must take into consideration the views of reality that have found currency in their day. Philo of Alexandria adapted the approach of Plato. The Talmud built its astronomical views on the teachings of Ptolemaic science. Maimonides adopted Aristotle's cosmological views, which were dominant in his day. Deists of the seventeenth and eighteenth centuries built their worldviews on Newtonian physics. In every major epoch of history, theological views have been overturned or reformulated according to the governing scientific models and metaphors of the time. Every new introduction of a paradigm introduces a new rethinking of the relationship between science and religion. This is no less true of the scientific and theological discourse of the twentieth century than it was in the days of Copernicus.

Fein's observations about the Jewish secular consciousness epitomize a worldview that is paradoxically "premodern." By the term "premodern," I mean a view of reality that is based on the scientific and theological thinking of the

---

9. Thomas Moore, *Care of the Soul* (New York: HarperCollins, 1992), p. xi.

seventeenth to nineteenth centuries. According to this kind of cognitive world-view, science and religion are considered two separate, contrary realities that are antithetical to each other.[10] This dualistic thinking owes its origin to the philosophical writings of the seventeenth-century thinker and mathematician René Descartes (1596–1650). Descartes emphasized the value of objective and observable dimensions of human experience while rejecting the relevance of nonobservable, aesthetic, subjective, intuitive, spiritual phenomena.

With Descartes (and those who followed after him), *the act of thinking was divorced from feeling, while morality was divorced from knowledge.* As Copernicus before him demonstrated, the senses were not to be trusted. All knowledge of the universe was based on hard physical evidence. Science was stripped of all of its metaphysical content, as the study and quantification of the universe became the sole source of all truth.

> . . . that all science was certain, evident knowledge . . . We reject all knowledge which is merely probable and judge only those things should be believed which are perfectly known and about which there can be no doubts.[11]

Descartes' world was a colorless, odorless, soundless, tasteless world of dead matter moving through space. It was a world in which the senses were devalued. He argued that the universe is composed of force and matter and operates solely according to impersonal mechanical laws. Nature was deterministic in that *mechanical causes* determined all natural events. To Descartes, there could be no spirituality in matter, nor could matter have any sense of purpose and meaning. In clear, one-sided terms, the Cartesian worldview suggested that humanity is divorced from nature as matter is divorced from spirit. Cartesian thought subscribed to a theory of reductionism, a doctrine that believes a system can be fully understood in terms of its isolated parts. According to the ancient Roman philosopher Lucretius, reductionism aims to reduce anxiety by analyzing the world in a certain way in order to control it. To know a phenomenon in its totality confers a power to control and predict its behavior.

The mechanical clock served as the model for how the natural processes of the universe worked.[12] The human body was also seen as a complex machine

---

10. The view of science and religion as antithetical is sometimes termed the "warfare thesis." This term is somewhat misleading, for Copernicus, Kepler, Galileo, Descartes, Newton, and numerous others all saw science as uncovering new pathways to God. The break between science and religion occurred primarily with the philosophers and scientists of the so-called Age of Reason, such as Hume, Comte, Voltaire, and Laplace.

11. René Descartes, *Discourse on Method*, Second Edition, part 1, ed. Laurence LaFleur (New York: New York Liberal Arts Press, 1956), p. 12.

12. Though the peoples of antiquity developed various ways of measuring time, the clock did not become the precision instrument it is today until the Renaissance.

equipped with all sorts of "mechanisms"—for example, pumps, springs, and all kinds of gadgetry.[13] Human beings, according to Descartes, were different only in that they possessed a rational soul. Animals were nothing more than machines bereft of consciousness and feeling—unconscious automata.[14] Performing a vivisection on a live animal, according to Descartes and his followers, was no different than dismantling a clock.[15] Mind (*res cognitas*) and matter (*res extensa*) represented two distinctive realities that were independent of one another.

In the premodern era, humanity belonged to the greater cosmos. The universe was (as Max Weber put it) "a place of enchantment." In the Middle Ages, the relationship with God was pivotal for any kind of self-knowledge. The self (or what used to be called the soul) could not be abstracted apart from God's relational Presence. Human beings were not alienated spectators, but were important participants in the unfolding of the Divine design. There was a spiritual wholeness and organicity that embraced every aspect of the premodern person's universe. Everything in the universe always embodied a nonmaterial inner principle that was seen as the essence of the particular phenomenon's reality. (Thus, for Aristotle and Maimonides, the planetary bodies were literally considered alive.) Nothing was what it seemed to be; the spiritual and material universes were intertwined. Prior to the Copernican revolution, the world believed that humanity could never thoroughly understand the universe; all that could be discerned were basic specific patterns. With the advent of the Copernican revolution, however, this ancient metaphysical view of the universe was challenged and was rapidly replaced by a world in which material "things" represented the sum total of reality, while the certitude of technology represented ultimate knowledge. The adaptation of the machine metaphor for describing the cosmos suggested that the world could be a wholly knowable phenomenon and that the construction of its individual parts could be analyzed.[16] The cosmology of the world was shaped and defined by the metaphor of the machine. Reality was no longer expressed in poetic and spiritual terms but instead was defined by the stoic language of science and technology. Seyyed Hossein Nasr correctly observed:

---

13. Cartesian medicine ignored traditional holistic wisdom that aimed to cure the total person. The new philosophical reductionism replaced the ancient interactive psychophysiology of Aristotle, Hippocrates, Maimonides, and the Renaissance.

14. René Descartes, *Discourse on Method*, part 2, *Great Books of the Western World*, vol. 31, pp. 75–76. "They do not have a mind, and . . . it is nature that acts in them according to the disposition of their organs, as one sees that a clock, which is made of only wheels and springs, can count the hours and measure time more exactly than we can with all our art."

15. The great Cambridge Platonist Henry More, who was one of Descartes' strongest critics, regarded Descartes' concept of *machina anima* as a "murderous doctrine."

16. For a brilliant critique of Descartes, see Robert Cummings Neville, *Recovery of the Measure—Interpretation and Nature* (Albany, NY: SUNY Press, 1989), pp. 31–38.

. . . the secularization of language and the attempt to substitute pure quality for the symbolic significance of language in the reading of a cosmic text also reflected upon the language of sacred Scripture itself, which until now had been considered as a gift from God. . . . But now that human language has been degraded and mathematics considered as the proper language of nature, the language of sacred Scripture began to appear as "more the slipshod invention of illiterate man than the gift of omniscient God."[17]

## *Babel Revisited*

The Enlightenment did its best to scour all language of any vestige of anthropomorphic nuances and meanings. Nature no longer revealed a God that was present in the world. Man had become a puny insignificant spectator in a vast cold, unfeeling universe that was silent and dead. Nature was like an open book that needed no commentary. The spirit of literalism affected not only the community of believers but also the savants of the new science. Nature existed as brute facts that required no interpretation. This dogmatic way of thinking is paradoxically similar to the way in which Christian Fundamentalists treat the Bible, for they too value the primacy of literalism over interpretation.

Like the mythic tower-builders of Babel, the philosophers and scientists of the Enlightenment and their twentieth-century descendents attempted to utilize a unitive and *unequivocal* language that would be free of any ambiguity, a language purged of all symbolic and mythic content— a language as precise and clear as mathematics. Such a language would have to serve the whims of technology and progress. Scientific language was (and still is) believed to hold the key to ultimate knowledge and societal evolution—and is religiously believed to be the Gateway to Heaven (the meaning of Babel in Assyrian).

The Rabbis of the Talmud refer to that fabled age of Babel as "the generation of *separation*" (*dor haflaga*); in modern terms we could say it was a generation of *estrangement* from God, from nature, and from each other. Spirit was divorced from human speech; words were reduced to the utilitarian status of bricks—the ancient symbol of technology. When God confused the speech of that generation, far from being a curse, it was actually a blessing. Language should never be the slave of technology or totalitarianism. The true gateway to Heaven must be discerned through developing a spiritual language that respects human integrity, nature, soul, and individuality. Humanity must discover God in many languages and dialects, for the Divine loves the subtlety, mystery, and majesty of words.

Though scientific language can inform and enlighten, it cannot nurture or enrich everyday life with meaning or purpose; it can describe *how* the universe

---

17. Seyyed Hossein Nasr, *Knowledge and the Sacred* (Albany, NY: SUNY Press, 1989), p. 47.

works, but it cannot tell us *why*. Scientific language cannot capture the mystery and ambiguity of human existence; only symbolic language can.[18] Nor can scientific language inspire love, connectedness, and meaning, nor help human beings transcend suffering or inspire hope. It is no historical accident that scientific language has often served as the instrument of power and exploitation, as evidenced by the horrors of the Holocaust.

It is ironic that the early scientific pioneers and thinkers of the sixteenth century were religious people who had a fascination with the matters of faith and theology. Copernicus, Kepler, Galileo, and Newton were deeply religious men who regarded science as the key to discerning the Divine Mind within nature. As the machine paradigm grew in popularity, God became more and more distant from the universe, standing at the periphery, uninvolved with the world and indifferent to the thoughts, concerns, and yearnings of humanity. With the development of positivism, more and more intellectual people began to view religion as a primitive stage in the evolution of humanity, superseded by the wisdom and critical open-mindedness of science. Jews and Christians alike came to believe that human beings could not know anything beyond the five-sensory world and that all talk concerning the spiritual world was literally and figuratively "none-sense."

But God was not the only casualty resulting from the great machine paradigm. Once a theology depersonalizes God, it will also diminish and depersonalize human beings. Had Descartes been more consistent, he would have applied his concept of radical doubt to human beings as well as animals and declared that human beings are also machines (human clockwork) and that soul, mind, and consciousness are illusions produced by the body's mechanical processes. Though he did not come to this radical conclusion, subsequent thinkers did.[19] By the eighteenth-century Enlightenment period, humanity became a part of the

---

18. Ricoeur observes, "The situation in which language finds itself comprises this double possibility, this double solicitation and urgency: on the one hand, purify discourse of its excrescences, liquidate the idols, go from drunkenness to sobriety, realize our state of poverty once and for all; on the other hand, use the most 'nihilistic,' destructive, iconoclastic movement so as to let speak what once, what each time, was said, when meaning appeared anew, when meaning was at its fullest. Hermeneutics seems to me to be animated by this double motivation: willingness to suspect, willingness to listen; vow of rigor, vow of obedience." (Paul Ricoeur, *Freud and Philosophy*, trans. D. Savage [New Haven and London: Yale University Press, 1970], p. 27.)

19. According to the philosophy of logical positivism, consciousness (that is, a mind or soul) was nonexistent. John Watson in 1903 attempted to establish psychology as a branch of natural science. He maintained that there is no such thing as mind or soul. Watson maintained that psychology could be reduced to physics and that psychological phenomena could be reduced to nothing more than molecular motions. Mind and soul (psyche) were nothing more than fictions. According to Watson, the body is the only human reality, and the existence of the soul and mind must be eliminated from science. Language was nothing more than a series of muscle spasms, while silent speech was "talking with concealed musculature." Watson took Cartesian reductionism to its ultimate absurd conclusion.

machine paradigm, whose operation could be explained without any reference to God. This materialistic worldview also made no place for consciousness or the existence of soul, which were both regarded as a subjective illusions.

### The Cry of an Alienated Being

Like Martin Buber in his critique of classical theology (the "I–It" relationship), Thomas Merton also noticed the dangers of objectifying God and our sense of soul that comes as a result of a purely intellectual faith:

> Nothing can be more alien to contemplation than *cogito ergo sum*—"I think therefore I am" of Descartes. This is a declaration of an alienated being, in exile from his own spiritual depths, compelled to seek comfort in a proof for his existence (!) based on the observation that he "thinks." If his thought is necessary as a medium through which he arrives at the concept of his existence, then he is in fact only moving away from his true being. He is reducing himself to a concept. He is making it impossible for himself to experience, directly and immediately, the mystery of his own being. At the same time, by reducing God as a concept, he makes it impossible for himself to have an intuition of the divine reality which is inexpressible. He arrives at his own being as if it were an objective reality, that is to say he strives to become aware of himself. And he proves that the "thing" exists. He convinces himself: "I am really some thing." And then he goes on to convince himself that God, the infinite, transcendent, is also a "thing," an "object," like other finite and limited concepts of our thoughts.[20]

In Merton's theology, the existential issue that confronts each human being is the spiritual dynamic of the "false self" versus the "inner self." It is the false self that appeals to the selfishness of the illusory ego. The "false self" sees the world and everything that is in it as a series of separate, detached entities estranged from God's love and reality. The more immersed a person is in his conventional self (*cogito*), the less awakened s/he is to his/her real self. The soul yearns for a truly human transcendence through the love of God.[21]

The Cartesian God is not a power that meets humanity or the world in relationships. Independent of encountering the world, Descartes' concept of the ego is entrapped in the mirror of its own creation and cannot see beyond its own egoic image. Cartesian thought observes rather than encounters the world. It functions as a voyeur rather than as a participant. The poet Rilke once wrote,

---

20. Thomas Merton, *New Seeds of Contemplation* (New York: New Directions, 1961), p. 8.

21. This theme of Merton has numerous parallels in hasidic mysticism, which also stresses the need for soul (*neshamah*) to triumph over the seductions of the *yesh hasheker*—the false self.

"Looking at, yet never out of, everything!" Cartesian thought is wholly intellectual rather than intuitive and feeling; Descartes' *monological* thought represents the polar extreme to Martin Buber's *dialogical* "I and Thou." In contrast to Descartes, Buber stressed that we discover God through relationships. The entire ethos of the Bible is to help humanity recover our shared rootedness in the Divine.

The spiritual and ethical implications of Cartesian dualism are immense and worthy of serious reflection. The separation of thinking and feeling allowed Nazi scientists to reduce Jews to objects of an experiment in order to study the limits of human pain. For centuries, science has had very little to do with matters of morality. By treating the world as in terms of mechanical parts, by insisting that science distance itself from values and issues of morality, it has become a dangerous tool in the hands of leaders who are completely indifferent to all human concerns and problems. By emphasizing a gospel of scientific objectivity, the belief in scientism has served humanity apart from the rest of nature. Our modern world is still suffering the ecological consequences of its dualistic gospel. Its impact upon society, and upon the modern secular Jew in particular, must not be ignored. Cartesian philosophy conceived and bequeathed to the modern age a philosophical legacy of fragmentation, alienation, and cosmic homelessness. The "loss of soul" that is so emblematic of today's times is due to the fragmentary worldview our epoch has accepted hook, line, and sinker. As we enter the year 2000 c.e., we may be facing a very different kind of apocalypse from the one our ancestors in the year 1000 c.e. anticipated. One millennium ago, the Western world believed God was going to bring this world to its final cataclysmic end culminating in the final judgment of humanity. Today's apocalypse threatens to come not from God but from science and technology. Without a spiritual and unitive worldview of God/world/soul, we may very well negate our very own existence.

## The New Physics and the Theology of Interrelatedness

The Cartesian/Newtonian scientific paradigm was overturned by the scientific discoveries of the twentieth century. Einstein's theory of relativity changed the way we view space, time, energy, and matter. Approximately fifteen billion years ago, there was absolute nothingness. Within a nanosecond the material universe came into being. The Big Bang theory demonstrated that the universe did have a genesis in time. Our mere presence in the universe is actually based upon a marvelous number of delicately balanced physical coincidences. Had the nuclear forces been slightly stronger than they presently are, hydrogen would be a rare element, and stars like the sun, which live a long time by slowly burning the hydrogen of their cores, could not exist. If the same nuclear forces had been substantially weaker than they presently are, hydrogen could not burn at all and there would be no heavy elements, and hence no life. There exists a hidden principle that seems to be organizing and structuring the cosmos in a coherent way. Many astrophysicists have observed that the entire creation of the universe seems to point to the existence of a Creator who has a biocentric interest in conscious life.

This cosmological approach has been called by some the *Anthropic Principle*. The Anthropic Principle suggests that there may be many regions of a single universe, each with its own structure and laws; only a few might have the conditions that exist on this world for the emergence of consciousness and intelligent life. Even more amazing and miraculous is how our conscious sense of personhood could ever have emerged out of the cosmic processes that began eons ago with the Big Bang.[22] As remarkable as the appearance of life is even on the most basic level, it is astounding that human consciousness has the ability to contemplate itself in relation to the universe. The Anthropic Principle shows that the organization of matter in the universe is not a slipshod or haphazard affair; the universe reflects symmetry and order. The British physicist Paul Davies observes that there are seven essential prerequisites that must be satisfied if life is to exist on the earth:

1. There must be an adequate supply of the elements that comprise our bodies, for example, carbon, oxygen, hydrogen, phosphorus, and calcium.
2. There must be little or no risk of contamination by other poisonous chemicals such as would be found in an atmosphere containing methane or ammonia.
3. The climatic temperature must remain within a narrow range of 5 to 40 degrees Celsius, which is a mere 2 percent of the temperature range within the solar system as a whole.
4. A stable supply of free energy must exist, which in our case is provided by the sun.
5. Gravity must be strong enough to keep the atmosphere from escaping into space, but it must be weak enough to allow us to move freely about on the earth's surface.
6. A protective screen must exist to filter out the Sun's harmful ultraviolet rays; in our case, the screen is provided by a layer of ozone in the upper atmosphere.
7. A magnetic field must exist in order to prevent cosmic subatomic

---

22. M. A. Corey, *God and the New Cosmology* (Lanham, MA: Rowan & Littlefield Publications, 1993), p. 232. According to the physicist John Wheeler, "observers are necessary to bring the universe into being."

particles from raining on the earth. Were the earth's circular orbit (a 3-percent variance) like the elliptical orbit of the planet Mars, which varies from 50 million kilometers to 4.5 kilometers, the earth would incinerate once a year when the earth is closest to the Sun.[23]

If the force of gravity was even slightly stronger, stars would burn out faster, leaving little time for life to evolve on the planets circling them. If the relative masses of protons and neutrons were changed by a tiny fraction, stars might never be born, since the hydrogen they burn wouldn't exist. If, at the Big Bang, some basic numbers—the "initial conditions"—had been shaken, matter and energy would never have formed into galaxies, stars, planets or any of the other platforms stable enough for life as we know it.

When we consider how precise each of these celestial developments is, we can only conclude that the Creator of the universe had a biocentric purpose in mind. Ben Sira's intuitive insight about how the "compassion of the Lord extends to all things much as the Shepherd guides his flock" seems to be an apt and perceptive metaphor full of cosmological wisdom. The physicist Stephen Hawking observes: "The odds against a universe like ours emerging out of something like the Big Bang are enormous. I think that there are clearly religious implications."[24] One astrophysicist poetically said:

> At this moment it seems as though science will never be able to raise the curtain on the mystery of creation. For the scientist who lived by his faith in the power of reason, the story ends like a bad dream. He has scaled the mountains of ignorance; he is about to conquer the highest peak; as he pulls himself over the final rock, he is greeted by a band of theologians who have been sitting there for centuries.[25]

The second great discovery that has altered our perception of the universe is the discovery of the inner world of the quantum universe. Reality is not as static or deterministic as the pre-twentieth-century scientific community once thought it was; instead, it is dynamic. The fundamental characteristic of matter is not bits of particles that make it up but, rather, a constantly changing process of energy events. The universe is in a state of constant movement and is an ever-changing process. According to Einstein, *matter is not a noun but a verb*; it is always active. This modern view has its antecedent in the ancient Greek philosopher Heraclitus (540–475 B.C.E.), who emphasized, "You cannot step twice into the

---

23. Paul Davies, *Other Worlds* (New York: Touchstone, 1980), pp. 143–144.

24. Cited in John Boslough, *Stephen Hawking's Universe* (New York: William Morrow, 1985), p. 121. In Stephen Hawking's *A Brief History of Time* (New York: Bantam Books, 1988), p. 120, he writes: "If the rate of expansion after the Big Bang had been smaller by even one part in a hundred thousand million millions it would have recollapsed before it reached its present size."

25. Robert Jastrow, *God and the Astronomers* (New York: Warner Books, 1978), p. 105.

same rivers; for fresh waters are ever flowing in upon you." The intuitions of the Jewish mystics (ancient and modern) were confirmed, for they, too, described creation as constantly recurring.[26]

The discovery of quantum mechanics blasted the Newtonian belief that science would enable us to predict everything if only we could know the complete state of the universe at any given moment. The new physics revealed that absolute objectivity is impossible. In the subatomic world, we cannot take a measurement without changing the particle we seek to measure. Our observations of the subatomic world alter our understanding of it. As we change the world, so, too, does the world change us. Erwin Schrodinger, one of the pioneers of quantum physics, suggests that consciousness is one of the basic building blocks of the universe.[27] The quantum theory does away with the old deterministic universe in which everything is preordained long before our birth. *Paradox seems to be consistent with how the subatomic world functions.*[28] *We might add that this phenomenon in nature also has profound spiritual overtones.*

The development of both modern cosmology and quantum mechanics has led many modern physicists to regard the behavior of the inner and outer world as more like that of an organism than that of a machine. All events and perceptions of the universe are interrelated, interconnected, and part of a unified whole. The new discipline of ecological studies has shown that the entire planet operates more in the manner of a living organism rather than according to the machine model scientists and philosophers once accepted. This century has abandoned the reductionist and mechanistic approach in favor of a more holistic view of the physical world and the principles of physics that underlie it. Reductionism has

---

26. Rabbi *Sholom Dov Baer* of Lubavitch explains: "Just as the human organism exists through the process of inhaling and exhaling and one cannot be conceived without the other, so too does the whole of creation experience the constant inhaling and exhaling of God." (*Sholom Dov Baer Schneerson, Sefer Mamamreem 1906, Vyechulu Hashayeem* reprinted by [Brooklyn, NY: Kehot Publications, 1974], p. 27.)

27. Schrodinger illustrated how consciousness affects reality with his famous paradox known as Schrodinger's cat. See Paul Davies, *God and the New Physics* (New York: Simon and Schuster, 1984), p. 114.

28. Amit Goswami, in his book *The Self-Aware Universe* (New York: Tarcher/Putnam, 1993), p. 9, observes:

- A quantum object (for an example, an electron) can be at more than one place at the same time (*the wave property*).
- A quantum object cannot be said to manifest in ordinary spacetime reality until we observe it as a particle (*collapse of the wave*).
- A quantum object ceases to exist here and simultaneously appears in existence over there; we cannot say it went through the intervening space (*the quantum jump*).
- A manifestation of one quantum object, caused by our observation, simultaneously influences its correlated twin object—no matter how far apart they are (*quantum action at a distance*).

added measurably to our understanding of the world we live in. Many great discoveries would have remained unrecognized were it not for the reductionististic approach. Yet, despite its virtues, it has flaws. Paul Davies writes:

> The distinction being made here is sometimes referred to as 'holism' versus 'reductionism.' The main thrust of Western thinking over the last three centuries has been reductionist. Indeed the use of the word 'analysis' in the broadest context nicely illustrates the scientist's almost unquestioning habit of taking a problem apart to solve it. But of course some problems such as [jigsaws] are solved by putting them together—they are synthetic or 'holistic' in nature. The picture on a jigsaw, like the speckled newspaper image of a face, can only be perceived at a higher level of structure than the individual pieces—the whole is greater than the sum of its parts. . . .[29]
>
> To say that an ant colony is nothing but a collection of ants is to overlook the reality of colonial behavior. It is as absurd as saying that the computer programs are not real, they are nothing but electrical pulses. Similarly, to say that a human being is nothing but a collection of cells, which are themselves nothing but bits of DNA and so forth, which in turn are nothing but strings of atoms and therefore conclude that life has no significance, is muddle-headed nonsense. Life is a holistic phenomenon.[30]

Philosopher and physicist Alfred North Whitehead is one of many modern scientists who have written extensively about the spiritual and theological implications of a cosmos that is in process and is organically related.[31] Life has three ingredients—self-enjoyment, creative activity, and purpose. To Whitehead, it would be wrong to consider the light of the sun, or the formation of mountains, as an abstraction, as a kind of setting or environment of life. Life is all pervasive, whether it be in the formation of a snowflake or the cry of an injured animal. Human beings, like the rest of nature, absorb what is outside themselves into their own being; all things are interrelated.

---

29. Davies, *God and the New Physics*, p. 61.

30. Ibid., p. 63. Davies' observation brings to mind the famous parable about the blind men in India who were examining an elephant. One person felt the leg and said, "It is a tree." Another felt the ear and said, "It is a fan." Another person felt the trunk and said, "It is a water pipe." The last blind man felt the tail and said, "It is a rope." We could say that the blind men's approach smacked of reductionism. Were we to put all the animal's parts together, we could conclude that the animal is an elephant. *Holisim teaches that the whole is always greater than the sum of its parts.*

31. Other modern exponents of this are Gary Zukav, *The Dancing Wu Li Masters: An Overview of the New Physics* (New York: Bantam Books, 1979); David Bohm's theory of the holographic universe is found in his book entitled *Wholeness and the Implicate Order* (London: Routledge and Kegan Paul, 1980). According to Bohm (p. 151), time and space are no longer absolutes and all fragmentation is an illusory abstraction of the implicate order, which is whole. The manifestations of matter, space, and time are called the explicate or unfolded order, and are highlighted forms contained within the totality of the implicate order. Bohm's conclusion is that wholeness is what is real and that all "parts" of the universe interpenetrate one reality, which is indivisible and non-analyzable. In Bohm's physics, mind and matter are not separate substances but "different aspects of one whole and unbroken movement."

Whitehead did not view the building blocks of the universe as tiny particles that are fixed and permanent. The underlying substance of matter is not a substance at all but, instead, is a system of interrelated events. Nature is composed of endless numbers of entities (protons, electrons, neutrinos, and so on) that share relationships with other entities while growing in infinite ways. Each atom, molecule, cell, organ, organism, and community receives from the other and in turn influences other patterns of activity. Each entity takes into account other events and reacts to them. The relationship between God and the universe is one of immanence and interpenetration. God presents novel possibilities for each creation, thus enabling even the smallest to reach its potential toward harmony and integration. This phenomenon is witnessed on the subatomic level (electrons, molecules, and cells), and is also the case with human beings.

French scientist/theologian Pierre Teilhard de Chardin (1881–1955) also argued for an organic view of the universe. He was profoundly influenced by Henri Bergson (1859–1941), who spoke of God as the driving force (*élan vital*) behind the evolutionary process. Teilhard taught that *there exists a degree of consciousness that is present at every level of reality.* The organization of matter becomes increasingly more complex, centered, and self-conscious with the appearance of humanity, which represents the first entity that has become conscious of itself. The cosmos is gradually evolving toward a profound mystical vision of God. This state is what Teilhard terms the Omega-point. He writes:

> All around us, right and left, in from and behind, above and below, we have only to get a little beyond the frontier of sensible appearances in order to see the divine welling up and showing through. But it is not only close to us, in front of us, that the divine presence has revealed itself. It has sprung up universally, and we find ourselves so surrounded and transfixed by it, that there is no room left to fall down and adore it, even within ourselves.
>
> By means of all created things, without exception, the divine assails us, penetrates us, and molds us. We imagined it as distant and inaccessible, whereas in fact, we live steeped in its burning layers. *In eo vivimus.* As Jacob said, awakening from his dream, the world, the palpable world, *which we were wont to treat with the boredom and disrespect with which we habitually regard places with no sacred association, for us, is in truth a holy place, and we did not know it. . . .*[32] (Emphasis added.)

In process theology, God is not only the "Ground of Being" as Tillich conceived, but also, as Charles Hartshorne describes, "the supreme reality is supreme creative *becoming, forever enriching itself.*"[33] There was a time when the sacred was regarded as a kind of transcendental wizardry that imposed itself

32. Pierre Teilhard de Chardin, *The Divine Milieu: An Essay on the Interior Life* (New York: Harper and Row, 1968), p. 112.

33. Charles Hartshorne, *Natural Theology* (La Salle, IL: Open Court, 1967), p. 104.

onto the world—*abracadabra!* Today, we can see its real nature—which is to give life from within through immanence, to be a constitutive part of all things, *yet never ceasing to be transcendent.*


### The God who Beckons

Jewish tradition teaches that the entire creative process emanates out of God's ceaseless love and goodness (*H'Mihadash b'tuvo b'kol yom tamid m'aasay berashit*).[34] Each moment of creation is a free, selfless act of love and compassion. Life is a continuous series of moments in which God is always present, luring us toward the unrealized possibilities that each moment presents. This call toward the fulfillment of the best possibility is where God's living Presence can be found. God speaks and the world responds (Psalms 33:9).

In every moment experienced by every entity, God is active and present.[35] God addresses each entity not as an it, but as a You, urging each entity to live according to its unique God-given potential. God's own activity (so-to-speak) in the world may be explained in the same context as other actualities and their relations. Human beings are constantly in the state of becoming. Life is a process of filtering out the negative while developing the positive aspects of our personalities. In a twin sense human beings and God are on a mutual journey toward oneness and individuation. The Hasidic masters have taught that though God is *Yachid* (Unique), He is not yet *Echud* (One). God's oneness will be apparent only when humanity accepts the yoke of Heaven. The Kabbalists dramatized this evolutionary process through a prayer calling upon God to unite His fractured Name in the world. Each *mitzvah* if performed with proper *kavanna* (intention) restores God's oneness in the world. This idea, though it may sound radical, has its antecedent in the commentary of Rashi (1040–1105) to the Shema prayer:

> *Shema Yisrael, Ado-noy Elo-hanu, Ado-noy Echud.*
> Listen Israel! The Lord is our God, the Lord is One.
> (Deuteronomy 6:4)

Rashi comments:

> The Lord who is now our God and not the God of other peoples of the world will at some future time be the One (sole) God, as it is said (Zephaniah 3:9), "*At that time I will change the speech of the peoples to a pure speech,* that all of them may call on the name of the LORD and serve him with one accord, . . ." and it is

---

34. Morning liturgy.

35. Cf. Shneur Zalman's *Tanya,* part 2, *Shaar Yichud HaYichud Veemeunah; Hayim* of Volozin's famous tract *Nefesh HaHayim,* chapter 2; and Nachmanides' commentary on Genesis 2:17.

furthermore written (Zechariah 14:9), *"And the* Lord *will become king over all the earth; on that day the* Lord *will be one and his name one."*[36]

God's love is the power that calls out and persuades each aspect of creation toward its best possible existence. Life is a continuous succession of moments in which God summons us to come forward and fulfill the best possibility that lies in the moment. Though we may not always respond (*hinenee*), we feel the pull toward the action God desires. This idea may help us discern the cryptic passage, found in the Talmud, in which God is portrayed as praying. Many students of the Talmud have long wondered: Why should an all-powerful God want to pray? What could God possibly pray for? Yet, as the talmudic sages have pointed out long ago, *God's prayer is a beckoning for humanity to embody and corporealize Divine compassion in the world.*[37]

Whenever we encounter a person, a family, or community that is in need of

---

36. The commentaries to Rashi wonder: Why did Rashi cite both verses when one verse would have sufficed? I would suggest an alternative interpretation. The Hebrew word *safah berurah*—"pure speech," cited in Zephaniah 3:9—denotes *purification of speech*. The journey toward God's oneness involves humanity's learning to purify its concept of God. Throughout history, many terrible deeds were perpetrated in the name of God. The second verse from Zechariah, 14:9 speaks of the end-time, after humanity will have purged its speech: on that day God shall become the sole God of the entire world. Therefore, Rashi cited the second verse from Zechariah 14:9 to indicate that God's oneness must become a historical reality in this world. (Eliahu Mizrachi and Shemuel Gelberd's commentaries.) In *Hilchot Melacheem* 11:4, Maimonides states that Christianity and Islam have a vital role to play in the purificiation of humanity's speech concerning God.

The kabbalists composed a special prayer to be recited before the performance of every *mitzvah* (precept): "For the sake of the unification of the Holy One, blessed be He, and His *Shechina*, behold I perform this *mitzvah* in fear and love, love and fear, through that Hidden and Concealed One, in the name of all Israel, and in order to give satisfaction to my Creator and Maker in order to raise the *Shechina* from the dust." It is important to note that the unification of God's name requires the blending of the masculine and the feminine qualities of Divinity. This earthly world is often called *Alma D'Paruda*—the world of Separation. Each *mitzvah* is designed to help restore God's Presence and unity in the world. Habad hasidic thought has always interpreted God's *Achdut* (oneness) as pertaining to *gilluyim* (revelation), and revelation is always tailored according to the limitations of the receiver. (See *Derech Mitzvotechar, Mmamr Achdut HaShem* and *Sefer Mamareem Kuntraseem Ma'mar Kol HaMaricheen B'Echud.*)

37. See *Eitz Yosef* and the *Hiddushei HaRashaba* in *Sefer Ein Yaakov*. According to the *Eitz Yaakov*, the notion that God prays has its basis in the Scriptures—for example, Deuteronomy 10:12: "So now, O Israel, what does the Lord your God *request (Shoale)* of you? Only to fear the Lord your God, to walk in all his ways, to love him, to serve the Lord your God with all your heart and with all your soul." Likewise in Micah 6:8 we find, "He has told you, O mortal, what is good; and what does the Lord *request (doresh)* of you but to do justice, and to love kindness, and to walk humbly with your God?"

R. Johanan says in the name of R. Jose: How do we know that the Holy One, blessed be He, says prayers? Because it says: *I will bring them also to my holy mountain of Jerusalem and make them full of joy within my House of Prayer.* It is not said, *'their prayer'*, but *'my prayer'*; This teaches you that the Holy One, blessed be He, says prayers. What does He pray? R. Zutra

help (as we see in many parts of our nation and world), God's love summons us to respond. In another Midrash,[38] God is depicted as longing for the prayers of Israel. Just as we yearn for God's nearness, so too does the Holy One desire our closeness. According to Shneur Zalman of Liadi, prayer is the time when God awakens the hidden love that yearns to come alive.

As Creator, and the Source of our being, God is always bringing our existence out of the abyss of nothingness (*yesh mayin*) into a new state of being and becoming. God's love and compassion is biocentric and embraces the universe in its totality. God's power is not all-powerful in the simplistic sense, nor is it coercive in achieving this end; rather, it is all-relational in His capacity to relate to the world—even suffer with it as well. God's love can initiate new beginnings and possibilities *ex nihilo* to a suffering people. God is always present with His people. In the Exodus narrative, God instructs Moses to tell the Israelites, "I will always be present as I will always be present" (*Eheyeh asher Ehehyeh*). Moses' announcement to the slaves contained a message of hope.[39] If human beings suffer, then the *Shechinah* suffers too, for we are a part of God's own life. Though the *Shechinah* freely embraces suffering, She is not overwhelmed or defeated by it. The *Shechinah* beckons us to redeem Her suffering through acts of compassion and the practice of justice.

Traces of Whitehead's, Teilhard's, and Hartshorne's ideas can be found in passages of the Talmud, Midrash, and Kabbalah dealing with the imagery of the *Shechinah*—God's feminine persona. The *Shechinah* represents a bold personification of God's participating Presence in the world. Even when the wicked of the world suffer, God's *Shechinah* identifies with the pain of Her errant children.

> *My head is heavy,*
> *My arm is heavy.*
> And if God is so grieved
> over the blood of the wicked
> whose blood is shed,
> how much more so

---

b. Tobi said in the name of Rab: "May it be My will that My mercy may suppress My anger, and that My mercy may prevail over My [other] attributes, so that I may deal with My children in the attribute of mercy and, on their behalf, stop short of the limit of strict justice." (Soncino translation.)

According to the fifteenth-century savant *Avudaraham*, God prays that His compassion overtake His attribute of justice. *Rashaba* sees in this talmudic dictum a very profound message. The thirteen attributes of Divine mercy found in Exodus 34:6–7 represent God's prayer to us to embody His characteristics (steadfast love, faithfulness, and so on) in the world. See also Rabbi Yonatan Steef, *Hadashim Gam Yashaneem* (Brooklyn, NY: *Ohel Blima* Foundation, 1964), *Halacha* 153–154).

38. *Midrash Tehillim* 116:1.

39. God's own being affirms life and existence. He will not allow those forces that are destructive to reduce the Jewish people to nothing. (*Seforno's* commentary on the Torah)

> is the *Shechina* grieved over
> the blood of the righteous.[40]

### *The Divine Feminine—The Theology of Immanence*

The concept of an organic universe is better understood in light of the new feminist theological movement. The new changes and developments in feminist theology have liberated men and women from the shackles of a pure masculine anthropomorphic spirituality and expanded their theological horizons. Every metaphor of God paints its own unique picture of how the Divine interrelates with the world. The metaphor of God as Mother reveals relationships that in some ways go beyond the limitations of paternal imagery. The fact that the Bible uses such language suggests that the feminine engendering of God is not necessarily a dangerous or syncretistic concession to the ancient Canaanite religions. The many feminine nuances found in the Scriptures indicate how dynamic God-language can actually be. The ancient prophets were not averse to using bold feminine imagery to convey the nature of God's pathos and concern. Maternal representations of God have long been embedded in Hebrew language that have been until recently, largely ignored.

> Can a woman forget her nursing child,
> or show no compassion
> for the child of her womb?
> Even these may forget,
> yet I will not forget you.
> Isaiah 49:15

Similarly, in Isaiah 42:14, the prophet depicts God's biocentric passion for justice in feminine terms:

> For a long time
> I have held my peace,
> I have kept still
> and restrained myself;
> now I will cry out
> like a woman in labor,
> I will gasp and pant.

The image of God acting as a mother giving birth to her child portrays a God who is present alongside those people who are trying to midwife a new world

---

40. *Mishnah Sanhedrin* 6:5.

where human degradation, apathy and suffering no longer exist. This organic depiction of God does not portray the Divine reality as being extrinsic or unaffected by the harsh presence of evil that is incarnated by malevolent people. The Talmud and the Midrash both describe the unfolding of the Messianic Redemption as the *Hevlay HaMashiach*—the birthpangs of the Messiah. According to the Talmud, the Messiah was born on the day of *Tisha B' Av*, the Ninth of Av for the number nine symbolizes birth and new life.

One of the most popular and intimate rabbinic names for God is *Rachamana*— The Merciful One. The Hebrew word for "compassion," *rahammem*, comes from the Hebrew word *rechem*—womb. God's compassion and mercy are not extrinsic to us, for we come from God's womb (so to speak). The womb is the place where all life is mysteriously conceived, carried and born. Later talmudic and midrashic depictions of the Sacred bring to consciousness what the Hebrew language has long unconsciously suggested—God creating the world out of Her own Self.

One of the oldest kabbalistic teachings is the radical belief that the entire creation forms God's very own "mystical body." The relationship of God and the world is thus organically interrelated. All this suggests a profound view that sees God's Presence as wholly inseparable from the world. It was later in the *Kabbalah* (and subsequently in Hassidut) that the creation of the physical and spiritual cosmos occurs through process of the *Tzimtzum*—Divine contractions. These contractions resemble the contractions and movements a mother has, culminating in the birthing process of a human being. The bond between mother and child continues beyond pregnancy. As the child grows, so, too, does the mother's love. As a spiritual metaphor for the divine, the mother/child imagery represents both interdependence and relatedness.

Isaiah's imagery of God as the nursing mother poignantly describes the organic nature of God's love for us. Just as the baby needs the mother for nurture, so too does the mother yearn to provide nurture for the suckling.[41] If the mother does not nurse the child, her body feels intense pain. Such imagery reveals an organic view of the universe where we as creation are a part of God's body (*kibyachol*). One of the most important maternal names of God, *Shaddai* is related to the Hebrew word for breasts (*shadayeem*) and field (*sadeh*). Both nuances signify sustenance and nurture. In Hosea we find:

> I myself taught Ephraim to walk,
> I myself took them up in my arms;
>> but they did not know that
>> it was I who was caring for them,
>> that I was leading them with human ties,

---

41. The Talmud states in tracate *Pesachim* 122a, "more than the calf wishes to suck does the cow desire to suckle."

with bands of love.
I was to them like those
who lift infants to their cheeks.
I bent down to nurse them.

Hosea 11:3–4

One of the most poignant verses in the Book of Isaiah reads:

For the mountains may depart
and the hills be removed,
*but my steadfast love*
*shall not depart from you,*
and my covenant of peace
shall not be removed,
says the LORD,
Who has compassion on you.

Isaiah 54:10

Earlier in this book, I cited the view of Arthur Green, who argued that the pastoral metaphors of Psalm 23 depict a God who is "out there" apart from the world,[42] and therefore is "dualistic." This view of the shepherd metaphor is sadly myopic. The very notion of dualism is not indigenous to Judaism *per se*; it is the legacy of the Greek philosophical tradition that posits a God that is apathetic to human suffering and degradation. Ever since the time of Aristotle, there have been continuous attempts to portray God as an Outside Prime Mover who stands apart from the processes of the universe. The biblical theological view of God suggests the very opposite paradigm of reality: God's transcendence is inextricably linked to God's relatedness to the world. *That is why the Psalmist exclaimed, "The Lord"* (transcendence) *"is my Shepherd"* (immanence and relatedness)—the Lord who created heaven and earth also shepherded and liberated an oppressed people out of bondage.

The imagery of Psalm 23 is compatible with a *relational* model of theology. God leads, directs, and is present with the flock even in times of danger and darkness, providing comfort and strength to those in need. Furthermore, God's life is never apart from our own (*For You are with me*). God's Presence is

---

42. This view is not original and has already been argued by many modern thinkers, including D. T. Suzuki, Joseph Campbell, Fritjof Capra, Gary Zukav, and Robert Tarnas, just to mention a few. All these thinkers portrayed the God of the Jewish and the Christian tradition as "the ruler who directs the world from above." Biblical spirituality has often been unfairly compared to Eastern mysticism and erroneously mislabeled "dualistic." Each has argued that such a "Western" notion about God must be replaced by the Eastern religious tradition that portrays God as the "principle that controls everything from within." It is questionable whether the reduction of God to an abstract "principle that controls everything from within" is an improvement on the personalism of God in the Bible.

inclusive and embraces all our experiences in the world. God follows creation with goodness and kindness, and human existence is an inseparable part of God's eternal life. The good shepherd must work with the instincts of the sheep and cannot force the flock to go where it does not want to go. As the supreme Shepherd, God works with our own unique instincts. He can lead, but it is up to us to respond and follow God's calling. God's power never violates human initiative and freedom.

It makes all the difference in the world how we look at ourselves in relation to God and the universe. The metaphors we use to describe our relationship with God exert a great influence on how we see ourselves and experience the world. The new physics suggests that the way to transcendence is to go beyond the boundaries of the ego, which sees the self as apart from God and the world. In an organic universe, to relate to any aspect of God's creation is to relate to the whole. This world is the place in which God is encountered and experienced. As the embodiment of persuasive and relational power, God's Presence beckons and prays for humanity to let compassion into the world. God's compassion (*rachmanut*) and love for the world are organically related, as the fetus is related to the womb. The more we see God as inseparable from the world, the more loving we will be in our own intimate relationships. The more distant we feel toward God, the more estranged we are from one another. All interpersonal relationships are profoundly shaped and influenced by the God-images we carry. Our relationship with the Transcendent is also a template for how we interact with other persons and the world.

### Healing Our Wounded Images of God

The immense suffering witnessed especially in this century alone has made it exceedingly difficult for many to think of the experience of God in personal or loving terms (for example, Shepherd). The pages of Jewish history have been written with the blood of its people. The tragedies of Jewish history over the millennia have produced a God-image that is wrathful, exacting, and punitive.[43] Our experiences shape the kind of images we have of God. The metaphors we use to describe God are of serious concern. They may inspire relatedness and love of

---

43. In the medieval period, Judah HaLevi and Maimonides both saw *galut* (exile) as a time when God's mercy has withdrawn, or, in the words of Maimonides, "they [the Jewish people] were left to chance" (*Guide to the Perplexed*, 3:51). Maimonides depicts accurately the feelings of a people that has been raped, persecuted, and battered; it was only natural for people to feel forsaken, since the historical realities did not reveal a God that was present in their shattered lives. Jews have long suffered from "battered people syndrome" and exhibit the same qualities as a battered wife.

God, or they may destroy or cripple a life of faith. The metaphors we use to depict our relationship with God are of crucial importance.

Rabbi David Blumenthal, in his recent book *Facing the Abusing God*,[44] describes how abusiveness is one of the fundamental attributes of the Divine personality. Not only has the shepherd image been discarded by Blumenthal and many modern Jews, but the dangerous image of God as an "abuser" has taken its place in light of the Holocaust experiences and centuries of continuous Christian and Muslim oppression. Indeed, Blumenthal has explicitly stated what many Jews have long suspected about their God but were afraid to admit candidly — God is abusive. Blumenthal's theology strikes a visceral note with many voices of the modern Jewish experience. Unfortunately, his book characterizes the severity of how dysfunctional and destructive God-images can be when God is portrayed as the Abuser Supreme.

The "wrath of God" theology, though ancient, is still very much alive regardless of religious ideation. After World War II, the rebbe of Satmere (St. Mary, Hungary), Yoel Titlebaum (1888–1979), was convinced that the Holocaust occurred because the Jews adopted Zionism instead of the Messiah; by insisting on a secular redemption, Israel became "prey" to their Nazi tormentors.[45] Titlebaum's reasoning is simple and clear. If Jews suffer, it is because of their sinful ways and attitudes. This idea finds expression in the Bible and especially in daily liturgy:[46]

> On account of our sins
> we were exiled from our land,
> and far removed from our soil.[47]

Rabbi Mordechai Gifter, another leading right-wing Orthodox thinker, has argued that the Holocaust should "become a source of inspiration and encouragement for us. We are assured that we do have a Father in heaven who cares for us and is concerned enough with our spiritual status to demonstrate His disfavor."[48] Though many of the Orthodox and hasidic Jews portrayed great courage in affirming their faith during the Holocaust, there were those who saw

---

44. David Blumenthal, *Facing the Abusing God* (Louisville, KY: Westminster/John Knox Press, 1993).

45. A clear account of this point of view is contained in Rabbis Yoel Schwartz and Yitzchak Goldstein, *Shoah* (Jerusalem: ArtScroll, 1990), pp. 127–141.

46. The Rosh Hashanah and Yom Kippur liturgy is replete with hundreds of metaphors depicting God's anger (or potential anger) toward his people. One congregant of mine, a young woman suffering from anorexia, was convinced, after reading the Yom Kippur liturgy, that God was "out to punish her."

47. Musaph Service in the Siddur.

48. Nisson Wolpin, *A Path through the Ashes* (Brooklyn, NY: Messorah, 1986), p. 59.

the Holocaust as a punishment for not observing Torah study and *mitzvot* (precepts). Consider Rabbi Mordechai Gifter's quotation from the Telshe Rav (rabbi):

> At the time when the Nazis took the Telshe community to their intended slaughter at the lake nearby, the Telshe Rav said in a *drasha* (homiletic commentary): "If we will be scrupulous in *kashrus*, in *Shabbos*, in *taharos hamishpacha* (laws of family purity), the enemy will have no dominion over us." And from that day on plans were changed; they were taken away from Telz and were confined in a ghetto. The entire community suffered no harm until the first breach in *kashrus* (kosher observance).[49]

Here is a personal anecdote to illustrate. Once at a Jewish singles event I attended at Congregation Beth Jacob in Beverly Hills, California, I heard a rabbi from the Jewish Learning Exchange speak about God and the Holocaust. One person asked the rabbi about something he had heard from an Orthodox rabbi:

> I heard that the reason the Holocaust occurred was that married Jewish women failed to cover their hair, and the Jews were consequently punished for that infraction. Is that really true? The rabbi thought for a moment and answered, "You can't say that is true, yet you can't say that it isn't true either!"

Most of the Orthodox Jewish singles present did not find anything objectionable in this particular theological view. Those who did find the answer offensive were ignored and silenced by the speaker. The belief in a retributional theology continues to be popular in many of the right-wing non-hasidic yeshivas in America and abroad. Moreover, this is not only an Orthodox problem; many "secular" Jews also share a similar viewpoint. Many nonobservant Jews have accepted a fearful image of a God who is out to "get them" if they fail to attend Rosh Hashanah services or fast on Yom Kippur! Across all religious denominations, whenever tragedy strikes a person or a family, a common response is, *"Why pick on me, God?"* or, *"What did I do wrong to deserve this?"* Statistics have shown that religious victims of domestic violence often feel that God is punishing them through their husbands for some past sin. Rape victims are often made to believe (especially in court cases) that they did something to lure the offender into attacking them. This attitude is even reflected in the etymology of the English word *pain*, which comes from the Greek word *poine*, meaning "penalty." In other words, if there is pain, then it must serve as a penalty for doing a misdeed.

It is no wonder that so many Jews across all denominations find it hard to

---

49. Ibid., p. 62.

relate to such a vindictive image of God. The God of retribution may inspire fear but cannot inspire a sense of security and healthy relatedness. Consider what Michael Shevack and Rabbi Jack Bemporad cleverly dubbed this theological view of God: the *"Marquis de God."*

> Wanted: Dominant deity for submissive person. Must be into pain and bondage. Willing to inflict human suffering in pursuit of satisfaction. Humiliation technique a plus. Sense of humor not required. Inquire P.O. Box G.O.D. . . .
>
> Get out the whips, the chains, the earthquakes, the pestilence. It's time for some good old-fashioned fun with a good old-fashioned god. Yes, this is the proverbial god of wrath. The Marquis de God, Ready to show you how much he cares by punishing you.
>
> For the Marquis de God is simply a god who hates. This is a deity who despises sins and sinners with such a passion that he'll murder in order to exterminate them.
>
> He forces his noblest creation to dance like a trained poodle on the brink of annihilation.[50]

According to Martin Buber, one of the great spiritual challenges of our time is to purge our faith of all imagery that portrays the Divine as either vindictive or abusive. In his short but insightful autobiographical book *Meetings*, Buber described a meeting he had with a very pious, learned, and observant Jew about the biblical story of King Saul and the war of genocide waged against Israel's ancient enemy, Amalek. After Saul captured King Agag of Amalek, Saul did not kill him. The prophet Samuel was enraged and personally hacked Agag to death. Afterward, Samuel told Saul to abdicate the throne. Buber told the man that, as a child, he had always found this story horrifying. Buber recounts:

> I told him how already at that time it horrified me to read or to remember how the heathen king went to the prophet with the words on his lips, "Surely the bitterness of death is past," and was hewn to pieces by him. I said to my partner: "I have never been able to believe that this is a message of God. I do not believe it."
>
> With wrinkled forehead and contracted brows, the man sat opposite me and his glance flamed into my eyes. He remained silent, began to speak, became silent again. "So?" he broke forth at last, "so? You do not believe it?" "No," I answered, "I do not believe it." "So? so?" he repeated almost threateningly. "You do not believe it?" And once again: "No."
>
> "What. What."—he thrust the words before him one after the other—"what do you believe then?" "I believe," without reflecting, "that Samuel has misunderstood God." And he, again slowly, but more softly than before: "So? You believe that?" and I: "Yes." Then we were both silent. But now something happened the like of which I have rarely seen before or since in this my long life. The angry countenance

50. Michael Shevack and Jack Bemporad, *Stupid Ways, Smart Ways to Think about God* (Liguori, MO: Triumph Books, 1993), p. 18.

opposite me became transformed as if a hand had passed over it soothing it. It lightened, cleared, was now turned toward me bright and clear. "Well," said the man with a positively gentle tender clarity, "I think so too." And again we became silent, for a good while.[51]

Buber, at the end of this anecdote, mentioned how people often confuse the words of God with the words of man. To speak of God as "abusive" is to speak of a man-made caricature of God. Buber was well aware of the power such images have over people in the formation of their own personal relationships.

Many psychological studies dealing with the pathology of religion have confirmed this. The seminal research of psychiatrist Ann-Maria Rizzuto, who argues (as Freud did) that images of God tend to be patterned after the image of the parents; children who have had strongly negative experiences with their parents (such as sexual abuse) tend to develop negative concepts of God's personality. Those children who have the lowest image of their parents reported having the lowest image of God.[52] According to Rizzuto, by the time a child is introduced to the house of God, s/he brings an image that is very difficult to reshape. Parents and spiritual leaders bear a great responsibility for the formation of a child's image of God. Not by words, but by deeds is how the child learns to cultivate a positive image of God.

Misrepresentations of God are a major reason why so many people lose faith in a personal God. When the God image becomes portrayed as anti-life, the symbolic message sent to society is devastating. Jews know this all too well. History is replete with diabolical images of God that have been a continuous source of human suffering in the world, as witnessed by the rising wave of religious terrorism in our time.

---

51. Martin Buber, *Meetings* (Lasalle, IL: Open Court, 1973), pp. 52–53.

52. Psychiatrist Ana-Maria Rizzuto has written extensively on this subject in her seminal, *The Birth of the Living God* (Chicago: University of Chicago Press, 1979). The type of image each individual develops comes from a medley of factors (parents, family, siblings, and other significant people) or circumstances (for example, a lightning storm or an earthquake). Prevailing conditions will alter a person's representation of God at any given time. Children project their internal parent images (both good and bad) onto their God-concept. If the child is sexually abused by the father, then the image of God as Father may have a negative meaning for the child. Rizzuto writes: "Reshaping, rethinking, and endless rumination, fantasies and defensive maneuvers, will come to help the child in his difficult task. This second birth of God may decide the conscious religious future of the child. This is the critical moment for those interested in cathechesis. If they want to understand the progress of an individual child, they must have some knowledge of the private God the child brings with him. No child arrives at the 'house of God' without his pet God under his arm," (Ibid., p. 8). See also Edward Stein, *Guilt: Theory and Therapy* (Philadelphia: Westminster Press, 1968), p. 139, who writes: ". . . *God is projected father (psychologically), and . . . this basis of trust is the sustaining, binding meaning that makes religion crucial to men. . . . It is perfectly possible that the way in which the Ground of Being makes himself known, revealed himself, was by making man biologically dependent upon his human parents and prone to such projections.*" (Emphasis added.)

Images of God that are anti-life inspire violent behavior and encourage human beings to perform wanton acts of destruction. Diabolical images of God also warp and destroy faith. We shall elaborate on this point later on when we examine the nature and primary source of Job's suffering. Modern theologians, spiritual teachers, and leaders must find a way to heal the dysfunctional and destructive images of God that inhabit all traditional religious orthodoxies today. In light of this, the war against idolatry still has special significance, for we must purge our understanding and faith on any image that falsifies how the Divine and the world are interrelated.

Here is the paradox of God's love as life force: the most profound wellspring of compassion is capable of transforming itself into a diabolical death force, capable of annihilating all life. Faith, the sweetest refuge and consolation, may harden, by a perverse miracle, into a sword—or a club or a torch or an assault rifle or even a nuclear bomb. Religious hatreds tend to be merciless, unyielding, undying, and absolute, and are seemingly capable of spontaneous generation.

Our images of God must inspire compassion, tenderness, concern, and hopefulness. Our images of God must engender a love for life and an avoidance of all wanton acts, words, and thoughts of destructiveness. Belief in God must instill in us a sense of dignity and respect for all of God's creation, and fill us with an inner sense of peacefulness. Healthy images of God must awaken our capacity to wonder and stimulate our ability to see beauty and goodness in ourselves as well as in others. It is for this reason that an examination of the positive depictions of God has profound implications for how the covenantal community translates faith into action.

# 6

# SPEAKING ABOUT GOD—
# REIMAGINING RELIGIOUS LANGUAGE

*If oxen and horses and lions had hands and could paint and sculpt with them like humans, then the horses would paint horselike, the oxen oxlike figures of the gods and would form such bodies as each species itself inhabited. The Ethiopians maintain that their gods have snub noses and are black; the Thracians, that their gods are blue-eyed and red-haired. Mortals believe that gods are born. But God did not become and is eternal.*

Xenophanes

*And gradually the philosophic God comes to permeate Jewish consciousness. The real God whom Adam feared and loved fades, to be replaced by a philosophical principle. The real estrangement between God and man has begun.*[1] (Emphasis added.)

Michael Wyschogrod

*The greatest impediment to the human spirit, on reaching maturity, results from the fact that the conception of God is crystallized among people in a particular form, going back to childish habit and imagination. This is an aspect of making a graven image or a likeness of God, against which we must always beware, particularly in an epoch of greater intellectual enlightenment.*[2]

Abraham Isaac Kook

---

1. Michael Wyschogrod, *The Body of Faith* (San Francisco: Harper and Row, 1983), p. 83.
2. *Abraham Isaac Kook*, trans. Ben Zion Bokser (New York: Paulist Press, 1978), pp. 262–263.

The problems many Jews have with the shepherd metaphor really underscores a far deeper problem—the modern Jew often does not experience God as a Personal Presence. There is a widespread attitude that regards all personal depictions of the Divine as *anthropomorphic depictions of God*. By the term "anthropomorphic," I mean any depiction of God that is said to resemble human beings.[3] Contemporary Jewry is reticent to use any kind of theological language that would suggest that God resembles human beings.[4] Such God-talk is generally associated with Christianity and not Judaism, as was mentioned earlier. Ever since the synthesis of Greek and Jewish thought, there has been a repeated emphasis on God's holiness and transcendence. Greek thought attempted to destroy all metaphors, depicting God's humanity and pathos, that implied a relationship with humanity.[5] In some ways, then, anthropomorphic presentations of God stress the theomorphic (in the form or image of *Theos*, "God") nature of our souls and their resemblance to God. This thought is well stated by Thorleif Boman, in his seminal study *Hebrew Thought Compared with Greek*, who wrote:

> Later generations, having failed to grasp the profound meaning of 'anthropomorphisms' have taken umbrage at their mere humanness, and have preferred more neutral means of revelation like word, spirit, and wisdom. The 'anthropomorphisms,' because of their profound descriptive power, continue to stand as peerless

---

3. Abraham Heschel writes: "We ascribe to Him not a psychic but a spiritual characteristic, not an emotional but a moral attitude. Those who refuse to ascribe a transitive concern to God are unknowingly compelled to conceive His existence, if it should mean anything at all, after the analogy of physical being and to think of Him in terms of 'physiomorphism.' " *Man Is Not Alone* (New York: Farrar, Straus and Giroux, 1951, reprinted 1990), p. 144.

4. Hermann Cohen comments on the verse "You shalt make no graven images" (Exodus 20:2–5): The absolute distinction between God and other essences vitiates at the ouset all attempts to portray God's image or likeness. Every portrayal of God appeals to the senses; it thus contradicts His uniqueness and only succeeds in removing Him from us. *"The it is the mark of the God of truth that He does not lend Himself to any likeness or image whatsoever"* (emphasis added); quoted from Natan Rotenstreich, *Jewish Philosophy in Modern Times—From Mendelssohn to Rosenzweig* (New York: Holt Rinehart Winston, 1968), p. 82. Part of Cohen's misunderstanding lies in his interpretation of idolatry. Idolatry was prohibited not because of the problems associated with images but because graven images allowed human worshipers to manipulate the deity for their own purposes, thus depriving God of His freedom. Cohen blurs the distinction between "portraying" and "defining." Scriptures abound with a plenitude of descriptions *portraying* God's Presence in the world. (For a view similar to Cohen's see Samson Raphael Hirsch's commentary on the above text.)

5. Despite the abhorrence in which the ancient Greek philosophers held anthropomorphisms, their philosophic writings often made use of anthropomorphisms in describing the nature of the soul, cosmos, God, and the universe. Aristotle's "Unmoved Mover" is one small example. The cosmos was still seen in broad anthropomorphic terms. For a sweeping critique of how anthropomorphisms have affected science and philosophy from ancient to modern times, see Stewart Elliot Guthrie, *Faces in the Clouds: A New Theory of Religion* (Oxford and New York: Oxford University Press, 1993), chapter 6.

expressions of the divine being; there is indeed, as P clearly understood, nothing in the sensible (not divine) world which comes so near divinity as man himself.[6]

## The Sensuous Language of Encounter

Despite the ban on images found in Exodus 20:2–5, the Hebrew Scriptures contains a wealth of metaphors that depict the anthropomorphic nature of God. Unlike the ancient Greek philosophers, the ancients of Judea did not perceive God as a philosophical construct, nor as an impersonal cosmic process, energy, force, or intelligence, and not as a sentimentalized ethical ideal, nor did they apologize for using human language in describing God. There was nothing epistemic or dogmatic about their faith. The Bible has no hesitation when it comes to using human language. When the ancient Psalmists gazed into the heavens, they did not behold an endless abyss of nothingness; they beheld a God whom they could audaciously and personally address as "You." All anthropomorphic imagery serves to convey God's Presence and closeness to the world, without which God could not be known. Martin Buber notes that in addition, anthropomorphic language reflects

> "our need to preserve the concrete quality evidenced in the encounter; *yet even need is not its true root: it is in the encounter itself that we are confronted with something compellingly anthropomorphic,* something demanding reciprocity, a primary Thou. This is true of those moments of our daily life in which we become aware of the reality that is absolutely independent of us, whether it be as power or as glory, no less than of the hours of great revelation of which only a halting record has been handed down to us.[7] (Emphasis added.)

The God of Israel is a "Living God" who loves and is literally in search of humanity: endowed with personality and sentience, transcendent (wholly Other), yet wholly immanent and related to the world—the supreme God of encounter. The God of Israel is a God worthy of emulation, a model for the community of faith. The Scripture's use of anthropomorphic language brings home the reality of God's Presence. The Scriptures bear witness to Divine–Human encounters that have moved people to speech. The psalmist felt a special intimacy with God and speaks of God belonging to him: "He is my Rock," "my Shepherd," "my Light," "my Husband," and so on. Biblical metaphors of God exemplify a familiarity and intimacy bearing witness to the personhood of God. Within the

---

6. Thorleif Boman, *Hebrew Thought Compared with Greek* (New York: Norton, 1954; reprinted 1970), p. 111.

7. Martin Buber, *Eclipse of God* (Atlantic Highlands, NJ: Humanities Press, 1952, reprinted 1988), pp. 14–15.

limits of human language, our ancestors expressed the inexpressible imaginatively and metaphorically.

The Scriptures describe the Presence of the Divine in tangible, humanlike terms. God was experienced not only with their minds *but also with their physical senses*. To the Israelites who crossed the Sea of Reeds, God appeared like a "mighty man of war" (Exodus 15:3). The Torah's depiction of the "glory of God," (*Kavod Adonai*),[8] was not a philosophical abstraction but just the opposite—an intensification and concentration of God's Presence. This phenomenon is what Rudolf Otto, in his classic work *The Idea of the Holy*, describes as the *numinous*. According to Otto, the numinous is best expressed through words like awe, terror, dread, mystery, mystical, fascination, astonishment, and wonderment.[9] An experience of the numinous leaves one in a state of humility. Thus, when Jerusalem was destroyed, God's numinous Presence (*Kavod*) was in a state of exile (*Shechina BeGalusa*). Yearning for return of the Divine Presence as the deer yearns for water in a parched land, the Psalmist experienced God not as an It but as the Eternal You. Martin Buber points out in *I and Thou*:

> Men have addressed their eternal You by many names. When they sang of what they had thus named, they still meant You: the first myths were hymns of praise. Then the names entered into the It-language; men felt impelled more and more to think of and to talk about the Eternal You as an It. But all names of God remained hallowed—because they had been used not only to *speak of* God but also speak *to Him*.[10] (Emphasis added.)

### The Contours of Mythic Reality

Whenever a close encounter with the numinous occurred, it was narrated in the language of myth. By the term *myth*, we do not mean a fictional account or ignorant notions, as is commonly assumed today. The contours of the mythic presents the world as an amalgam of existential meanings. Myth tries to answer the great questions humanity has asked since the beginning of time. *What does life mean? How do we all interrelate? What is the purpose of human existence?* Myth is a symbolic story that describes how human beings are related and integrated to the Godly presence that suffuses the universe. Myths also proclaim a truth and message about how human beings are to live in the world. Whereas

---

8. Cf. Exodus 24:16–17. "The *glory* of the LORD settled on Mount Sinai, and the cloud covered it for six days; on the seventh day he called to Moses out of the cloud. Now the appearance of the *glory* of the LORD was like a devouring fire on the top of the mountain in the sight of the people of Israel."

9. Rudolf Otto, *The Idea of the Holy*, first pub. 1923 (reprint Oxford and New York: Oxford University Press, 1958), pp. 5–12.

10. Martin Buber, *I and Thou*, trans. Walter Kaufmann (New York: Scribners, 1970), p. 123.

myth only points to the existence of a spiritual reality, rituals enable the community to embody its mythic essence. Throughout history, the faith community would participate in the unfolding of its mythical tradition by re-enacting its primal roots through ritual and sacred drama.

An excellent example is the panorama of rituals experienced at the Passover Seder. The Seder provides the framework by which the original Exodus is re-enacted, thus linking the present with the past and future. In the Passover Seder, for example, the rituals seek to integrate all the senses through the participants' partaking of various symbolic foods, clothes, and songs, all of which form a sacred play by which the mythic message is conveyed to a new generation. All religious rituals point to the presence of a mythic and spiritual reality.

Myth was never meant to explain empirical facts about the natural world but, instead, was intended to disclose the sacred meaning present within the natural observable universe. To the mythic person, reality is experienced as a living presence and process. According to Eliade, by entering the ritual, by retelling the sacred myth, by creatively reinterpreting the symbol, we can escape the ordinary "profane" world and enter the realm of sacred time. The symbol, the ritual, the myth reveals a sacred or cosmological reality that no other manifestation is capable of revealing.

Without symbols, myths, and rituals the human being is a fragmented being apart from the universe. In a broader sense, a symbol is never a mere pointer, unrelated to human behavior; it always aims to integrate meaning into human existence. By participating in the ritual, the symbol, the retelling and redramatization of the myth, we can belong to a realm that is hidden and transcendent. Mythic reality helps us regain a sense of belonging to the universe.

Myths, symbols, and rituals help us get in touch with the mystery of our innermost being. They enable us to transcend the narrow confines of the ego. Mythic reality possesses a special transpersonal quality that connects us with the deepest part of our souls and God. The absence of myths, rituals, and symbols reflects an impoverishment of our spiritual epicenter.

The early period of Greek philosophy attempted to correct the earlier mythic view of the world by introducing rational paradigms that could measure and explain worldly phenomena. The ancient Greeks taught that the universe was an ordered cosmos that could be rationally grasped by the human mind. The universe reflected a transcendental intelligence that could be seen in all things. The world existed as an object to be contemplated and understood.

According to Plato, the true structure of the universe is not revealed by the senses but by the power of reason. Knowledge is not derived not from the gods but is actively cultivated by the human intellect. The Greek consciousness taught that truth must be discovered through empirical and objective observation. All natural phenomena of the world draw their reality from impersonal and physical causes. In Plato's vision of the perfect society, the archaic poetic, artistic, mythical, and supernatural explanations had to be rejected. Greek philosophy went out of its way to discredit the mytho-poetic language that was in currency for thousands of years by introducing its own cognitive myth. Ironically, despite Plato's disdain of myth and poetry, his own theories about the pre-existence of the soul, women's roles, and the archetypal world of eternal forms, as well as his theory of numbers, and so on, were no less mythic (and poetic) in content and in substance than the old worldviews Plato tried to displace and correct.[11] Like other Greek philosophers, Plato, in effect, exchanged one mythic view of reality with another.

Plato's star pupil, Aristotle, went even further and called for an even greater degree of objectivity, less imagery and storytelling. Aristotle disregarded Plato's penchant for describing the transcendental reality in ethereal images. Knowledge had to be pursued in practical, objective, earthly terms. Aristotle introduced a *reified* view of the universe. Reification (derived from the Latin *res*, "thing") is the belief that reality must be understood substantively in terms of entities and objects rather than in terms of spirit. To Aristotle, myth and philosophy were polar opposites. This, I believe, is where Aristotle erred. Myths disclose something existential about the universe that cannot be expressed in scientific or logical reasoning. Myth is not necessarily the opposite of logic or philosophy, as Aristotle contended; it is just a different way of interpreting our place in the universe. Even scientific theories have their own mythic and existential underpinnings. Conversely, mythic reality has its own philosophical dimension. Paul Ricoeur is certainly correct in saying *it is in the interpretation of the myth that we come to understand its internal logic (logos).*[12] Myths like dreams, contain their own kind of intelligibility, which needs to be deciphered.[13]

We must remember that the Bible does not pretend to be a philosophical discourse about the nature of the cosmos. Halevi, Creacas and Pascal were correct—the God of Abraham *is not* the God of the philosophers. The biblical narratives about creation, the flood, the patriarchs, and the Exodus do not depict a God who is asensual or indifferent to the suffering of human beings and the world. Biblical language is richly mytho-poetic and intensely metaphoric. The Bible portrays the Divine Reality in subjective and relational metaphoric terms—for example, father/son, king/subject, shepherd/sheep, husband/wife,

---

11. The same may be said of Aristotle's concept of God as the Prime Mover or his principle of noncontradiction.

12. Ricoeur writes: "Every mythos involves a latent logos *which demands to be* exhibited. That is why there are no symbols without the beginning of interpretation; where one man dreams, prophesies, or poetizes, another rises up to interpret. Interpretation organically belongs to symbolic thought and its double meaning." (*Freud and Philosophy*, p. 19.)

13. T.B. *Brachot* 55b.

planter/vineyard, potter/earthenware, mother/fetus, and so on. Though some metaphors are more intimate than others, nearly all the biblical metaphors of God emphasize relatedness with His creation. The Bible concerns itself with the primal origins of our world and with the existential meanings of the living world; it is a *Sefer HaAdam*—a book that articulates how we are to relate to God and the world. Such relationships cannot be described in the cold, precise language of science, nor can they be conveyed in the obtuse formulas of a mathematician; they can best be expressed in the language of myths, symbols, poetry, and metaphors.

## The Metaphoric Imagination

When speaking *about* images and symbols, we use metaphors to give *verbal* representation of the images, pictures, and symbols that are latent in myths.[14] Like the symbol, the metaphor transfers meaning from one domain to another. Like the symbol, the metaphor does not lend itself to literal, statistical, or reductionist thinking.[15] The purpose of a metaphor is not merely informational; *it is the language of meaning.*

Metaphors tease[16] the imagination, arousing it from slumber. They are evocative and create tension.[17] Metaphors pulsate with movement and activity. The boundaries of the written word are transcended by metaphors. They serve as the bridges that link us with the realm of mystery. Metaphors create attention and propel human speech to new meaning while going beyond the ordinary boundaries of language. Metaphors give rise to new visions of reality that ordinary words would be incapable of portraying. Metaphoric speech makes accessible images and ideas that would otherwise be beyond linguistic grasp.

---

14. According to the 1993 edition of the *American Heritage Dictionary*, a metaphor denotes: "**1.** A figure of speech in which a word or phrase that designates one thing is applied to another in an implicit comparison, as in 'All the world's a stage.' (Shakespeare). **2.** One thing conceived as representing another; symbol [ME *methaphor* < OFr. *metaphore* < *metaphora* < Gr., transference, metaphor < *metaperein*, to transfer: *meta-* + *pherein*, to carry.]"

15. John Watson, founder of Behaviorism, shifted the focus of psychology from dealing with the inner processes to the external observation of human behavior. This approach dominated the psychological community until the 1960s. See Dr. Michael Samuels' excellent work, *Seeing with the Mind's Eye* (New York: Random House, 1975) for a history of imagery in civilization.

16. Marcus Jastrow notes in his *Sefer Mileem* that the Hebrew word for metaphor is *Miltzsa*. *Melitza* is derived from the same word that denotes laughter or teasing. It is also used to designate an enigma or interpretation, or anything that is obscure (*Gensenius' Hebrew–Chaldee Lexicon to the Old Testament*). Ricoeur points out metaphors have a "cunning distortion" that is much more subtle than ordinary analogic language (*Freud and Philosophy*, p. 17).

17. For an outstanding illustration of how biblical metaphors create tension, see Robert Alter, *The Art of Biblical Poetry* (New York: Basic Books, 1985), pp. 163–184.

Metaphors compel us to encounter the image. To fathom the metaphor's meaning, we must breathe its vitality into our very being. Spiritual metaphors in particular, as Paul Ricoeur suggests, give rise to thought processes that impart our knowledge of God.[18]

Augustine of Hippo (354–430 c.e.) correctly observed that one of the major reasons people have difficulty in understanding the figurative expressions of the Bible is that most people do not understand the subtle meaning of metaphors. A personal knowledge of the individual metaphor provides a far deeper appreciation of the reality it is alluding to. Metaphors provide a pictorial view of reality. Each metaphor tells a story and is not a mere adornment to the text. Augustine gives an example:

> Many, again, by reason of their ignorance of hyssop, not knowing the virtue it has in cleansing the lungs, nor the power it is said to have of piercing rocks with its roots, although it is a small and insignificant plant, cannot make out why it said, "Purge me with hyssop, and I shall be clean" (Psalms 51:7).
>
> Ignorance of numbers, too, prevents us from understanding things that are set down in Scripture in a figurative and mystical way.[19]

Thus, to Augustine, if the biblical metaphors seem foreign or obscure, it is because we have not yet grasped the content of their imagery. In addition, without the knowledge of the original Hebrew, the reader will never go beyond a facile understanding of the Holy Text. Augustine adds that the fact that the Bible's metaphors and euphemisms are ambiguous is not happenstance: the Bible is purposely ambiguous so that we may uncover its deeper meanings. The rabbis of the Midrash are in perfect agreement with Augustine on this point. The very purpose of midrashic interpretation (as its root-word *Doresh* "search out," suggests) is to uncover the meanings suggested by the different nuances suggested in the Hebrew language.

The ninth-century Jewish philosopher and biblical translator Saadia Gaon observed that all religious discourse is bound by the limitations of human speech and experience. Saadia observed that all human language (whether secular or religous), is inherently anthropomorphic. Saadia patiently instructed his readers:

> These and similar expressions show the tendency of language to broaden the meaning of words. Each of the above expressions covers a certain range of

---

18. Paul Ricoeur in his book *The Symbolism of Evil* (Boston: Beacon, 1967), pp. 347–357, notes: ". . . metaphor, far from being limited to a linguistic artifact, is characterized by its epistemological function of discovering new meanings. What is at stake is still knowing in process but considered in its nascent moment. In this sense, metaphor is a thought process before being a language process."

19. St. Augustine, *On Christian Doctrine*, II, chapter 16:23, published in the Great Books of the Western World, vol. 18, trans. J. F. Shaw (Chicago: Encyclopedia Britannica, 1952), p. 644.

meaning, and their allegorical meaning is established by their use in contexts in which *there is no reference to God*. We know that it is an essential feature of language to extend meaning of words, to use metaphors and images.[20] [21] (Emphasis added.)

The use of anthropomorphism goes far beyond the Bible and theology. The poetic imagination utilizes metaphors that describe the heavens as "speaking," or a storm as "raging" or a wall as "listening." From a modern perspective, Saadia's understanding of language is remarkably astute. Anthropomorphisms abound in every human field of endeavor, including art, literature, poetry, and even advertising (for example, the Chiquita Banana or the Spuds McKenzie dog).[22] Halachic language occasionally uses anthropomorphic[23] imagery, as do physics and philosophy.[24]

---

20. Saadia Gaon, *Book of Doctrines and Beliefs*, trans. Alexander Altmann, reprinted in *Three Jewish Philosophers* (New York: Harper and Row, 1965), pp. 87–90.

21. The outstanding tenth-century Jewish philosopher Bahya Ibn Pakuda had a sympathetic view of anthropomorphic expressions. Bahya understood that human beings require such language for relating to God; without them, we would have no way of relating to God. Bahya saw anthropomorphisms as a necessary step in humanity's spiritual evolution. In the spirit of Saadia, Bahya wrote:

> Necessity compels us to describe the Creator in corporeal terms that we might conceive in our souls the idea that the blessed Creator exists. Therefore the prophetic books express His nature in words drawn from the physical world which are near to man's intellect and his power of understanding. Were they to describe in a manner suitable to Him, i.e., by using only spiritual words and ideas, no one would understand either the words or the ideas. It would be impossible to worship the unknown for how can one serve that which is uncomprehended?
>
> Therefore, it was necessary for the words and ideas to be used in accordance with the listener's mental capacity so that, at first, the idea is comprehended in a corporeal sense through words that are drawn from the physical universe. Afterwards, we can increase his wisdom by encouraging him to grasp all that is figurative and symbolic until the true idea is more refined, elevated, and remote than one can possibly understand by virtue of its true nature. (Shaar HaYihud, chapter 10, trans. Moshe Hyamson (Jerusalem: Feldheim, 1963).

22. The current debates about artificial intelligence continue to raise difficult questions regarding the nature of human personality and consciousness. The character Data, from the television series *Star Trek, The Next Generation*, raises the old question: Are we only the sum of our parts (as reductionism advocates), or is being human a holistic phenomenon?

23. Inanimate objects in the *Halachah* are sometimes described as having human-like qualities. For example, the *Hallah* is covered when the *Kiddush* over wine is recited so as to "spare it from embarrassment"; it is customary to stand before the Torah as it is brought around the synagogue, as a sign of respect; the altar of God is said to "weep" whenever a husband and wife divorce. *T.B. Gittin* 90b.

24. Guthrie notes that, despite the Greek philosophical criticism of anthropomorphisms, *nearly every Greek philosopher utilized anthropomorphic language when describing the nature of the universe, the soul, and God.* According to Guthrie, anthropomorphisms represent a *perceptual strategy* of how humanity perceives itself in an uncertain world. If, for instance, we mistake a dark shape in the forest, it is better to assume it is a bear and not a boulder. Guthrie's innovative idea is

Though Saadia was critical of anthropomorphic language, he knew that the popular religious imagination could not subsist without it. Saadia knew that people need a functional language of faith to make the Presence of God more meaningful to worshipers. He recognized how the metaphor can awaken the poetic and emotional faculties of the human heart. Without a feeling language, any spiritual discourse about the Sacred would be impotent and meaningless, for the heart can not be aroused by prose alone. Saadia also added that ambiguity of language is paradoxically a wellspring for revelation and insight. The biblical authors purposely invite the reader to explore, decipher and interpret the words of the Sacred text. The hidden meanings of the biblical words lend themselves to a multiplicity of interpretations. Were we to insist on a precise language in Scriptures, if we were to eliminate metaphoric language, Saadia notes,

> . . . it would be a poor instrument of expression. It would not be able to convey even a fraction of what we think. Thus if we wanted to speak of God in exact language, we would have necessarily to refrain from describing Him as hearing, seeing, being merciful, desirous, so that the only activity we could assign to Him would be existence.

The use of anthropomorphic language is not a concession to the popular imagination, as some philosophers would have us believe. The prophetic imagination never uses the noetic language of logic or prose, *but instead employs the rhetoric of poetry and hyperbole.* We could even say that prophetic speech would be ineffective without it. Sensuous and symbolic, prophetic vision appeals to the receiver's imagination.[25] God's revelation grips the listener's attention, tantalizes the prophet's senses, and inspires dramatic speech. Walter Brueggemann adds an insight that dovetails with Saadia's shrewd remarks:

---

patterned after the famous wager of Pascal. If what we are observing truly resembles human behavior, then our use of anthropomorphic language is correct; if we are wrong, then what did we lose by employing anthropomorphisms? In a world in which scientific analysis fails or is severely limited, human beings consciously and unconsciously gravitate toward imagining the universe in the likeness of themselves (Guthrie, *Faces in the Clouds*, chapter 6).

25. Even Maimonides admits that the anthropomorphic imagery that the prophets encountered serves as a means (not as an end) by which God's message to the prophet becomes known. Similarly, Maimonides writes:

> All of these metaphors are meant to relate to human thought processes which can only grasp [spiritual ideas] through somatic imagery — this is because the Torah speaks in the parlance of human beings and therefore must be understood as metaphors. . . . Evidence of this concept [in Scripture] — One [prophet] says that he saw the Holy One, *clothed in snow white* (Daniel 7:9), while another [prophet] envisioned Him coming *in crimson stained garments from Batzra* (Isaiah 63:1). Moses, our teacher, envisaged Him at the Red Sea as a mighty man, waging war, and at Mount Sinai, he saw Him as the leader of a congregation wrapped in a tallit. All these are simply idioms of prophetic vision and imagery. (Maimonides, *Hilchot Yesodie HaTorah 1:9*).

By prose I refer to a world that is organized in settled formulae, so that even pastoral prayers and love letters sound like memos. By poetry, I do not mean rhyme, rhythm, or meter, but language that moves like Bob Gibson's fast ball, that jumps at the right moment, that breaks old worlds with surprise, abrasion, and pace.[26]

Often in the prophetic encounter, God presents the prophet with an image that conveys God's pathos with Israel (see Exodus 3:2, 25:8; Amos 8:1–3; Jeremiah 1:11–15). When the people hear the prophet, they hear and see God's Presence. The anguish of the prophet mirrors God's own anxiety and concern over the fate of His people. The prophet, in turn, transmits God's concern and pathos to the community through provocative images and symbols (see Zechariah 11:4–17).[27]

Occasionally, the prophet's personal life *becomes the very image and the metaphor of God's message to the people*—for example, the prophet Hosea was commanded to marry a whore (Hosea 1:2-9). The story of Jonah illustrates how the life of a stubborn prophet reflected the stubborn nature of the people he represented. The book of Jonah is replete with imagery and metaphors depicting God's own "stubborn" love and forgiveness. In a pedagogical sense, the prophet became a living embodiment of God's word. The prophet revealed God's humanlike character to the world.

## Anthropomorphisms—The Language of Humanity

In addition, anthropomorphisms portray the special bond between God and people and serve as models for the community of faith. God's humanity is the source of our own humanity. One of the most basic teachings of the Torah is that God *images, molds and fashions* humanity out of His own Being.[28] The hasidic masters have long noted that the term "image of God" is a way of mirroring God's Presence to the world. Image in this sense is not necessarily a noun, but may also be interpreted as a verb—a way of acting. Thus to *image God* is to sculpture out of our own being and nature a likeness of God. Since God's being cannot be fixed in any object or thing, we can only be depict our likeness by imitating God's ways and deeds.

---

26. Walter Brueggemann, *Finally Comes the Poet* (Minneapolis: Fortress, 1989), p. 3.

27. The great eighteenth-century Italian Kabbalist, Moshe Hayim Luzzato, writes, "In many cases, prophets are instructed to perform a certain act in conjunction with their prophecy. The prophet Jeremiah was thus instructed to wear a linen loincloth (Jeremiah 13:1), and, in another instance, to place a yoke around his neck (Jeremiah 13:27). The prophet Ezekiel was similarly told to trace a map of Jerusalem on a brick (Ezekiel 4:1)." (Moshe Hayim Luzzato, *Derech Hashem*, "Way of God," 3:4:7–9, trans. Aryeh Kaplan [New York: Feldheim, 1977], p. 221).

28. The word "image," according to the *American Heritage Dictionary*, is not always a noun, but may also be a verb, as in "to make or produce a likeness."

The Scriptures are full of such examples: When the eyes of God notice cruelty and corruption, they serve as a model for human beings to be observant of cruelty and corruption in all its subtle and obvious forms. The just society cannot close its eyes to injustice or brutality.[29] The ears of God that hear our prayers call upon us to give ear to the oppressed, the powerless, the marginalized, and anybody else who suffers. The human hand that gives charity becomes a conduit for the Divine hand that dispenses sustenance and life. Depictions of God's wrath instruct human beings to be angry when the poor or the defenseless are oppressed. The *Tenach* utilizes human language so that the covenantal community will image God in their lives. The prophet Isaiah emphasized how God's own humanity is to become the model and template of our own.

> Is not this the fast that I choose:
>     to loose the bonds of injustice,
>     to undo the thongs of the yoke,
>     to let the oppressed go free,
>     and to break every yoke?
> Is it not to share your bread
>     with the hungry,
> and bring the homeless poor
>     into your house;
> when you see the naked,
>     to cover them,
> and not to hide yourself
>     from your own kin?
>                                     Isaiah 58:6–7

As we move into the talmudic era, we discover that the Talmudists, like their biblical ancestors, also described God in very humanlike, relational terms: Feeder of all, Friend of the world, Searcher of hearts, Healer of all flesh, the One who knows all thoughts, the God of consolations, the Height of the world, Eye of the world, the Heart of Israel, the One who understands, the Rock of the world, Hearer of prayer, Peace, and so on.

The rabbinic teachers taught their students to discern God in all reality—that there is no place that is ever void of God's Presence. The rabbinic imagination has no less than ninety metaphors that describe God. Like their biblical ancestors, the ancient talmudic sages intuited a fundamental truth concerning the nature of all religious discourse: "The Torah speaks in the language of ordinary people."[30]

---

29. When God *went down* "to see" how the people of Sodom and Gomorrah were conducting themselves, this, according to the talmudic rabbis, serves to remind human judges that all legal decisions must be based on the hard evidence and not hearsay. (See Rashi and the Targum.)

30. The rabbis also understood the need for faith to be grasped in intelligible human terms. Thus

These rabbis stressed that God-talk has little meaning unless it can inspire, change, and improve human behavior. All human depictions of God function as models for human beings.

In summary, the biblical/midrashic use of anthropomorphisms introduced to an oppressive and cruel society a new, radical, politically subversive way of speaking about God and the earthly realization of the Heavenly Kingdom. These narratives depicted a God who was and is concerned with the wellbeing of His people. The God of Exodus challenges dictators and all who oppress human beings. God is a Liberator, Lawgiver, and Redeemer of widows and orphans who expects humankind to imitate the Heavenly path through observance of Torah. It was only centuries later that this rabbinic dictum came to describe *how people spoke about God as a philosophical abstraction*. In the next section we shall examine how and why this change took place.

---

we find: *Dibra Torah Clshon Adam*, "The Torah speaks in the language of human beings." There is a classic discussion (*Bava Metzia* 31a) between Rabbi Akiva and Rabbi Ishmael regarding how to interpret Hebrew phrases that are occasionally repeated. Rabbi Akiva interpreted the extra words as denoting some additional insight from the sacred text. Rabbi Ishmael argued that it is common for people to repeat words when trying to stress a particular point, and this is why "the Torah speaks in the language of people." Thus, according to Rabbi Ishmael, one should not deduce new *halachic* (legal) meanings from superfluities in the Torah. It would appear that the stages *did not* expound the *Dibra Torah Clashon Bnei Adam* principle philosophically.

According to Heschel in his seminal work on revelation, *Torah Min Hashamayeem B'Asplakalaria Shel HaDorot*, the controversy between Rabbi Akiva and Rabbi Ishmael goes beyond the sphere of determining *Halachah*. Their argument is relevant to the *Agaddah* as well. Rabbi Akiva saw the Torah in a platonic sense in which every word, every crown, represents a higher spiritual truth that is hidden in the text itself. Rabbi Ishmael maintained that the Torah needs to be understood according to the context of *peshat* (its simple meaning). According to Rabbi Ishmael, the words of the Torah serve to make the Divine more accessible to common people according to their own understanding. From Akiva's perspective every metaphor serves as a symbolic re-representation of a higher esoteric truth. Illustrative of this is Akiva's view regarding the Song of Songs, which, under his influence became an accepted part of the canon. According to Akiva, this book is more than just an erotic tale about two lovers; the Song of Songs represents the mystery of God's love of Israel. Though Akiva was not unaware of the simple meaning of the *peshat*, he argued that one needs always to go beyond the surface level of interpreting the Torah.

According to Arthur Marmostein, the issue of anthropomorphisms was a debated subject among the talmudic sages. Some were embarrassed by it (as reflected in the Targum), whereas others were not so intimidated by its use and sanctioned a more literal interpretation (Arthur Marmostein, *Old Rabbinic Doctrine of God*, vol. 2, Essays in Anthropomorphism [London: 1937]. Max *Kaddashin* argues that the rabbis were not concerned with such abstract philosophical subjects. For a recent exposition of the problem of anthropomorphism, see David Stern's brilliant *Parables in Midrash: Narrative and Exegesis in Rabbinic Literature* (Cambridge, MA: Harvard University Press, 1991), pp. 97–100. His thesis is similar to mine. Stern argues that philosophical thinking has dominated the discussion concerning anthropomorphisms. Seldom has the subject been explored as a way of defining the personality of God. All the parables in the Midrash and Talmud have one common aim: to define the nature of God's personality (and, I might add, *relational Presence*).

## Maimonides' Grammar of Faith

Until the rise of Islam, the issue of anthropomorphisms did not concern mainstream Jewish communities. Though the Septuagint, the Targum[31] and the philosophical teachings of Philo[32] all wrestled with the implications of anthropomorphic language, mainstream Judaism was not interested in pursuing this new philosophical enterprise. Instead, the ancient rabbis approached biblical metaphors not as theological abstractions, but as models for ethical human behavior.

A shift in attitude occurred in the early medieval period when the Church fathers[33] and Muslims accused Jews of being anthropomorphists.[34] Judaism was

---

31. Onkelos's Aramaic translation (better known as *Targum Onkelos*) was not always consistent in the way he treated anthropomorphic expressions, but he was usually careful to use language that divested God from any corporeality. Here are some examples: God did not *smell* the sweet smell of an offering, *but accepted it with pleasure*; on Passover night He did not *pass over* the Israelites, but *spared them*; He did not *go out* before His people but *leads them*; instead of God *hearing* or *seeing*, it is said that *it was revealed before Him*. Instead of *coming down* Mount Sinai (Exodus 19:20), *He revealed Himself at Mount Sinai*; the finger of God (Exodus 8:15) becomes *a blow before Him*. God's feet are *His glorious throne*. All actions that were considered inappropriate for God also became redefined in the Targums. Thus, when God meets Moses to slay him (Exodus 4:24), it is not God who wants to slay him but, instead, God's angel. Moreover, whenever the original Hebrew Bible speaks of a revelation of God as He is perceived by man, the Targum of Onkelos inserted the term *Shechina*; the Targum thus distinguishes between God's transcendence and His Immanence. *Shechina* thus becomes a reflection of God's Presence here on earth. Some scholars maintained that Onkelos may have had the simple worshiper in mind, that would account for some inconsistencies in his translation of anthropomorphisms. Perhaps Maimonides felt that Onkelos did not go far enough, for Onkelos never compromises the metaphors that describe God's love for His people.

32. Philo taught that the attributes of God could best be described in the negative—that is, one can say that God is not unjust but not that God is just. Philo observed, over a thousand years before Saadia and Maimonides, that all attributes serve to make God more intelligible to us but must not be understood as divine predicates. God's essence is unnameable and ineffable. God Himself is nameless; He cannot be defined. The root meaning of *define* is "to limit"; the more one attempts to define God, the more one limits Him. We may know of God's existence, but we cannot know of His essence. (See Philo, *The Changing of the Names*, chapters 11, 14.) Like Maimonides, Philo taught that all biblical anthropomorphisms describe nothing more than God's ability to act. God never pauses in His activity; He is ever active; *God's nature is to act:* "It is impious and false to conceive of God as in a state of 'complete inactivity.'" What, then, are the purposes of anthropomorphisms? According to Philo, anthropomorphisms are needed "for the sake of instruction and admonition, and not because God is really such by nature" (*The Unchangeableness of God*, chapters 53–56). Philo, like Maimonides, was critical of traditionalists who rejected philosophical interpretation: "they are like unthinking persons who have not examined themselves and are full of inconsistencies." (Cited in Harry Austryn Wolfson's classic study *Philo* [Cambridge, MA: Harvard University Press, 1947], vol. I, pp. 59–60.

33. For a modern Christian view advocating the belief in divine corporeality, see Terrance Fretheim, *The Suffering of God* (Philadelphia: Fortress, 1984), pp. 79–106. It must be stressed that Fretheim is attempting to use the biblical belief in corporeality in order to make belief in the incarnation of God more plausible for Christians. For an interesting and provocative work arguing the

regarded by many of its critics as an inferior brand of monotheism when compared to the monotheism of the Muslims and the Christians. When an anthropomorphic sect appeared in Muslim history, they were grouped with the Jews who believed in the anthropomorphisms of the Bible. When similar accusations were made against the Koran, the Muslim thinkers were quick to point out that these expressions were not to be interpreted literally but figuratively.[35]

The Muslim and Christian allegations against the Jewish communities were not completely ungrounded. Maimonides himself describes how widespread the belief in a corporeal God actually was throughout much of the Jewish world. Moreover, those who held this belief maintained that the Scriptures warranted such a view and that to suggest otherwise would be like denying the whole Torah. He writes:

> . . . people were led to think that He exists in the same way as a body. Likewise, it was made believable that He lives by presenting Him as animated. The crowd, you see, will not regard any object as existing beyond doubt if it is not physical.[36]

---

belief in Divine corporeality in rabbinic tradition, see Jacob Neusner, *The Foundation of the Theology of Judaism* (Northvale, NJ: Jason Aronson, 1991), pp. 137–170. It is a pity that Neusner did not take the historical role of the Targum into consideration when writing his otherwise fine book.

In the second century, the rabbis introduced the Aramaic translations (*Targumim*) to deliteralize biblical anthropomorphisms. The most famous of these translations is attributed to Onkelos/Aquilas, a nephew or relative of the Roman Emperor Hadrian and a convert to Judaism. According to one tradition, Rabbi Akiva (second century) encouraged Aquilas, a relative of the Emperor Hadrian, to make a new Greek translation of the Bible, since there were many corrupt versions of the original Septuagint. All that has remained is the Aramaic translation of the original Greek. In ancient times, during the Sabbath, the Aramaic translation was read in the synagogue together with Hebrew text, so that every person would understand the reading. Aquilas's translation also served as a commentary to the ancient biblical text. The ancient sages of Judea clearly understood the spiritual implications of the new translation. Passages in the Scriptures were softened so that the Torah would be more intelligible to the average Jew. Already at this early period of Jewish history, there is ample evidence that the talmudic sages did *not* ever subscribe to a physical view of God. In addition, just as biblical language needs to be interpreted symbolically and metaphorically, this same manner of interpretation must also be applied to the midrashic and talmudic metaphors of God.

34. Harry Wolfson, *Repercussions of the Kalam in Jewish Philosophy* (Cambridge, MA: Harvard University Press, 1979), pp. 41–46.

35. The first development of philosophy in Islam (c. 757) was the school of *Mutazilites*—that is, Seceders—who denied the eternity of the Koran. Though they had great respect for Islam's holy book, they maintained that where it or the *Hadith* contradicted reason, the Koran and its subsequent traditions had to be interpreted allegorically. Intellectual Muslims had difficulty accepting those Koranic passages that ascribed hands and feet, anger and hatred, to Allah. They gave the name *Kalam*, or logic, to this effort to reconcile reason and faith. The *Mutazilites* were sometimes called by their critics *Mu'attilites*—"Those who emptied the conception of God."

36. Maimonides, *Guide to the Perplexed*, Freidlander's translation, chapter 46.

This was not only a problem of the uneducated masses; many of the elite talmudic scholars also literally subscribed to anthropomorphisms. Indeed, much (if not most) of Maimonides' cricticism was squarely aimed at the rabbinical establishment for endorsing a philosophy of literalism with regard to how the Bible, the Talmud, and the Midrash ought to be interpreted. In his commentary to the Mishnah, Maimonides writes:

> The worst offenders are preachers who preach and expound to the masses what they themselves do not understand. They ought to be silent about matters they do not know as it is written: *If you would only keep silent, that would be your wisdom!* (Job 13:5). It would be far more honest for them to admit "We don't understand what precisely our sages intended in this statement, we don't know how to explain it." Thinking that they do understand, they vigorously interpret to the people what they think rather than informing them of what the sages actually said. They therefore give lectures to the masses on the [aggadic passages] found in tractate *Brachot* and chapter *Helek* [of *Sanhedrin*] which they interpret [in the spirit] of literalism.[37]

The world of Saadia, Halevi, and Maimonides was profoundly affected by religious wars and conflicts in all segments of life. It was an age in which Judaism had to struggle mightily to observe its ancestral traditions. Christianity and Islam adapted Greek philosophy and utilized its teachings for spreading their own religious message to the world. Many of the brightest Jewish minds found the message of Judaism to be irrelevant and anachronistic. Not even the exciting talmudic debates seemed to answer the philosophical and existential questions people were asking about God and humanity and the meaning of existence. The new Jewish intelligentsia found the monotheistic teachings of Judaism to be inferior to their Muslim counterpart. Saadia, Bahya (ninth and tenth centuries), and Maimonides all sought to restate and redefine Judaism's most sacred teaching—the belief in monotheism.

After having observed the models of faith utilized by the Muslims,[38] Maimonides decided to define the fundamentals of the Jewish faith. Maimonides sought to help refine the Jewish understanding of faith by elevating such understanding to the status of a *mitzvah* (a religious precept). Like Philo, the Septuagint, and Onkelos before him, Maimonides believed that philosophy was necessary for every Jew who wanted to understand the real meaning of the Torah. Maimonides knew that the survival of Judaism was at stake. The average Jew had to upgrade his/her understanding of faith. Ignorance was no excuse. Maimonides

---

37. *Maimonides' Commentary to the Mishna, Introduction to Perek Helek of Sanhedrin.*

38. Maimonides may have also been influenced by the Apostles' Creed, which was formulated by the Church around the year 400 C.E.

sought to educate his generation by going back to the basics of faith and introducing a new and proper *grammar* of faith.

By the term "grammar," we mean an aspect of language by which means we communicate to the world around us. In order for language to be clear and precise, words must adhere to specific rules and syntax that help make the proper communication of ideas and information possible. When language is haphazardly used, words lose their meanings and become ineffectual tools for communication. Improper grammar impedes the flow and exchange of ideas. What is true regarding secular language is especially true of the language of faith. The first section of Maimonides' *Guide to the Perplexed* is dedicated to defining the proper language for speaking of God in the Torah. Maimonides was convinced that an improper understanding of anthropomorphic language could endanger the beliefs shared by all Jews, that the belief in God's incorporeality was pivotal in eradicating idolatry from the world, and that the daily spiritual language of the Jew had to reflect this. In his commentary to the Mishnah, he explains in detail:

> The third principle: God's incorporeality. This is the belief that this Unity is neither a body nor the power of a body and that nothing occurs to bodies, such as motion and rest. That is why our sages said: "On High there is neither sitting nor standing, desire or fatigue." He has no constitution nor does He have any separation as witnessed in the Scriptures. It is regarding this thought the prophet said: *To whom then will you compare me, or who is my equal?* (Isaiah 40:25). If God were a body He would be like other bodies. Wherever Scriptures speaks in terms of God having the attributes of a body, e.g., walking, sitting, speaking, standing, etc., it speaks in the parlance of humanity.[39]

Maimonides was convinced that any false image of God was in a sense more harmful than idolatry. For Maimonides, sculptured images were not the only ones forbidden in the Torah; wrongful spiritual images conceived by the human intellect were also forbidden and certainly much harder to eradicate! Maimonides committed his whole life to deliteralizing the Bible. In modern terms, we could say that Maimonides was concerned with *demythologizing* all the mythic content and imagery of the Scripture. He was determined to show that the various anthropomorphisms of Scriptures had to be understood within a philosophical context. In this way, Maimonides sought to safeguard the oneness of God from being compromised by unintelligent people and, at the same time, to distinguish Judaic monotheism from the Christian belief in God's incarnation through Jesus.

Today's controversy concerning God's "gender" underscores the difficulties many people have when they take anthropomorphisms too literally. Despite Maimonides' criticism of anthropomorphic language, he invariably referred to

---

39. *Maimonides' Commentary to Mishnah Sanhedrin,* 10:1, ed. Yosef David Kapach (Jerusalem: Mosaad HaRav Kook, 1965), pp. 135–136.

God as a "He," as Judith Plaskow has already observed.[40] On other occasions, Maimonides sometimes invoked "God's wrath" against the very people he argued were guilty of believing in the corporeality of God. (For more details of Maimonides' critics see Appendix, Excursus 1.)

### Speaking of the Ineffable

In addition to Maimonides' war against anthropomorphic language, Maimonides boldly answered that the negative attributes of God are the true attributes.[41] Thus, when we say that God exists, that means to say that He is not nonexistent; when we say that God is wise, that is another way of saying that God is not foolish. When we describe God as "knowing," that is another way of saying that God is not ignorant, hearing and seeing excludes ignorance, and so on; in no way is God circumscribed by the qualities that we share alike. This approach is sometimes called the *via negativa* (the way of negation). Maimonides regarded all biblical predicates about the personality of God as *homonyms*—that is, when referring to God, all anthropomorphic descriptions denote an entirely different reality than is commonly assumed by humankind.

Maimonides taught that we cannot know anything about God *per se*; God is completely incomprehensible. Human beings at best can only describe *what God does* in the world but will never be able to discern *what God is.*[42] In all

---

40. Judith Plaskow has written eloquently about this problem. She writes:

Maimonides, for an example, considers it illegitimate ever to characterize God in positive terms, for this might imply that God is similar to other existing things. Yet, throughout his discussion of negative and positive attributes, Maimonides continually refers to God as He and Him without ever taking note of the fact that maleness is a positive trait or applying to this attribute his doctrine of negation. In recent times, the anger and fear awakened by feminist attempts to alter male God-language similarly bespeak a profound, often previously unarticulated, attachment to this image, and a dread of losing along with it the very nature of God. . . . The claim that only male language may be used for God—whether defended explicitly or disguised behind a liberal "what difference does it make anyway?"—attributes ultimacy to particular male symbols."

(Plaskow, *Standing Again at Sinai* [San Francisco: Harper and Row, 1990]), pp. 127–128.

41. The tradition of negative theology (or, as it is oftentimes called, apophatic theology) goes back to Xenophanes, Plato, Philo of Alexandria, Plotinus, Proclus, Dionysius the Areopagite, Meister Eckhart, John of the Cross, the anonymous author of *The Cloud of Unknowing*, Saadia Gaon, *Bahya Ibn Pakuda*, and the mystics of the Kabbalah to name just a few.

42. This idea is not new; it was stated long ago by one of the great Palestinian sages of Israel, R. Abba Bar Memel, who taught:

The Holy One, blessed be He, said to Moses: "What does thou seek to know? I am called according to My acts. Sometimes I am called *El Shadday* [Almighty God], or *Tse'va'ot*

likelihood, Maimonides would have agreed with Otto's statement that God is "wholly other" in that the Holy utterly transcends the bounds of human reason. According to Maimonides, God cannot be categorized by human thought. The way we represent God to ourselves cannot adequately describe the nature of the Divine reality. Maimonides' "negative theology" emphasizes the discontinuity between God and the world. Though God's Presence (*Shechina*) is intimately and organically related to the cosmos, God is also sovereign over the world. "If the Heavens cannot contain You" (1 Kings 8:27), how much less can philosophical categories adequately represent the nature of the Divine continuum?

With the *via negativa* every idea, however lofty and spiritual, nevertheless remains a mental picture and thus limiting. Without the *via negativa,* God becomes a creature of our mind. Maimonides warned his generation that we must be careful never to define God in any image or metaphor.[43] All positive affirmations of God, when pushed to the limit, must always bow in silence before God's mysterious nature and being. Maimonides recalls the talmudic story about how once the rabbis heard a man praying,

> "God that is great, powerful, awesome, strong, forceful, feared, courageous, reliable, and revered." After he had finished, the rabbi told him a parable. Suppose a king owned a thousand myriads of gold coins, and someone were to praise him for owning some silver coins, would it not be perceived as an insult?[44]

---

[Hosts], or *Elohim* [God], or *YHWH* [Lord]. When I judge mankind I am called *Elohim*, when I make war against the wicked I am called *Tse'va'ot*; when I suspend man's sins I am called *El Shadday*, and when I have compassion on my world, I am called *YHWH*, for the Tetragrammaton signifies none other than the quality of mercy, as it is said: O *YHWH, YHWH*, God merciful and gracious."—I am that I am. This is the meaning of the verse. אהיה אשר אהיה, [I am that I am]—*I am named according to my acts* [that is, *manifestations*].

In the spirit of Maimonidean theology, the *Tsemach Tsedek* emphasizes that every name attributed to God does not refer to God's person (His Essence) *per se* but to His manifestations in the world. It is what God does that determines what we call Him, but God's own being is beyond our capacity to define or describe.

43. It is interesting to speculate how Maimonides might have responded to the twentieth-century Protestant thinker Paul Tillich, who argued for the radical depersonalization of God. Tillich was opposed to the belief that God is personal. In his words:

> The concept of a "Personal God" interfering with natural events, or being "an independent cause of natural events," makes God a natural object beside others, an object among others, a being among beings, maybe the highest, but nevertheless a being. This indeed is not only the destruction of the physical system but even more the destruction of any meaningful idea of God.

(Paul Tillich, *Theology and Culture* [New York and Oxford: Oxford University Press, 1964], p. 129.)

44. Maimonides, *Guide* I, chapter 59 (Pines translation). The Jewish liturgy would certainly seem to substantiate Maimonides' criticism of human language when describing God: "Even if our mouths

Maimonides argued that it is inappropriate to employ even all the attributes ascribed to God in the Bible; we may use them in context when we come to them, but it is unbecoming and even sinful to speak of God's possessing humanlike characteristics. According to Maimonides, human language falls short whenever it speaks of God. Words are devalued and cannot hope to contain the profundity of God's mysterious Being and Presence. Human language falters and proves impotent. If words have difficulty describing the beauty of a classic work of art like Michelangelo's Sistine Chapel, how much more so will words be clumsy and ineffectual in describing the reality of God.

The most apt phrase concerning the subject is the dictum occurring in the Psalms, "Silence is praise to Thee" (Psalms 65:2), which interpreted signifies: silence with regard to You is praise. This is a most perfectly put phrase regarding this matter. For of whatever we say intending to magnify and exalt, on the one hand we find that it can have some application to Him, may He be exalted, and on the other we perceive in it some deficiency. Accordingly, silence and limiting oneself to the apprehensions of the intellects are more appropriate.[45]

Where Maimonides ends his *via negativa* is mysticism.[46] Maimonides might well agree with the words of Lao Tzu in the *Tao Te Ching*: "One who speaks, knows not, one who knows speaks not."[47] The word "mystical" comes from the

---

were full of song like the seas, and even if our tongues could express the proper praise for the God of the universe . . ."

45. Ibid., chapter 59.

46. Some scholars (Isaac Frank, Keneth Seeskin) argue that Maimonides did not believe that the unknowability of God necessarily leads to mysticism. Many Jewish mystics and hasidic thinkers of the Habad dynasty, however, have argued that Maimonides' negative theology ends in the mystical experience. Suffice it to say that the debate is hardly new. The reader should choose which view s/he finds preferable. For a fascinating article on Maimonides' relationship to the Kabbalah see Moshe Idel, "Maimonides and Kabbalah," in *Studies in Maimonides*, ed. Isadore Twersky (Cambridge, MA: Harvard University Press, 1990), pp. 31–81. See also Sholom Dov Baer of Lubavitch's *Sefer Mamaareem* 5670 Discourse I–III.

47. *Tao Te Ching*, trans. Ellen M. Chen (New York: Paragon House, 1989), p. 188, Hexagram 56. It is intriguing to compare Maimonides to the *Advaita Vedanta* mystic and philosopher Sankara (seventh–eighth centuries C.E.). Sankara taught that *Brahman* (the Hindu name for God) cannot be described by word or idea: "It [Brahman] is the One as the Scripture says: 'Before Whom words recoil.'" A comparison of Maimonides with Sankara goes far beyond the scope of this study. It is fascinating to note, however, that there are many similarities between Maimonides and Sankara even in the language they use. Sankara characterized Brahman as without form, unknowable by philosophical reflection, free from all relationships with the illusionary world we live in. Like Maimonides, Sankara also advocated the *via negativa* when describing Brahman. Like Maimonides, Sankara described Brahman as the *Knower, the Known, and the act of Knowing*. For an excellent summary of Sankara's monistic teachings see Rudolf Otto's classic study *Mysticism East and West: A Comparative Analysis of the Nature of Mysticism* (first pub. New York: Macmillan, 1932; reprinted by Quest, 1987).

Greek word *muein* (to close the lips). Related to the word "mystery," the mystical represents the secret teachings that are only for the initiated—clearly, not for everybody. Thus, God's own transcendence must always be something that is shrouded in Mysterium. Some scholars speculatively suggest the Greek word *mysterion* actually comes from the Hebrew word *masteer*—"hidden."[48] The term *mystery* as used here does not denote an unsolved puzzle or a gap in our knowledge. Rather, it refers to something that is inherently unknowable and inexplicable. No amount of knowledge can ever diminish or eliminate the sense of mystery. On the contrary, it intensifies the sense of mystery, which is the source of all wonder and lies at the root of true worship and devotion. This sense of mystery evokes questions that point us toward ultimate issues and ultimate concerns. Maimonides himself speaks of this in the beginning of his halachic *magnum opus*:

> What is the path to attaining love and awe of Him? When a person contemplates His great, wondrous deeds and creations, seeing through them His boundless, infinite wisdom, he immediately loves, exults, and is ecstatic with a passion to know the great Name. That is what King David meant when he said, "My soul thirsts for God, for the living God." (Psalms 42:2).
>
> When one thinks about these things, he immediately becomes awed and abashed. He realizes that he is but an infinitesimal creature, lowly and unenlightened, standing with his diminutive mind before the Perfect Mind. David thus said, "When I see Your heavens, the work of Your fingers . . . what is man that You consider him?" (Psalms 8:4–5).[49]

Maimonides taught that the true praise of God must come through the silence of the contemplative experience. Any attempt to define God affirmatively by any metaphor[50] will lead to a procrustean theology.[51] Cognitive faith (faith that is

48. See Jonathan Smith's provocative *Drudgery Divine* (Chicago: University of Chicago Press, 1990), pp. 62–63. The *Shorter Oxford Dictionary* lists seven different meanings of mystery: "**1 n.** (pl. -ies) 1a secret, hidden, or inexplicable matter (the reason remains a mystery). **2** secrecy or obscurity (wrapped in mystery). **3**(attrib.) secret, undisclosed (mystery guest). **4** the practice of making a secret of (esp. unimportant) things (engaged in mystery and intrigue). **5** (in full mystery story) a fictional work dealing with a puzzling event, esp. a crime (a well-known mystery writer). **6a** a religious truth divinely revealed, esp. one beyond human reason. **b** RC Ch. a decade of the rosary. **7**(in pl.) **a** the secret religious rites of the ancient Greeks, Romans, etc. **b** archaic (the Eucharist) make a mystery of treat as an impressive secret.mystery play a miracle play.mystery tour (or trip) a pleasure excursion to an unspecified destination. Etymology ME f. OF *mistere* or L *mysterium* f. Gk *musterion*, related to the word *mystic*."

49. Maimonides, *Hilchot Yesodei HaTorah* 2:2, trans. Aryeh Kaplan in *Meditation and the Kabbalah* (York Beach, ME: Samuel Weiser, 1978), pp. 132–133.

50. This would seem to negate even Tillich's concept of God, as "the Ground of Being."

51. Procrustes was the evil innkeeper of Greek mythology who forced his guests, big and small, to fit the bed they slept in, either through torture or mutilation. Tall folks were cut short to size,

defined by solely intellectual criteria) will lead to skepticism and spiritual estrangement. The mystical experience cannot be properly defined because it is an experience of the Ineffable. Any attempt to define the Sacred diminishes God by lessening His own Mystery. No words can ever portray the wonder of the Divine reality. No theological discourse, however elevated and inspired by the passion of love,[52] can ever do justice in depicting God's indescribable Being and Presence.[53]

Maimonides' *via negativa* may be expanded in a variety of different ways. When we say that God is Personal, we must be careful not to mean in the way human beings are personal. For God is more personal than we are to ourselves. God's own personhood is transpersonal—infinitely beyond what we understand as personal. God is just and moral, but He is not just in the arbitrary way in which we define justice and morality. This, according to Maimonides, is the entire point of God's response to Job. When we say that God loves, we must say that it is in a manner that is different and transcends all of our categories of what we perceive love to be. In short, the Holy One's immanence is just as incomprehensible as is His transcendence. The ancient rabbis intuited one of the most important truths concerning God's character: "in the place that you find God's *greatness*, there you will find His *humility*."[54] God's greatness is revealed in His relatedness to creation.[55] This would explain why the shepherd metaphor conveys such an important theological message about caring and about love.

---

whereas short people were stretched to fit. As a metaphor for theology, procurstean theology attempts to mutilate and stretch truth by forcing data to fit preconceived notions.

52. Rational worship will only help sensitize us to God's radiance in the higher spiritual realms. True closeness to God comes if we transcend the limitations of the intellect through the commitment of the physical *mitzvoth*. For, it is for that reason the soul descended into the earthly realm. Shneur Zalman of Liadi (1745–1813), *Torah Or, Parshat Noach* (Brooklyn, NY: Kehot, 1985).

53. Maimonides elsewhere explains the mystery of God's consciousness of the world: "The Holy One blessed be He, recognizes His truth and knows it as it is. He does not know with a knowledge that is external to Him in the way that we know, for we are not one. The Creator, however, may His name be blessed, is one from every side and every angle, in every way of unity. . . . You could say that He is the Knower, the Known, and the process of Knowing. All [this exists within God's] Oneness. We are incapable of verbally describing what this reality is. Our ears cannot begin to understand, nor is it within the heart of humanity grasp it properly" (Maimonides, *Hilchat Yesodei HaTorah*, 2:10).

54. T.B. *Megillah* 31a.

55. The idea behind this talmudic teaching is that God "humbles" Himself to be involved in this world and its problems. One hasidic rebbe, *Tsemach Tsedek*, explains that, though we regard God's greatness in terms of His creative power, the truth is just the opposite! From God's perspective, creation is barely a minuscule expression of God's true power; the entire physical and spiritual universes are like a ray of light before God's Infinite Being. Where, then, is God's greatness? God's greatness lies in His humility. See Rabbi Menachem Mendel *Schneersohn, Derech Mitzvotecha, Ma'mar Shoresh Mitzva Tefila* (Reprint, Brooklyn, NY: Kehot, 1992), chapter 9, p. 236.

Why does it state *The LORD is my shepherd, I shall not want?* Rabbi Yossi ben Hanina said, "You will find no craft more despised than that of the shepherd, yet David called God 'shepherd.' The meaning for this: *I have gained understanding from my elders* [Psalms 119:100], for Jacob too identified God as "shepherd" [Genesis 48:15].[56]

Though God transcends the world, He infuses it with soul and existence. He is paradoxically close yet infinitely distant. He is closer to us than we are to ourselves. He is not perceivable even when His Presence is encountered yet He is present even when His absence is most felt. He is inherent in the world and yet not contained in it; He embraces it and nevertheless is not confined by it. His knowledge of us surrounds us in ways we can never fully know or understand.

### Flavorless Faith

Though Maimonides' struggle against anthropomorphic language did not succeed during his lifetime, his ideas eventually became popular. Utilizing the new philosophical hermeneutic, Jewish thinkers of the medieval period portrayed God in terms that reflected the Greek way of thinking. One of today's most eminent Jewish theologians, Louis Jacobs, catalogs some of the names of God used in the medieval period: *Illat Ha-Ilot*—"Cause of Causes"; *Illah Ha-Rishona'* — "First Cause"; *HaSiba Rishonah*—"The First Cause" (or "Reason"); *Matzui Rishon*—"The Prime Being"; *HaBore*—"The Creator"; *HaShem*—"The Name; Blessed Be He"; *Tehillot Ha-tachalot*—"The Beginning of Beginnings"; *Matzil*—"The One Who Produces Emanations."[57] Each of these metaphors reflected a spiritual distancing from the biblical/rabbinic God of relationship experienced by our forebears. The medievalists went from a relational faith to a cognitive (Greek) model of faith. God-language became stilted, analytical, detached, passionless, and ultimately depersonalized. Even Maimonides' own lofty words became distorted and misunderstood. The mere word "God" became a source of theological and spiritual discomfort—a social taboo nobody introduced in pleasant conversation. Far from being a handmaiden to faith, as Philo and Maimonides both envisioned, philosophy became instead faith's mistress—a complete role reversal.

This point may be illustrated by a personal story Martin Buber tells about a man who once asked him how he could mention God so casually, as though he were familiar with Him.

---

56. *Midrash Tehillim*, ed. Buber, p. 198.
57. Louis Jacobs, *Jewish Theology* (New York: Behrman House, 1973), pp. 146–151.

How can you bring yourself to say "God" time after time? How can you expect that your readers will take the word in the sense in which you wish it to be taken? What you mean by the name of God is something above all human grasp and comprehension, but in speaking about it you have lowered it to human conceptualization. What word of human speech is so misused, so defiled, so desecrated as this![58]

The man of Buber's anecdote reflects the dramatic impact of Maimonides' religious agnosticism. Unfortunately, for the modern Jew, Maimonides' negative theology has mutated into plain, simple agnosticism. With the birth of modern secular consciousness, God seemed to disappear into the great void where all mythologies died, as Eliade pointed out (see page 37). If God existed, He dwelled only at the periphery of universe. In an age of lost innocence, the modern Jew stopped identifying God as a personal or loving Presence. Such affective attributes implied that God possessed sentience, a naïve and "primitive" belief moderns could no longer accept. This point was well articulated by the Reconstructionist theologian Mordecai Kaplan, who claimed that anthropomorphism was on a par with "an animistic fetishism."

We cannot *conceive* of God any more as a sort of invisible superman, displaying the same *psychological* traits as man, but on a greater scale. We cannot *think* of Him as loving, pitying, rewarding, punishing, etc. Many have therefore abandoned altogether the conception of a personal God, and prefer to think of ultimate reality in terms of force, energy and similiar concepts. . . .[59]

Modern man is able to *conceive* the godhead only as immanent in the world; man is incapable of entering into a relationship with the supernatural.[60] (emphasis added)

Note the cognitive words Kaplan uses to describe his point: *conceive, psychological, think.* To Kaplan, there is no Divine Mysterium. In the Kaplanian model of faith, religion must be subordinated to the dictates of reason. Mystery is annoying to rationalists who insist on neat solutions, precision, and exactitude. Uncertainty, shades of gray, paradoxes unsettle the rational mind. The aspects of faith that embrace the symbolic, the intuitive, and the transpersonal are completely excluded from Kaplan's spiritual worldview. There is no joy, humor, no irony, no sense of wonder, or mystery. Nor is there a cadence of poetry; nor

---

58. Martin Buber, *Eclipse of God* (Atlantic Highlands, NJ: Humanities Press, 1952 [Reprinted, 1988]), p. 7.

59. Mordecai Kaplan, *The Meaning of God in Modern Jewish Religion* (New York: Jewish Reconstruction Press, 1962), pp. 87, 88.

60. Ibid., p. 26.

is there any kind of radical amazement in Kaplan's noetic metaphysical system. His theology is emotionally decapitated and cannot ever depict the miracle of God's love or pathos. Kaplan misrepresented Maimonides' negative theology far beyond anything Maimonides ever intended, for Mamonides' theology leads to an encounter with the Numinous. Though Kaplan's thinking reflects the positivistic thinking and spirit of the nineteenth century, it also reflects a theological and spiritual distancing that came as a result of misreading one of Maimonides' most profound and subtle teachings.

Despite Kaplan's disdain of anthropomorphisms, he doesn't hesitate to use them when describing God as the source of all positive human affections. With a touch of irony, one critic[61] dubbed Kaplan's theology as "pananthropomorphic." Kaplan's view of God as an amalgam of *human* virtues is, in effect, a deification of "certain aspects of the human personality."[62] In Pickwickian style, Kaplan attempts to define the belief in God "as the power that makes for salvation." How did Kaplan define salvation? Salvation is another way of describing how people grow toward fullest potential. What Kaplan and his followers fail to notice is that any depiction of God as the source of human values is no less anthropomorphic than the views of the traditionists Kaplan was criticizing. Kaplan's opinion is indebted to his older contemporary John Dewey, who, like Kaplan, attempted "to reconstruct" and redefine the meaning of God for his time.[63] One of the criticisms made against Dewey could be applied to Kaplan:

> Is not Mr. Dewey, in effect, attempting to exploit the traditional prestige of words that he has emptied of nearly all their traditional meaning? Certainly his religiousness will strike the orthodox as something extremely attenuated, the extract

---

61. See Eliezer Berkowitz, *Major Themes in Modern Philosophies of Judaism* (New York: Ktav, 1974), pp. 182–184.

62. Berkowitz, op. cit.

63. According to Dewey, the definition of God should be revised to stand for all the forces in society that bring about an ethical transformation of humanity. Dewey notes: "It is this active relation between ideal and actual which I would give the name 'God.' I would not insist that the name must be given. There are those who hold the association of the term with the supernatural are so numerous and close that any use of the word 'God' is sure to give rise to misconception and be taken as a concession to traditional ideas." (John Dewey, *A Common Faith: Later Writings, 1925–1953*, ed. Jo Ann Boydston [Carbondale: Southern Illinois University Press, 1990], pp. 79–80.) In the same manner, Kaplan attempted a definition of God that would accommodate even the most agnostic point of view. The best modern example of Kaplanism is Harold Schulweis's "predicate theology," which attempts to create a theological grammar based solely on the use of predicates and which clearly ignores objects. See Kenneth Seeskin's stunning critique of Schulweis in *Judaism* (Winter 1986), pp. 117–119. Seeskin correctly shows how Schulweis's work is profoundly based on the atheism of Ludwig Fuerbach's *Essence of Christianity*.

of an extract, having the same relation to old-fashioned religion as beef bouillon poured through a filter has to beef.[64]

The analogy of the "beef bouillon extract" is more perceptive than Dewey's critic could have imagined, for the spiritual life is characterized by flavor: "O taste (*ta'am*) and see that the Lord is good" (Psalms 34:8). The Hebrew word *ta'am* may mean reason, understanding, or flavor. *Ta'am* denotes perceiving with the sense of taste and usually refers to a food that is tasty, pleasant, and enjoyable. According to the laws of *Kashrut*, the flavor defines the character of a questionable substance (*ta'am k'ikar*)—the taste is the essence.[65] If the flavor is excessively diluted, radically altered, or destroyed, the character of a forbidden substance is considered changed. In terms of prohibited foodstuffs, the flavor must be intact in order to be considered *asur* (forbidden).

As a spiritual metaphor, once a faith is purged of all of its taste and sensuality, then what remains is of negligible value. It is, in a sense, bereft of *ta'am*. After God's personhood has been stripped and laid bare, we are like the lady who popularized the famous question, "Where's the beef?"

Stripping faith bare of all its anthropomorphic language has created some serious logistical problems in other areas of Jewish life and observance— especially with regard to prayer. Prayer is, in effect, *a way of doing theology*. Our theological beliefs all come out in the wash with prayer. Many modern Jews wrestle with the liturgy, for it speaks of a God who is "compassionate," "merciful," "angry," and "forgiving." The liturgy is a kaleidoscope of anthropomorphic depictions. If prayer is to be personally meaningful, we must see through its words and allow ourselves to hear and experience its spiritual message. Prayer forces us to examine our deepest primal beliefs in a Supreme Being. The act of praying says something immeasurably important about who we are and what our spiritual vocation and destiny may be. Its spiritual implications are too profound, too weighty, too challenging to ignore.

---

64. Cited in James Campbell, *Understanding Dewey* (La Salle, IL: Open Court, 1995), p. 278 n. 20.

65. According to the *Halachah*, the Torah regards the flavor of a nonkosher substance as like the prohibited substance itself. See Tractate *Chullin* 97a, *Shivii't* 7:7, *Terumot* 10:1, Maimonides' *Ma'acalot Arusot* 15:1, *Tur Yoreh Deah* 81:1, *Safer Hachinuch Mitzvah* 368. For example: May fish or carrots (which are *pareva*) that are boiled in a dairy pot be eaten on a meat dish? Is the flavor of the dairy pot considered as a mere secondary residue (*nat-bar-nat*) *and therefore permitted?* See the *Rosh*'s commentary to *Chullin* 8:30, and *Shach* 95:4, who permit fish that is boiled in a meat pot because of a triple transfer. Others rule that even a secondary flavor is permitted regardless of whether the cooking occurred through boiling or through roasting. Cf. *Beit Yosef*'s interpretation of Maimonides cited in *Yoreh Deah* 95:4. These examples show that once flavor is diluted, the identity of the substance is altered—the same could be said of faith.

### *Prayer and Our Images of God*

W. W. Meissner summarizes the importance of prayer:

> In this activity, the believer immerses himself [*sic*] in the religious experience in a
> more direct, immediate, and personal way than in any other aspect of his religious
> involvement. Thus all the unconscious and preconscious as well as conscious and
> reflective elements in the individual's relationship to God and the characteristics of
> his god-representation come into play.[66]

From Meissner's insightful comments, it is not hard to see why so many
modern Jews find it difficult to believe in God. Prayer is an activity where we
come face to face with our deepest beliefs and convictions. We can either face our
questions of faith or run away from them. Unfortunately, many Jews have run
way from prayer. If human speech is denigrated, *what can a Jew prayerfully say
to God?* The modern Jew does not have available to him/her any imaginative
picture of how God and the world are interrelated. Few seem to know what
God-talk means in terms of the individual's own personal spiritual formation.
The theological jargon of the past and present will not capture their imagination,
nor will it mesh with the rest of their spiritual sensibilities. The modern Jew is
caught in the web of a mechanistic and dualistic universe in which God can only
stand at the periphery of existence. God has become portrayed either as distant
or virtually nonexistent. This quandary has imperiled the modern Jew's ability to
*effectively speak to God.* This loss of speech has in turn contributed to a loss of
experienced presence, or spirituality—especially in the sphere of prayer. This
phenomenon is reflected by the widespread absenteeism that is pervasive in
contemporary synagogue worship. Jews are among the least likely to attend
regular religious service. According to one recent study, only 41 percent of all
American Jewish households attend or affiliate with synagogues (most of whom
attend synagogue services only twice a year). These studies have shown that Jews
are among the least likely to attend regular religious services.[67] Elliot Dorf, a
leading Conservative theologian, poignantly describes the awkwardness and
muteness the modern Jew often experiences when opening the pages of the
prayer book:

> The language and the prescribed form of Jewish prayer are matters at issue for a
> large number of contemporary Jews, but their fundamental philosophical problem
> with it centers around their lack of belief in God. Many Jews are professed

---

66. Cited in Andrew Greeley, *Religion as Poetry* (New Brunswick, NJ: Transaction Publishers,
1995), p. 157.

67. Barry Kosmin, *Highlights of the CFJ. National Jewish Population Survey* (New York: Council
of Jewish Federations, 1990), p. 53.

agnostics or atheists, and most of those who believe in God have moments of doubt, sometimes lasting a long time and penetrating to the core of their beings. My own belief in God has certainly not been immune to such periods of doubt. How, then, can one engage in prayer without a firm, fairly specific belief in God, when both the act and the texts of Jewish prayer assume it? Part of the answer stems from the fact that prayer is a multifaceted phenomenon, as described above, and some of its features are less directly tied to its underlying theology than are others. Without a belief in God, one can clearly reaffirm communal and historical roots, and one can also learn about the tradition, and its texts. Even some of the moral and emotional effects of prayer are independent of faith in God. . . ."[68]

Prayer assumes a sentient relationship with God. God must be no less real than myself for me to pray. Prayer also assumes that God must be more than a theological construct. If God has no power to communicate with people, how can spiritual people prayerfully communicate with God? When the modern Jew reads in the liturgy about God's love for Israel, s/he reaches an impasse. The *Siddur's* words seem awkward and foreign. Some Jewish thinkers have suggested it is possible to retain the act of prayer though the belief in a personal God has been discarded. These advocates see prayer as a dialogue with the self. Some see prayer as a way of affirming the historical and communal roots of the Jewish people (cf. Dorf). Eugene Kohn, one of the leading theologians of Reconstructionist/Conservative Judaism, viewed prayer as a soliloquy with the impersonal cosmic processes of the universe. Kohn's thinking is full of contradictions, for he tries hard to keep the traditional language of Jewish prayer, but without the meaning ascribed to it by Jews throughout history. Thus when a Jew recites *Blessed art Thou* . . . (second person), Kohn attempts to define "Thou" *in the third person*. This not only shows a poor, vacuous understanding of spiritual grammar; it is also theologically delusional.[69]

The theological ambivalence concerning the efficacy of petitional prayer is a spiritual problem that confronts modern Jewish thinkers and laypeople alike (see the story of Joe Price in chapter 4). The questions moderns ask concerning the validity of prayer is not a new problem that was introduced by the forces of modernity. Jewish, Christian, and Muslim philosophers have all wrestled with the meaning of prayer. Maimonides' own view on petitional prayer is hazily defined. Despite numerous attempts of scholars to purge the use of anthropomorphism, the fact remains that the liturgy is still intensely anthropomorphic. The rabbis of the Talmud have long insisted, "When you pray, know *before Whom you stand*." God is a Presence Who confronts us as we enter into the arena of prayer.

Maimonides' disdain of anthropomorphic language helped create many of the

---

68. Elliot Dorf, *Knowing God*, pp. 186–187.

69. See Eugene Kohn, *Religion and Humanity* (Philadelphia: Reconstructionist Press, 1953), pp. 121–142 for the definitive view of Kaplanistic prayer.

problems moderns have with prayer. If the praise of God is humanly impossible because we lack the proper spiritual vocabulary to speak of Him in a meaningful way, how can we engage God in prayer? To petition God in prayer, to suggest that God can somehow be persuaded to "change His mind" or show "sympathy" and "mercy," is from a strict Maimonidean perspective theologically pointless—even ridiculous. Is prayer no longer possible for the modern consciousness? The communal prayers beseeching God to take notice of us (as we find in the Psalms of lament) suggest that God is affected by prayer! Not only is this true of biblical prayer; it is no less true of rabbinic prayer also. Yet, if we were to follow Maimonides' Aristotelian thinking, we must say that God is completely apathetic and unaffected by the common problems human beings face. We would be better off to throw ourselves to the discretion of God who knows what we need even before we pray.

In a famous passage of the *Guide*, Maimonides as much as confesses that petitional or intercessional prayer (*bakasha*) is only a relative improvement over the animal sacrifices our ancestors offered in ancient times. As a religious pragmatist, Maimonides knew that purging the liturgy of all its anthropomorphic metaphors would be regarded as a scandalous act. It would be like Moses attempting to eradicate the Israelite's desire to offer sacrifices as a way of worship. Had he done so, he would have met stiff resistance. Maimonides writes:

> . . . it would in those days have made the same impression as a prophet would make at present if he called us to service of God and told us in His name that we should not pray to Him, nor fast, nor seek His help in time of trouble.[70] Your worship should consist solely in meditation without any works at all. (Guide III, chapter 32)

Though petitional prayer is a concession fraught with linguistic pitfalls, Maimonides recognized that most human beings are incapable of experiencing the grandeur of contemplative meditation. The true worshiper knows the limitations of the spoken word and realizes that there is no earthly analogy that can do justice in describing the Creator. Yet, were we to eliminate petitional prayer from the liturgy, the very fabric of our religious and spiritual life would unravel and disappear.

Regardless of Maimonides' ambivalence about petitional prayer, he accepted its place in the spiritual evolution of human consciousness. Perhaps Maimonides felt that this was a small price for the eventual good that it would eventually germinate. God does not work against human nature but, instead, patiently prods

---

70. Thus far I have followed Michael Friedlander's translation of Maimonides, *Guide for the Perplexed* (London: Pardes, 1904). The remainder of this passage is from Shlomo Pines' translation of Maimonides, *Guide of the Perplexed* (Chicago: University of Chicago Press, 1963).

it along, directing it toward its ultimate destiny. Perhaps, as human beings developed, simplistic prayer would eventually be replaced with the silence of the contemplative meditative experience.

On a postive note, the prayers of *bakasha* enable us to acknowledge our needs and concerns. These prayers helps us realize how dependent we are on God's continuous tender mercies. *The prayers of bakasha help us realize that it is God who is the Source of all good things, and this leads us to prayers of gratitude and thanksgiving.* Along these lines, Nachmanides (1195–1270) writes:

> God demands naught of the lower creatures with the exception that man should acknowledge and be grateful to his God for having created him. The purpose of raising our voices in prayer in synagogues as well as the merit of public prayer is precisely this: that people should have a place to assemble and express thankfulness to God for having created and sustained them, thus saying before Him, *"We are Your creatures."*[71] (Emphasis added.)

Nachmanides' Christian contemporary Thomas Aquinas stated similarly:

> God loves his creatures, and he loves each one the more, the more it shares in his own goodness, which is the first and primary object of his love. Therefore he wants the desires of his rational creatures to be fulfilled, *because they share most perfectly in the goodness of God.* And his will is an accomplisher of things, because he is the cause of things by his will. . . . So it belongs to the divine goodness to fulfill the desires of rational creatures that are put to him in prayer. (Emphasis added.)

The problems moderns have with petitional prayer underscore the conceptual and semantic difficulties moderns have with traditional God-language. Today's generation requires a different theological and spiritual approach. In the next section we shall examine alternative ways of using religious language that honors the human capacity to speak *of* as well as *to* God. A re-evaluation of anthropomorphic language fills a void that needs to be filled if modern Jewry is ever to regain its spiritual sensibilities. A new assessment of the pictorial dimension of language is vital for understanding our faith's most important mythic images. It is ironic that Aquinas' concept of analogical language, remarkably, comes closer to the aggadic thinking of our ancient rabbinical sages than does Maimonides' negative theology. Indeed, Aquinas' positive use of divine predicates found numerous sympathetic voices among our own sages. I believe his insights provide the key to re-examining one of our most primal images of faith—the image of God as Shepherd—as we shall shortly see.

---

71. *Nachmanides' Writings and Discourses*, trans. Charles Chavel (New York: Shilo, 1978), p. 68 and *Nachmanides' Commentary on the Torah*, vol. 2, Exodus, trans. Charles Chavel (New York: Shilo, 1973), p. 174.

### Breaking the Language Barrier—Aquinas' Doctrine of Analogy

Maimonides' age (like our own era) was preoccupied with the problem of God-talk. Judaism's claim of being the preeminent monotheistic religion was rigorously challenged by its daughter religions. Enamored of Greek wisdom and its Muslim and Christian permutations, the young intellectual community wondered: how could they speak intelligently about God when Judaism seemed to be so full of archaic anthropomorphic descriptions of the Deity. More than any Jewish philosopher before him, Maimonides sought to redefine his generation's faith by safeguarding the utter transcendence of God. He did it by emphasizing the hidden aspect of God's "Otherness" but at the expense of His immanence and relatedness. Maimonides is surprisingly silent when speaking about God's love for Israel. At no point does Maimonides ever elaborate on this vital and important theme.

The subtle dangers we now see in Maimonides' negative theology were anticipated by the great Christian theologian Thomas Aquinas (1224–1274). Aquinas was well aware of the possibility that Maimonides' negative theology (*via negativa*) might be distorted and lead to agnosticism. Though Aquinas had great respect for Maimonides' *via negativa* (and even agreed with it in principle), Aquinas concurred that we must be careful not to be misled by the linguistic pitfalls contained in human language; yet he also foresaw the shadow side of the *via negativa*. Aquinas was convinced that the *via negativa per se* could lead to a spiritual impoverishment of faith. There were Jewish thinkers who also had serious reservations about Maimonides' disdain of positive predicates. One of the most important critiques was expressed by Hasdai Creacas (1340–1410). Creacas agreed with Aquinas that the limitations imposed by Maimonides' penchant for the *via negativa* could lead to a spiritual emptiness that is more offensive to God than the ordinary use of anthropomorphic expressions.[72]

If we lack a sensitivity to the subtle meaning of images, symbols, and metaphors, our capacity to relate personally and *prayerfully* to God becomes stilted as we become estranged from feeling God's Presence. The whole point of any kind of God-talk (God as Person) is to inspire human beings to emulate the qualities of the Divine.

Aquinas objected to Maimonides' view that we can only speak of God in negative terms. Aquinas taught that though human language is limited, the use of

---

72. Levi Gershonides (1288–1344) also maintained that the use of positive attributes was essential for any kind of discourse concerning God. See Ledvi Ben Gershon's controversial *The Wars of the Lord*, book 3, chapter 3, trans. Seymour Feldman (Philadelphia: Jewish Publication Society, 1987). See also Louis Jacob's excellent book *A Jewish Theology* (New York: Behrman House, 1973), pp. 40–41, and Julius Guttman's classic summary of Jewish philosophy, *Philosophies of Judaism* (New York: Schocken, 1963), pp. 254–281.

anthropomorphisms does have one important use, for they imply that there is *literally* a relationship between God and His creation. The purpose of all divine predicates is to give concrete expression to how God's personhood might be realized in this earthly world. The metaphors we use to describe God do not have to be viewed as negations (as Maimonides argued), *but rather as symbols and analogies.*[73] Rather than eschewing all mental images of God, Aquinas advocated a theology that distinguishes between appropriate and inappropriate paradigms of God's Being and Presence.

Every divine predicate beckons us to search for its deeper analogical meaning and must not be taken at face value. If Maimonides were right that the names that are said positively about God are applied in a purely equivocal sense (that is, having literal meaning when said of creatures, but when speaking of God are strictly metaphoric) then, it would follow "that from creatures nothing at all could be known or demonstrated about God." If we were to purge all human language of anthropomorphic language, human beings would never have a context with which to speak about God. Aquinas writes:

When we say that a man is wise, we signify his wisdom as something distinct from the other things about him—his essence, for an example, his powers or his existence. But when we use this word about God we do not intend to signify something distinct from his essence, power or existence. When 'wise' is used of a man, it so to speak contains and delimits the aspect of man that it signifies, but this is not so when it is used of God; what it signifies in God *is not confined by the meaning of our word but goes beyond it.* Hence it is clear that the word 'wise' is not used in the same sense of God and man, and the same is true of all other words, so they cannot be used univocally of God and creatures.[74] (Emphasis added.)

Language is circumscribed by the way human beings experience the world. Whenever we speak about something of which we have no direct experience, we must think by analogy or abstain from thinking. Even the most abstract scientific theory must be expressed in terms of pictures, metaphors, and analogies.[75] If God

---

73. The use of analogy in theology and philosophy goes back to antiquity. According to Aristotle, metaphor is the result of a transference in language (*epiphora*). Such a transference of name can take place in four different ways: (1) from the genus to the kind; (2) the kind to the genus; (3) from one kind to another; or (4) according to analogy. According to Aristotle, analogy (*analogia*) is predicated on the similarity of two relationships between quite dissimilar things (Aristotle, *Poetics*, chapter 21, 1457b).

74. Thomas Aquinas, *Summa Theologica*, Great Books of the Western World, vol. 19, trans. the Fathers of the Dominican Province, rev. Daniel J. Sullivan (Chicago: Encyclopedia Britannica, 1952), Summa 1a. 13:5.

75. Ian Barbour in his book *Religion in an Age of Science* observes that analogical language is not only vital for understanding religious language; it is also essential for discerning scientific truths about reality. (1) The most abstract mathematical truths can best be expressed by scientists through

were fully unknown within the world and its human language, then responsible talk about God on the basis of analogy would be impossible. Aquinas stated a profound epistemological truth—knowledge corresponds to the person's ability to know. All our religious, moral, and sense perception is shaped by our cognitive software.[76]

> And in this way some things are said of God and creatures analogically, and not in a purely equivocal nor in a purely univocal sense. *For we can name God only from creatures. Hence whatever is said of God and creatures is said according as there is some relation of the creature to God as to its principle and cause,* wherein all the perfections of things pre-exist excellently.[77] (Emphasis added.)
>
> For the words of *God is good,* or *wise,* signify not only that He is the cause of wisdom or goodness, but that these exist in Him in a more excellent way. Hence as regards what the name signifies, these names are applied primarily to God rather than to creatures, because these perfections flow from God to creatures.[78]

In kabbalistic terminology we could say that *light is tailored to the structure of the receptacle.* Every divine predicate beckons us to search for its deeper analogical meaning and must not be taken literally. The ancient biblical writers used metaphors that described their own particular relationships with God. I will return to this point since it is most relevant to the pastoral imagery of Psalm 23, as it will become abundantly clear.

Aquinas maintained there are statements about God in the Scriptures that must be taken literally and other expressions that must be interpreted metaphorically. For an example, when we say that "God is a Rock," we are using a metaphorical description and not a literal depiction. How is God like a rock? A rock is firm and stable; in that sense the Scriptures are teaching us that God is firm and stable.

> Some words that signify what has come forth from God to creatures do so in such a way that part of the meaning of the word is the imperfect way in which the creature shares in the divine perfection. Thus it is in part of the meaning of 'rock' that has its being in a merely material way. Such words can be used of God only metaphorically. There are other words, however, that simply mean certain perfections without any indication of how these perfections are possessed—words, for an

the medium of analogies. (2) All models of science are analogical and contribute to a deepening knowledge of already existing theories. (3) Models provide a mental picture whose unity can be more readily understood than that of a set of abstract equations. *Religion in an Age of Science* (San Francisco: HarperCollins, 1990), pp. 41–45.

76. Thomas Aquinas, *Summa Theologica* II/II, Question 1, Article 2.

77. Ibid., I Question 13, Article 5.

78. Ibid., I Question 13, Article 6.

example, like, 'being,' 'good,' 'living,' and so on. These words can be used literally of God.[79]

A modern illustration to Aquinas may be drawn from the philosopher Ludwig Wittgenstein (1889–1951); it is based on Wittgenstein's concept of family resemblance:

> Consider for an example the proceedings that we call 'games.' I mean board-games, card-games, ball-games, Olympic games, and so on. What is common to them all?—Don't say: "There must be something common, or they would not be called 'game'"—but look and see whether there is anything common to all.—For if you look at them you will not see something that is common to all, but similarities, relationships, and a whole series of them at that.[80]

Thus, according to Aquinas, we could say there is a family resemblance between God and His creation; God and humanity may be both compared without actually hedging. Since all creatures come from God, we as His creatures share a "family" resemblance to our Maker. We can only interpret in terms of patterns that stem from our own individual experiences. Aquinas taught that religious language *must* facilitate relatedness to God. If religious language is opaque and non-analogical, it could lead to an overall diminishment of faith.

Our metaphors, images, and symbols of God must provide an imaginative picture of how God, humankind, and the world are all interrelated. The way we experience the world will be determined by the imaginative pictures we develop of God. Our pictures of God contain a metaphorical narrative and analogue of how we are to live in the world. That is why the metaphors and images of God are so important: they color each of our thoughts, words, and deeds.

Our metaphors of God become the template for all human behavior. An image of God that is hateful induces hatefulness in human behavior. Images of God that emphasize "distance" or transcendence can cause a society or an individual to feel that the world is "God-forsaken." Images and stories of God that emphasize love and tenderness can influence a society or individual to see a God that is present and concerned with the quality of interpersonal relationships. In summary, Aquinas argues that all God-talk should be grounded in a language that is theologically human. When speaking about the divine reality, we shouldn't be ashamed to utilize human speech—especially since human beings need a spiritual language that can inspire.

---

79. Ibid., Ia. 13.3 ad. I.

80. Ludwig Wittgenstein, *Philosophical Investigations*, trans. G. E. M. Anscombe (Oxford, England: Oxford University Press, 1968), para. 66.

## Imitation as the Path to Enlightenment

In fairness to Maimonides' position, we can say that there is a danger when anybody attempts to develop an immaculate conception of theology. The real anthropomorphism, according to Maimonides, occurs when the human intellect attempts to define the nature of God's essence and being. It is the height of human arrogance that presumes reason can grasp the Infinite. The old medieval Jewish saying: "If I knew Him, I would be Him" (*e'lu ya'da'teev, ha'yee-teev*) applies especially here.

Maimonides' critique of God-talk (despite Aquinas' analogical theology) shows that ultimate reality cannot be arrived at by speculative means. The mystery of God's reality transcends *all analogies*. Theology must bow its head to the Mysterium of God's Being. Maimonides stresses that when we construct a theology "about" God, we must be careful not to take our metaphors and categories of faith too literally. Maimonides himself *did acknowledge the importance of analogical language* and its importance as a model for emulating God's ethical conduct (*imitatio Dei*). Contemplation of the Divine can only reveal to us God's behavior (but not His essence) and relationship to the world. Contemplation alone, however, can produce only a flawed understanding of God. To know God is to follow God's moral ways (Exodus 33:13). Maimonides further taught it is in the emulation of these models we come to know God. Maimonides observes:

> We are commanded to follow these intermediate paths—and they are the good and decent paths alluded to in the Torah when it states [Deuteronomy 28:9]: *And you shall walk in His ways.* Our sages define this precept in the following manner: Just as He is called "Gracious," so shall you be gracious. Just as He is "Merciful," so shall you be merciful. Just as He is called "Holy," so shall you be holy. In a similar manner, the prophets called God by other titles: "Slow to anger," "Abundant in kindness," "Righteous," "Just," "Perfect," "Almighty," and so on. These metaphors serve to inform us that these are good and worthy paths. A person is obligated to accustom himself to these paths and emulate Him to the extent of his ability. (Maimonides, *Hilchot Deaot* 1:5–7.)

At the end of his *Guide* (III: 34), Maimonides concludes that the philosophical knowledge of God means little if anything if it does not inspire humaneness, justice, and compassion. Our experience and knowledge of God is mediated through acts of love and compassion for our fellow beings. Wisdom must engender a reverence for life. Any knowledge that places wisdom above works of compassion cannot know the God of Israel. It was here Maimonides politely parted company with Aristotle and the Greeks. The love or knowledge of God can never exist solely in the realm of *nous* (thought). When Moses sought a personal theophany from God, he was shown the thirteen attributes of mercy. Moses learned that to know God is to emulate His compassionate ways. Otherwise, our knowledge of God becomes a caricature and a mockery. To profess a knowledge of God that ignores the welfare of all its members is idolatrous.

Despite their differences, Maimonides and Aquinas helped set the stage for the twentieth century's renewed interest in symbolism. What Aquinas called analogical, many modern theologians and philosophers have rephrased as symbolic. In the next section we will show how Aquinas' doctrine of analogy and Maimonides' doctrine of *imitatio Dei* can help us decipher the spiritual meaning behind the Shepherd metaphor of Psalm 23.

# 7

# THE SPIRITUAL MESSAGE OF

# PSALM 23

*Once a kid escaped from the flock, and when Moses followed it, he saw how it stopped at all the water courses, and said to it: "Poor kid, I did not know that you were so thirsty! I see that you are tired," and he carried it back to the herd on his shoulder. God then said, "Since you have shown compassion with a flock belonging to a man of flesh and blood, as you live, so shall you pasture my flock, Israel."*

*Shemot Rabbah 2:2*

To better understand the theological, the spiritual, and social message of Psalm 23, we must observe it through the eyes and heart of the shepherd. The life of the Middle Eastern shepherd sheds considerable light on the shepherd imagery contained in Psalm 23. Many of the comments and insights on the life of the shepherd are adapted primarily from Phillip Keller's excellent book, *A Shepherd Looks at Psalm 23*,[1] as well as the Reverend Faddoul Moghabghab's *Shepherd's Song*, written almost one hundred years ago. The experiences both men relate provide a wonderful analogy for how the shepherd imagery can serve as a model for an active and healthy faith.

---

1. Phillip Keller, *A Shepherd Looks at Psalm 23* (New York: Harper & Row, 1970).

## *Psalm 23 through the Eyes of a Shepherd*

Before elaborating on the details of this hypothesis, it is essential to make a cursory sketch of the ancient shepherd who roamed Judea. The shepherd was a peaceful person who avoided strife as much as possible; his life was often fraught with danger. The shepherd came to realize that his occupation symbolized the way and manner God cared for him. When he said, "The Lord is my shepherd," he did not come across the shepherd metaphor by happenstance. His life experiences as a shepherd inspired him to see God as the Shepherd of all creation. His occupation as a shepherd became an analogy for the spiritual processes that govern the universe.

Though many consider shepherding a masculine profession, it must be noted that female shepherds were also common in the biblical period. As a metaphor for the Divine, the shepherd image is gender inclusive and is not merely gender specific (see Genesis 29:6 and Exodus 2:16). For men, shepherding was one of the first occupations that enabled men to get in touch with their feminine nature by being nurturers to God's tender creation.

Ensuring that the sheep were comfortable in lying down was no easy task. Keller notes that there are four factors that inhibit a sheep from lying down:

1. Sheep are anxious creatures; their timid nature stems from fear.
2. They must be free from strife with their fellow sheep.
3. If sheep are tormented by flies or parasites, this could inhibit them from lying down. Since parasites are a common problem among sheep, the shepherd must look for fresh areas that will provide respite from the parasites.
4. Sheep will not rest when they feel hunger. The considerate shepherd must see to it that these problems are reduced to a minimum in order to provide rest and peace of mind for the flock.

The presence of the shepherd inhibited the sheep from fighting. The more aggressive the sheep, the more they were inclined to be anxious and disturbed, whereas the less aggressive sheep were more likely to be content and satisfied. The shepherd must have a soothing personality and know how to help his flock relax. In ancient days, the shepherd used to play his flute to help calm the nervous flock. Of all the ancient professions available to men, shepherding best enabled men to develop their maternal persona.

Keller also notes that green pastures were not the product of chance but were the result of the shepherds' efforts in farming. Most shepherding lands in the world are in dry, semiarid areas. David for instance, shepherded his sheep in Bethlehem, a dry barren land.

The Hebrew word for "still waters," *menuchot,* means motionless waters in contrast to running waters. Sheep are afraid of fast-running waters, and for good reason. Sheep know they cannot swim in a swift current because of their heavy fleece. It would be like a man attempting to swim with his heavy overcoat on. If the waters are moving rapidly, there exists a danger that the sheep may fall in and drown. If there are no still waters available, then the good shepherd will gather stones and make a temporary dam so that even the smallest lamb might be able to drink from the stream.

How important are still waters for a sheep? When an animal feels thirsty, it is a sign that his body is undergoing dehydration. Keller notes that since the sheep's body is composed of 70 percent water, the shepherd must make sure that the sheep do not dehydrate themselves. Dehydration can cause damage to the sheeps' tissues, making the sheep sickly and depleted of their life energy.

Sheep are very stubborn creatures who will on occasion drink water from filthy water holes, even though the shepherd is leading them to drink clean water. Keller notes that water can come from three sources—dew on the grass, deep wells, and streams. If the sheep are not led to clean, pure water, they will drink from any water hole, even if it is dirty and full of parasites. Keller writes:

> Most people are not aware that sheep can go for months on end, especially if the weather is not too hot, without actually drinking, if there is heavy dew on the grass each morning. Sheep, by habit, rise just before the dawn and start to feed. Or if there is bright moonlight they will graze at night. The early hours are when the vegetation is drenched with dew, and sheep can keep fit on the amount of water taken in and with their forage when they graze just before and after dawn.[2]

One of the most poignant scenes seen in the life of the shepherd is that in which he carries the young sheep to the water and holds it so that it may drink. The Reverend Faddoul Moghabghab describes the scarcity of water in Judea and notes that the shepherds are responsible for securing their own wells for their sheep. He writes:

> About noontime one flock after another comes down from the mountains to these wells. When they have all gathered, the shepherds unite to lift the stone lid that covers the mouth of the well, descend ten or twenty steps to the very bottom, fill their buckets with water, and empty them into the stone troughs at the surface until they are full. Then the shepherds bring a few sheep at a time to the still water, or "waters of rest" in the trough, repeating this performance until they have all drunk.[3]

The good shepherd could not look after the health of the sheep while standing afar. He had to be close at hand. There were many qualities the good shepherd

---

2. Ibid., p. 49.
3. Faddoul Moghabghab, *Shepherd's Song*, p. 71.

excelled in: diligence, persistence, care, and love. The shepherd had to have not only a strong, forceful personality to guide and discipline the sheep; he had to be gentle and nurturing. Shepherding was one of the few ancient professions that enabled men to develop their maternal qualities. Here is a passage that describes the soft, maternal side of the shepherd:

> He will feed his flock like a shepherd, he will gather the lambs in his arms, he will carry them in his bosom, and gently lead those that are with the young.
>
> Isaiah 40:11

The shepherd gathers the newly born lambs and holds them in his arms. These little lambs do not yet respond to the shepherd's voice. They have to be gathered. The young lambs' legs are not yet strong enough to walk; therefore the shepherd must patiently wait for the lambs to walk slowly with the flock.

### He restoreth my soul. . . .

The Hebrew word for soul, *nefesh*, is not to be understood in the Cartesian sense of "body" and "soul." The Hebrew word does not recognize the distinction between the physical and the spiritual; they are as one unit.[4] In pastoral terms, this would indicate that pastoral care must address the total person's well-being—the physical, the emotional, and the spiritual.

Keller describes a common problem in the art of shepherding, helping the "cast sheep." A cast sheep is a sheep that has turned over on its back and cannot get up. This incapacity may be due either to the sheep's large, heavy fleece or to the position in which the sheep finds itself when lying down on an opening inside the earth; the animal, because of its weight, may not be able to maneuver to its feet and may be in danger, especially in the summer. A cast sheep is also prone to predator attacks from vultures or coyotes. The shepherd has to make regular inspections to make sure none of his sheep is cast. The shepherd takes considerable pride in restoring the sheep back to its feet. According to Keller:

> There is something intensely personal, intensely tender, intensely endearing, yet intensely fraught with danger in the picture. On the one hand there is the sheep so hopeless, so utterly immobilized though otherwise strong, healthy and flourishing;

---

4. *Nefesh.* This word may mean: self, soul, life, person, and mind, and is also related to the word *naphash* which means to breathe, catch one's breath, to be refreshed. In general, *nefesh* represents the life principle by which something lives. *Nefesh* is often rendered in Latin as *anima*, "life." In Exodus 21:23, we read about "one who smites a soul"—what does "smites a soul" mean? To smite a soul is to diminish the quality of life.

while, on the other hand, there is the attentive owner quick and ready to come to
its rescue—ever patient, tender and helpful.[5]

Unlike the dog or the cat, who if lost can find its way back, sheep have no
sense of direction. Their vision is poor, and the most they can see is ten or fifteen
yards ahead. Sheep depend on the shepherd to guide them to streams and pasture
lands. To avoid the problem of wandering sheep, the shepherd had to count the
sheep as he gathers them to their holding-pen (see Leviticus 27:33, Jeremiah
33:13). If any sheep are lost, it is his duty to go out and restore the straying sheep
(see Ezekiel 34:11–12). Sheep are gregarious animals, and the shepherd had to
be vigilant and alert at all times. The Reverend Faddoul Moghabghab describes
the joy and tenderness the shepherd feels about finding his lost sheep:

> The news is enough to awaken in a shepherd's heart all the feelings of affection, all
> the powers of action. He can never sleep nor be comforted until his lost sheep is
> brought back safely to the flock. Unless one has experienced the same loss, he
> cannot fathom the depths of the good shepherd's anxiety.

The good shepherd will take a straying sheep and point him to the correct way
in which he is to go. Moghabghab relates a poignant story about his brother and
he, who were looking for two lost sheep:

> At last, after a long and careful search, we discovered a trail of the sheep on the soft
> sand, and at once we ascended the hill and cried out, "Ha, Hoo, Ta, Ta, Ta!" and
> after we had listened for a while, the faint voices of our sheep were heard on the
> distant hill, "Maaaaa!" Poor creatures, they had been wandering blindly on the hills,
> and had waited long for help to come. "I lift up my eyes unto the mountains from
> whence shall come my help?" (Psalms 121) At once we rushed to their side; thank
> God, both were safe. We led them home with great joy; and as we neared the town,
> our father, who was waiting anxiously for our safe return, saw the lights descending
> the hill, and immediately called us again, "Have you found them?" The answer we
> sent back to him, "saved, both saved," was enough to fill that little house of ours
> with great rejoicing. Rejoicing did I say? Why every member of our family asked us
> to tell again and again the story how our sheep were sought for, found, and saved.[6]

The above story serves as an explanation why the ancient leaders of Israel
were originally shepherds. In nearly all ancient civilizations, the leader was
ideally compared to the shepherd for that reason. A leader who treated animals
with sensitivity was worthy of being a spiritual and political leader. Moghabghab's personal anecdote is similar to the midrashic interpretation that describes
why Moses and David were worthy of being leaders of their people:

---

5. Keller, *A Shepherd Looks at Psalm 23*, p. 54.
6. Moghabghab, *Shepherd's Song*, pp. 77–79.

He would prevent the adult sheep from heading first to the pasture lands. He would lead the younger sheep out first so that they would graze off the soft, juicy grass. Then he would take the older sheep to graze off the medium-grade grass; finally he would take the young robust sheep and let them graze off the tough graded grass.

The Holy One said: Let he who knows how to shepherd sheep according to their needs come and shepherd my people. It is regarding this that the Psalms states: *From tending the ewes that had young he brought him to be the shepherd of Jacob his people, of Israel his inheritance. With an upright heart he tended them, and guided them with skillful hand.* (Psalms 78:71–72)[7]

*He leads me in the paths of righteousness for His name's sake. . . .*

The shepherd always walked ahead of his flock. He was the first to face the dangers that awaited the flock. His boots had a steel spike for crushing snakes that stood in the way. He used his sling to frighten wolves away and keep the flock away from dangerous spots. He always looked out for hidden marshes and swamps. His life was always on the front line.

Sheep are creatures of habit; sheep will overgraze a piece of land until the land becomes wasted and incapable of sustaining life. It is interesting to note that one of the terms for overgrazing in Hebrew is *ra'ah*,[8] a term that is distantly related to the Hebrew word for evil, *ra*. Overgrazing is an ancient problem that still affects many nations in the world today. To avoid it, the shepherd cannot afford to be indifferent. The good shepherd must be ever vigilant in watching over his flock. The shepherd also had to be careful not to let the sheep graze without a permit beyond the territory of their owners, which was defined by landmarks. If the shepherd did not carefully watch the flock, he risked having his flock confiscated (see Job 24:2).

Areas that are overgrazed also will make the animals sick with parasites and worms. The good shepherd was mindful of the effect overgrazing had on both his sheep and the land. The sheep needed to be periodically moved from place to place to prevent this problem from occurring. As I mentioned earlier, sheep would often go back to the old pasture land whether it was good for them or not.

The neglectful shepherd not only harmed the sheep he was responsible for looking after; he also damaged the land. The sheep would get parasites and flies and suffer from various diseases. To such a custodian, it did not matter whether the sheep suffered; the bad shepherd was indifferent. He would just dispose of the sick if they prove to be too difficult to manage. Keller notes:

It is worth reiterating at this point that sheep can, under mismanagement, be the most destructive livestock. In short order they can ruin and ravage land almost

---

7. *Shemot Rabbah* 2:2.
8. Cf. Micah 5:5, Job 20:26, Jeremiah 22:22.

beyond remedy. But in bold contrast they can, on the other hand, be the most beneficial of all livestock if properly managed. Their manure is the best balanced of any produced by domestic stock. When scattered efficiently over the pastures it proves of enormous benefit to the soil. The sheep's habit of seeking the highest rise of ground on which to rest ensures that the fertility from the rich low land is redeposited on the less productive higher ground. No other livestock will consume a wide variety of herbage. Sheep will eat all sorts of weeds and other inedible plants which might otherwise invade a field. For an example, they love the buds and tender tips of Canada thistle which, if not controlled, can quickly become a most noxious weed. In a few years a flock of well-managed sheep will clean up and restore a piece of ravaged land as no other creature can do.[9]

*Though I walk in the dark valley,*
*I fear no evil*
*for You are with me.* . . .

In ancient Judea, the good shepherd would take the sheep on long journeys through the ravines and the wadis where the steep and narrow slopes keep out the light. Sometimes, the shepherd had no choice but to lead his flock through the wadis. Avalanches, flash-floodings, poor weather conditions, rock-slides, poisonous plants, and predators were perennial dangers the shepherd faced with his flock. Overexposure to the sun could be very dangerous to the well-being of the flock. The shepherd had to be prepared so that none of these things would deter him. He had to know the paths so that the flock would not be swept away in a flood. The good shepherd preferred the valleys, since they had a great deal of fresh rain water and vegetation left from the winter. The earth was remarkably rich, and the foliage was lush.

The Hebrew word for valley is *gei*. This word is used in the Bible to designate particular kinds of valleys. *Gei Hinnom* was where human sacrifices were offered to the pagan god *Molech*. It was a place that was full of hyenas and wolves. *Gei Melech*, the Valley of Salt, situated in the Dead Sea area; there are neither trees nor any kind of life that flourishes there. *Gei Zevoim* is the "Valley of Wolves" (see 1 Samuel 13:18). *Gei* in Arabic denotes a depressed, barren tract in the mountains, or a deserted valley or well where brackish rainwater settles. In short, the creatures that inhabit the *gei* are dangerous and predatory. The shepherd must always be mindful as to where he was leading the flock.

As the thick fog settled in, the sheep would follow the shepherd by the sound of his voice and shepherd song. The shepherd's voice and presence gave comfort and confidence to the sheep. The sheep have an instinctual trust in their shepherd. If a wolf attacked a lamb, the shepherd's voice gave comfort to the sheep as he

---

9. Keller, *A Shepherd Looks at Psalm 23*, pp. 129–130.

rescued the lamb from its clasp. The experienced shepherd could tell what kind of animal attacked the sheep. Keller notes that a lion will attack a sheep by biting into the throat with its teeth. Unlike the horse, or the cow, the sheep is defenseless against the predator. The well-being and safety of the flock is up to the shepherd. The shepherd's arms, body, and feet were often scarred with the wounds he suffered for his flock while fighting predators who attempted to destroy them.[10]

*Your rod and staff, they comfort me. . . .*

The rod was also used to keep the sheep away from the edge of a cliff. The shepherd carried a rod and a staff. The rod is called in Arabic *nabbutt*. It is used to ward off predators that would harm the sheep. The young shepherd learned to handle and throw this staff with high speed and accuracy. The reflexes of the shepherd were quick, since he never knew what kind of danger might be awaiting him and his flock. The rod was seldom used to discipline the sheep, unless they wandered astray. Keller writes that the rod would sometimes be flung at a sheep that was about to eat some poisonous berries. In the biblical narrative, Moses used his shepherd's rod to punish the Egyptians. It was a symbol of strength and power. There was also a practical application with regard to determining the condition of the sheep's skin, Keller notes:

> But the skilled judge will take his rod and part the sheep's wool to determine the condition of the skin, the cleanliness of the fleece and the conformation of the body. In plain language, "One just does not pull the wool over his eyes."[11]

The rod was also used in the management of the sheep. As each animal is coming out of the gate, the sheep is stopped by the shepherd's rod as he carefully inspects his sheep. The shepherd made it a point to know the animal's hidden problems. The experienced shepherd had to be skilled in finding out the hidden problems that lay beneath the surface of the sheep's wool.

The staff was what the shepherd leaned on while he walked. The staff was used for discipline. Occasionally, it was used to remove the sheep when it got entangled in a thorn bush. A staff was used to guide the flock. More than any other instrument, the staff identified the role of the shepherd. Its shape was especially made for sheep and no other kind of animal. It gave the shepherd strength as well as support.

The staff was also used to assist the sheep when it gave birth to its young. Keller describes its use:

---

10. Cf. Zechariah 13:7.
11. Keller, *A Shepherd Looks at Psalm 23*, p. 89.

The shepherd will use his staff to gently lift a newborn lamb and bring it to its mother if they become separated. He does this because he doesn't wish to have the ewe reject her offspring because it bears the odor of his hands. I have watched skilled shepherds moving swiftly with their staff among thousands of ewes that were lambing simultaneously. With deft but gentle strokes the newborn lambs are lifted with the staff and placed side by side with their dams. It is a touching sight that can hold one spellbound for hours.[12]

One of the common problems shepherds are faced with is how to extricate the young lamb when it gets stuck in a hole or pit. Pits are a part of the wilderness. There are pits that are open and visible, whereas others are concealed from the naked eye, as with pitfalls and traps (as in Psalms 35:7). In the Scriptures, the pit was often associated with the place of the dead (Sheol). When a person is stuck in the pit, he is virtually trapped and cannot get out. The shepherd's staff was made to help lift the lamb out of places the shepherd could not easily reach.

*You prepare a table before me. . . .*

Scholars have debated why the psalm switches from the shepherd imagery to the host imagery. There are many answers to this question. One answer intimates that the shepherd is not only a protector of the sheep; he is also a protector of the traveler who seeks refuge from the dangers of the desert. The practice of hospitality can still be seen in the Middle East today.[13] Jewish tradition records that Abraham practiced this kind of nomadic hospitality.

The land shepherds sought preferred the mountainous highlands and plateaus known as *mesas*, the Spanish word for "tables." The shepherd had to prepare "the table" for his flock to eat.[14]

The Middle Eastern shepherd looked hard for these mesas, since they were not always obvious to the eye. Finding them required high energy and diligence. Before the sheep embarked on their quest for grazing, the shepherd had to decide which lands would be best suited to the flock's needs. The shepherd had to have a discerning eye as he surveyed the environment. Many bushes looked alike, and some were poisonous, whereas others were not. The neglectful shepherd caused much of his herd to suffer if he failed to "prepare" the land. If the streams were full of twigs and debris, the shepherd had to see to it that the streams were clean. Moghabghab writes that when he was a young shepherd boy, he had much

12. Ibid., pp. 93–94.

13. Bernard Anderson, *Out of the Depths: The Psalms Speak for Us Today* (Philadelphia: Westminster, 1983), p. 208.

14. Keller, *A Shepherd Looks at Psalm 23*, p. 99.

difficulty distinguishing many of these desert plants and shrubs. Some flowers were as beautiful as a rose yet deadly when consumed by the sheep. The good shepherd prepared the land and removed any poisonous weeds that would harm the sheep. Keller notes:

> My youngsters and I spent days going over the ground plucking out these poisonous plants. It was a recurring task that was done every spring before the sheep went on these pastures. Though tedious and tiring with all of the bending, it was a case of "preparing the table in the midst of my enemies." And if my sheep were to survive, it had to be done.[15]

According to Moghabghab, the "table" referred to in Psalm 23 may refer to the common "table" that was shared by shepherd and flock alike. The shepherd removed his coat, laid it down on the ground, and fed his sheep as he ate (see Matthew 22:7–8). The responsible shepherd saw to it that he loaded up on bundles of fresh herbs and grass so that the young ewes being born would be provided for. Moghabghab adds:

> Sometimes the ewes will give birth to lambs while he is on the mountains. He places these young lambs, or those of them that have broken legs, right inside his coat; every now and then will be seen gathering the tenderest grass to feed them. It is both amusing and pathetic to see these lambs raising their heads and bleating, while the mothers are following his tracks. "He shall feed his flock like a shepherd. He shall gather the lambs with his arm, and carry them in his bosom, and shall gently lead those that are with the young" (Isaiah 40:11).[16]

### In the presence of my enemies. . . .

According to biblical scholar Bernard Anderson, once a guest is received by his Bedouin host and has the table spread before him, he is guaranteed sanctuary from his enemies. Anderson adds:

> This divine hospitality is not just a temporary reprieve but a limitless protection from the powers that threaten one's existence. The Hosts's tent is none other than the Temple, as in Psalm 17:1–6 which closely parallels the thought of Psalm 23.[17]

The responsible shepherd had to inspect the caves and pits that could harbor wild predatory animals. The shepherd would seal off the cave and thus protect the flock. If the caves were empty, the shepherd would utilize the caves as a

---

15. Ibid., p. 101.
16. Moghabghab, *Shepherd's Song*, p. 107.
17. Anderson, *Out of the Depths*, pp. 210–211.

temporary sheepfold for his flock, while going ahead of them to inspect the land. The good shepherd inspected the holes in the grass to see whether there might be poisonous snakes awaiting. If there were bears, wolves, and coyotes, the shepherd would hunt them down and remove their threat to the flock. Keller writes that one of the most difficult, crafty animals he had to contend with were the cougars. After describing the nature of their attack, Keller adds:

> Yet despite the damage, despite the dead sheep, despite the injuries and fear instilled in the flock, I never actually saw a cougar on my range. So cunning and so skillful were their raids they deftly defy description.[18]

### You anoint my head with oil; . . .

There were several reasons a shepherd would administer oil on the sheeps' heads. The oil served as a medicine. If a sheep bruised itself on a briar patch, the good shepherd would apply healing oil to ward off infection. The oil also served to keep the male sheep from harming one another and to keep parasites away from the sheep. When the sheeps' heads were dipped in oil, the oil would overflow on a sheep's body if the sheep dipped its head too deeply.

Keller notes that oil over the head also served another purpose. During mating season, it is not uncommon for male sheep to fight over possession of the ewes. Keller would put grease on the rams' heads; the grease served as a natural repellent, thus minimizing the harm they would inflict upon each other.

The good shepherd had to anticipate a solution to the problem of parasites. According to Keller, the shepherd would take homemade oil made out of sulfur mixed with linseed or olive oil, spices, and tar, and then smear the ointment over the sheep's nose to keep the flies away. The sheep were less fidgety and restless. To rid a sheep of scabs, the shepherd would smear the sheep's entire body in oil. This kept the animal blemish-free.

Although the sheep may be resting beside still waters or grazing in green pastures, their contentment could be threatened by a host of different parasites that can harm and irritate them. Keller notes:

> For relief from this agonizing annoyance sheep will deliberately beat their heads against the trees, rocks, posts or brush. They will rub them in the soil and thrash around against woody growth. In extreme cases of intense cases of infestation a sheep may even kill itself in a frenzied endeavor to gain respite from the aggravation. Often advanced stages of infection from these flies will lead to blindness.
>
> Because of this, when the nose flies hover around the neck, some of the sheep

---

18. Keller, *A Shepherd Looks at Psalm 23*, p. 104.

become frantic with fear and panic in their attempt to escape their tormentors. They will stamp their feet erratically and race from place to place in the passage trying desperately to elude the flies.[19]

The Middle Eastern and African flies often created havoc for the whole herd. When one sheep would run amok, the other sheep would do the same. Keller adds that if the mother is disturbed by these pests, she will leave her young languishing for milk while she is off trying to get rid of the parasites.

## My cup overflows

If a lamb was freezing because of the cold weather, the good shepherd would provide the lamb with an occasional drink of whisky and water mixed in together. Shortly afterward, the lamb would renew its energy and vitality.

*Surely goodness and love*
*shall follow me all the days of my life;*
*and I shall dwell in the*
*house of the Lord forever.*

The shepherd's life was far from idyllic; nor was it carefree and easy. Comfort and luxury were sacrificed to give care and comfort to his sheep. His sheep were his life. He lived with them, and engaged them daily. The ancient Judaic shepherd placed himself in routine danger on their behalf. His destiny was with the flock.

Regardless of the difficulties and dangers his occupation brought him, the good shepherd was determined to treat his flock with goodness (*tov*), and with loving-kindness (*hesed*). The good shepherd did not distinguish between his flock; he loved his flock like his own children. The shepherd endured the climatic changes of the four seasons; he suffered with his flock when they suffered. It is for this reason that, if a sheep is well managed, it will generally remain with the fold. The sheep is content so long as its needs are met. Once the sheep's needs are provided for, it will stay with the good shepherd until its last dying days. Thus, from Psalm 23, we have a living model and analogy (*mashal*) as to how the Supreme Shepherd relates us to us and how we are to serve as shepherds to our neighbors (as in love your neighbor, *re'eh'cha*).

---

19. Ibid., pp. 112–113.

# 8

# THE BIBLICAL NARRATIVES
# THAT MIGHT HAVE INSPIRED
# PSALM 23

Portraying the psalm from the perspective of the shepherd adds considerable meaning to the metaphors contained in this psalm. While it is possible a shepherd may have composed this psalm, it is also possible that this psalm may have been inspired by certain collective memories shared by the Jewish community as a whole. The meaning of the shepherd metaphor may be discerned through the scriptural narratives that inspired it. Many of the midrashic sources see this psalm as having a close affinity with the narratives of the Exodus. Other commentaries consider Psalm 23 to be based on the life of King David. Both narratives share certain common themes dealing with the themes of suffering, wandering through the wilderness, hope, and personal redemption. In this chapter we shall explore the theological implications of the Exodus and Davidic narratives and how each contributes to our general understanding of Psalm 23 as a whole.

## Psalm 23 as a Poetic Midrash of the Exodus

In a recent study[1] the distinguished Bible scholar David Noel Freedman traces the psalm's roots to the tradition of the Exodus, the crossing through the wilderness, and the entry into Canaan.[2] Freedman believes that an unknown poet of the sixth century B.C.E. composed it at a time when Israel had been exiled and that the poet had implicit faith that, at some future date, the Israelites would eventually return from their captivity.

Freedman adds that the verse, "You prepare a table before me in the midst of my enemies," must be understood in light of Psalm 78:19, which, although stated by an individual, was probably recited by all Israel. This psalm might have been liturgically said at the pilgrimage holidays of Passover, Shavuot, and Succot (this possibility could help explain the close relationship between Psalm 23 and Psalm 27; see Appendix). Here is a synopsis of his interpretation:

Psalms 23:1 "The LORD is my shepherd, I shall not want," corresponds to:

> Surely the LORD your God has blessed you in all your undertakings; he knows your going through this great wilderness. These forty years the LORD your God has been with you; you have lacked nothing.
>
> Deuteronomy 2:7

Psalms 23:2, "He makes me lie down in green pastures; he leads me (*vehahalanee*) beside still waters," corresponds to:

> In your steadfast love you led (*nacheeta*)
> the people whom you redeemed;
> you guided (*nahalatcha*) them by your strength
> to your holy abode.
> Exodus 15:13

Psalms 23:3, "He restores my soul. He leads me in right paths for his name's sake," corresponds to:

> I will restore Israel to its pasture,
> and it shall feed on Carmel and in Bashan,
> and on the hills of Ephraim
> and in Gilead its hunger
> shall be satisfied.
> Jeremiah 50:19

---

1. David Noel Freedman, "The Twenty-Third Psalm," in L. L. Orlin, ed., *Michigan Oriental Studies in Honor of George G. Cameron*, pp. 139–166.

2. Freedman's observations pertaining to Psalm 23 and the Exodus were also anticipated by the Jewish biblical commentator Rabbi David Kimchi (1160–1235). Cf Kimchi's Commentary to Psalm 23.

Psalms 23:4, "Even though I walk through the darkest valley, I fear no evil; for You are with me; your rod and your staff, they comfort me," corresponds to:

> They did not say, "Where is the LORD who
> brought us up from the land of Egypt,
> who led us in the wilderness,
> in a land of deserts and pits,
> in a land of drought and deep darkness,
> in a land that no one passes through,
> where no human being lives?"
>
> Jeremiah 2:6

Psalms 23:5–6, "You prepare a table before me in the presence of my enemies; you anoint my head with oil; my cup overflows. Surely goodness and mercy shall follow me all the days of my life, and I shall dwell in the house of the LORD my whole life long," corresponds to:

> They spoke against God, saying, "Can God spread a
> table in the wilderness?"
>
> Psalms 78:19

Freedman concludes that the entire psalm corresponds to the life of a human being. The experiences listed in this psalm are about the trek of the ancient Israelites in the wilderness. Just as God guided Israel through all its travails, so, too, God leads each person accordingly through his or her own life's journey through the wilderness. All the tribulations and deliverance Israel experienced are reflected in the spiritual journey of the ordinary person of faith.

### Psalm 23 as a Description of David's
### Journey through the Wilderness

According to Jewish tradition, King David composed this psalm based upon the stories of his flight from Saul[3] and from his rebellious son Abshalom[4] (2 Samuel 15–19). According to one nineteenth-century Jewish commentator, Psalm 23 represented all the events of David's life that ultimately led to his ascent to the

---

3. According to Rabbi Meir Loeb Yechiel (Malbim), Psalm 23 is a depiction of all the events that led to David's ascent to the throne. Faced with numerous foes and adversaries, David managed to survive. Every incident of David's life reflected how God shepherded him from danger to safety.

4. Among modern critical scholars, the vast majority do not believe David composed this Psalm. One notable exception is Aubrey Johnson, who is quoted in J. Hastings, ed., *Dictionary of the Bible*, second revision, by F. C. Grant and H. H. Rowley (London: Scribner's, 1963), p. 819.

throne. Both these episodes in David's life and those of the Exodus contain several similarities, especially the wilderness experience, which is basic in each of the accounts. Modern scholarship does not believe David composed the psalm[5] (I might add just because they maintain such a view does not necessarily mean it is correct). Whoever wrote the psalm, the psalmist personally identified with David's life experiences and clearly saw his own life as analogous to David's.

In the first story, God provides David with all the help he needs to escape Saul. Through the help of Michal (1 Samuel 19:12–15), David barely managed to escape the guards of Saul. Afterward he went to Ahimelech, who provided him with food while he himself starved. David received several loaves of bread, as well as a sword to use for self-defense. David later hid in the land of Ziph (1 Samuel 23:14–28), where the Ziphites informed Saul of David's general whereabouts. After a brief fight with the Philistines, David became acutely aware that it was God who distracted Saul so that he and his men could escape. This may be the reason Psalm 23:3 states, "He leads me in right paths for his name's sake." God guided David's steps, enabling him to escape from King Saul.

David went to the wilderness of Ein Gedi, a place known for its peaceful waters. This episode may be alluded to in Psalm 23, which speaks of quiet waters. There, David and his six hundred men hid in a cave that was adjacent to Saul's cave. As Saul went to the bathroom, David cut a part of his cloak; he later confronted Saul with the possibility that he might have been killed by David and his men. Saul finally came to his senses, and reconciliation was achieved. A similar story occurs later, in 1 Samuel 26:1–27. In all probability, the second story was probably based on the original story in chapter 19. In chapter 25, David and his men were well received by Abigail, who provided his men with food and drink. In chapter 26, David and Abishai spared Saul's life; Saul was once more confronted by David:

> Why does my lord pursue his servant?
> For what have I done?
> What guilt is on my hands?
>                         1 Samuel 26:18

---

5. It was not unusual for the ancients either to dedicate a psalm in honor of a great person, (David Kimchi, thirteenth century) or to ascribe authorship to a famous person to popularize the composer's work. Some scholars argue that the Twenty-third Psalm was composed after the building of the Temple (the House of the Lord) and may have been recited during the pilgrimage holidays. See Jon D. Levenson, *Sinai and Zion: An Entry into the Jewish Bible* (San Francisco: Harper and Row, 1985), pp. 176–177. *Yaakov Bazak* in his *Mizmorei Tehillim Be' Tefillot Hashabbat* ([Tel Aviv: Yavnah Press, 1991], pp. 151–156), notes the parallels between Psalm 23 and Psalm 27, which I cite at the end of this book's Appendix.

The king admitted his poor behavior and gave up the chase. David kept himself at a safe distance from Saul, knowing that the king was psychotic and could not be trusted.

In 2 Samuel chapters 15–19, David's troubles reached a climax as Abshalom, with the help of Ahitophel, David's closest advisor, rebelled and proclaimed Abshalom king. Once again David ran for safety. Here too, David did not have to wait long for God to provide him with all his needs. Mephiboshet, the lame son of Jonathan, met David and provided him with two hundred loaves of bread, one hundred bundles of raisins, one hundred bunches of summer fruit, and a skin of wine. As in the story of Abigail, David found sustenance before his enemies, who were in hot pursuit of him. Shortly afterward, David and his men were rudely greeted by Shimei ben Gera, a former patriot of the late King Saul, who cursed David and pelted him and his soldiers with stones. When David's men wished to punish Shimei for his attack, he told his men:

> But the king said, "What have I to do with you, you sons of Zeruiah? If he is cursing because the LORD has said to him, 'Curse David,' who then shall say, 'Why have you done so?'" David said to Abishai and to all his servants, "My own son seeks my life; how much more now may this Benjaminite! Let him alone, and let him curse; for the LORD has bidden him. It may be that the LORD will look on my distress, and the LORD will repay me with good for this cursing of me today." So David and his men went on the road, while Shimei went along on the hillside opposite him and cursed as he went, throwing stones and flinging dust at him. The king and all the people who were with him arrived weary at the Jordan; and there he refreshed himself.
>
> 2 Samuel 16:9–14

David perceived Shimei ben Gara as God's instrument of discipline, as foretold by Nathan the prophet.[6] According to other Jewish commentaries, this may have been the reason David recited: "Your rod and your staff, they comfort me." David was convinced that God was still with him regardless of Shimei's curses and attacks, even though God's Presence had withdrawn from him.[7]

David's spiritual sensitivity enabled him to see beyond the "dark valley" in which he was situated. He learned to perceive God's Presence in all his life's experiences. In the midst of evil, he did not give up his trust in God's ability to help orchestrate a newness in his position.

As David and his company entered Jordan, they found themselves comforted by the peaceful waters of the Jordan River. The mention of paths that are

---

6. This is according to Malbim's Commentary on 2 Samuel 16:9–14.

7. One fifteenth/sixteenth century Spanish Jewish commentator noted that when Shimei cursed David over the Batsheba affair, all David could do was humbly accept the Heavenly decree (Abravanel's Commentary on 2 Samuel).

righteous (or "right paths," as rendered by the *New Revised Standard Version of the Bible*) may also be rendered as paths of *tsedek*—'deliverance.'

> When David came to Mahanaim, Shobi the son of Nahash from Rabbah of the Ammonites, and Machir son of Ammiel from Lo-debar, and Barzillai the Gileadite from Rogalim, brought beds, basins, and earthen vessels, wheat, barley, meal, parched grain, beans and lentils, honey and curds, sheep, and cheese from the herd, for David and the people with him to eat; for they said, "The troops are hungry and weary and thirsty in the wilderness."
>
> 2 Samuel 17:27–29

This may have inspired David to recite, "You prepare a table before me in the presence of my enemies. . . ." In every instance in which the wilderness is experienced in the Bible, it always represents a crucible of change and discovery for all who traverse it. David, like the ancient Israelites, had to learn that survival in the wilderness (both physically and spiritually) was possible. God never forsakes His people, and will see to it there are always good individuals who would guide and nourish them even in their darkest hour; no one is ever left forsaken.

Not only was David left unharmed; eventually his kingdom was restored to him. David's immense faith in God kept him going until the very end. When David wrote Psalm 23, he wished to convey that no matter what kind of wilderness experience a person may happen to go through, we must always believe that we are never forsaken. The presence of evil is not absolute, nor does it have the final word. Righteousness and faith must triumph—even if it does not today. A reversal of fortune is always possible, and regardless of the circumstances, God is able to work a newness in all things.

Despite David's bitter experiences, he recognized God's sustenance through His earthly messengers. The experiences of David serve to show how sustenance and guidance come to us from God in hidden and unexpected ways. On a transpersonal level, the reader of the psalm is invited to see how one's own spiritual journey corresponds to the life of David. The Davidic narratives also underscore how decent human beings must act toward those in dire need, and help them. God's shepherding becomes revealed through human shepherds. This biblical theme runs like a continuous stream of consciousness throughout the Bible—especially in the prophetic writings, as we will see later.

### Deciphering the Wilderness Metaphor

Shepherding is inextricably related to the wilderness. Since wilderness imagery figures prominently in the narratives of the Exodus and King David, it is important to examine why the wilderness metaphor is fundamental in discerning the deeper spiritual and psychological meaning of shepherding. The Hebrew word *midbar* is usually rendered as "wilderness" or "desert." The King James Version, New King James, The Jewish Publication Society, New English Bible, New Revised Standard Version, and Revised Standard Version translations render *midbar* as "wilderness"; the New American Standard Version, New International Version, and New Jerusalem Bible render *midbar* as "desert." Although the terms are similar, there are some distinctive connotative differences. Among the definitions of the word "wilderness," the *American Heritage Dictionary* lists:

An extensive area, such as a desert or an ocean, that is barren or empty; a waste. **2.** Something characterized by bewildering vastness, perilousness, or unchecked profusion. [ME < OE * widderones, prob. < wildeor, wild beast: wilde, wild + deor, wild animal.]

According to the *American Heritage Dictionary*, the word "desert" means:

**a.** A region of permanent temperatures, and sparse vegetation. **b.** region of permanent cold that is largely or entirely devoid of life. **2.** An empty or forsaken place; a wasteland. **3.** Archaic. A wild, uncultivated, and uninhabited region. —adj. **2.** Barren and uninhabitable, desolate. [ME , OFr. < LL. desertum, neut. p.part of deserete, to desert.]

The Hebrew word *midbar* includes both definitions. According to several modern scholars, the Sinai technically is not a desert. Dr. Jacob Milgrom notes, "although its scant rainfall cannot support cultivation, it can provide adequate pasturage for the flock."[8] However, since *midbar* can mean both definitions, the word is sometimes used to denote a desert.

From both translations of *midbar*, we may surmise it is a place of bewilderment, perilousness, isolation, detachment, wandering, desolation, and homelessness. In the *midbar,* we feel cut off from the world. The *midbar* is a place of loneliness and desertion. In addition, in the wilderness, the Israelites made a journey into the unknown.

The wilderness was the symbol of chaos and nothingness (see Deuteronomy 32:10, Job 6:18). It was the place of demons, confusion, and wild creatures that preyed on helpless victims. The wilderness represented certain death to the unwary traveler because of its many dangers. Earlier, one of the definitions for wilderness was "profusion." The ancients feared the wilderness invading their

---

8. Jacob Milgrom, *The JPS Torah Commentary—Numbers* (Philadelphia: Jewish Publication Society, 1990), Numbers 1:1.

ancestral land and regarded the profusion as the symbol of chaos and disorder. The wilderness was also a place of madness, confusion, emptiness, and rage. One loses the sense of time in the wilderness. Formless and lifeless, the wilderness is the arena of chaos. The wilderness is both unknown and unpredictable; where there are no shortcuts and ready-made paths. Since the wilderness can provide pasturage, shepherding is also inseparably related to the wilderness.

The wilderness experience of the Israelites served as a paradigm for all subsequent experiences dealing with the trauma of destruction and exile. The imagery of the Exodus served as a symbol that out of the ashes of *Hurban* (destruction) God would orchestrate a new future that would restore the Jewish people to their ancestral home—despite the prevailing political conditions and realities.

The images of the wilderness are vivid and real. In today's terms, the wilderness can serve as a metaphor for those who have experienced loss, sickness, homelessness, loneliness, divorce, transition, substance abuse, and especially meaninglessness. Viktor Frankl, the founder of logotherapy, believed that the central human need—more basic than the drives for pleasure, food, or power—is the need for meaning. Human beings require a pattern and purpose that will make sense of our experiences and of the world around us. Meaninglessness threatens not only the inner world of the individual, but also the identity of a society. Later, we will elaborate on the image of the wilderness and its relevance to sickness and loss, and how Psalm 23 represents the best response to those undergoing the journey through the wilderness.

### The Wilderness as a Place for Shepherding

Though the biblical image of the wilderness is a symbol of bewilderment and death to the Israelites, the wilderness became a place of faith, promise, and hope. Abraham discovered his God through wandering in the desert, as did the other patriarchs. God's revelation demands that we leave the comfort of our homes and our cities. In the wilderness, the Israelites came to discover that God could provide for all their needs. As in the narratives of Sarah, the wilderness narratives illustrate how God can create life out of seemingly impossible circumstances. To others, the wilderness was a place of death and chaos; to the Israelites, the wilderness is the place where they learn, "The Lord is my shepherd, I shall not want" (Psalms 23:1).

One connotation of *midbar* does not exist in the English equivalent "wilderness" or "desert." The term *midbar* also denotes an uninhabited land *fit for pasture.* It is derived from its Hebrew root, *davar*, which among numerous other definitions, means "to pasture."[9]

Though the wilderness is a metaphor of spiritual homelessness and feeling out of place, the return to old slavish habits and dispositions, it is also the place where sheep are shepherded. The *midbar* is also where revelation (theophany) occurs. In the spirit of midrashic interpretation, the Hebrew word *midbar* is a cognate cousin of the Hebrew word for speaker, *midabar*. The Hebrew root word of *midbar* is *davar*, which means "word." It may be no coincidence that it is the barren pasture land in which God chose to speak with His people. Despite the adversity, there was promise and hope and theophany. Faith was discovered in the *midbar*—wilderness. Likewise, it is in the *midbar* that the Israelities were first commanded to make a *Mishkan*—a dwelling place for God's Presence to be manifested. Throughout Jewish tradition, the *Mishkan* represented God's triumph over the forces of chaos. Creating a sacred place within the hostile precincts of the wilderness is a spiritually suggestive metaphor for moderns for, even as we enter our own personal wilderness, we are beckoned to make a holy space for God to dwell with us as we traverse the *midbar*.

In ancient times, the prophets, and later the Essenes, had their communities in the wilderness where they could be more receptive to God's Presence.[10] The early Church fathers built monasteries in the wilderness to help them develop their sense of the Sacred. The Baal Shem Tov, Rav Nachman of Bratzlav, and others all recommended that the worshiper find God in the uninhabited areas apart from civilization.

The wilderness experience taught the ancient Israelites that "Human beings live not on bread alone but on every word that comes from the mouth of God" (Deuteronomy 8:3). The miracle of the manna taught the Israelites that God is capable of nourishing and guiding a people despite external circumstances and conditions.

The miracle of the manna is fundamental to the Judaic worldview of

---

9. Cf. Jeremiah 23:10, Isaiah 1:19, Psalms 65:13 and Joel 2:22.

10. Philo asked why God did not give the Ten Commandments in a city. Why did He choose the desert? Philo's answer may be paraphrased briefly as follows: (1) The city is not a safe place; it is full of crime. (2) The city is a symbol of vanity, which is the source of many civil conflicts, whereas the desert, by comparison is characterized by simplicity. (3) Life in the desert had fewer distractions; being in the desert enabled a person to purify him/herself and become a more suitable vehicle for receiving the Divine oracles. (4) In the desert, the Israelite people learned that the Ten Commandments were not the products of human beings. It was in the desert that the people came to know God through the various miracles of the manna, the quail, the making of sweet water, and so on. Philo observed, "For he who gave abundance of life's necessaries also granted the resources for the good life; for living they needed food and drink, which they found without making any preparations." (Philo, *Decalogue*, 2–7.)

sustenance, for all food is manna (מן = from) *from God*.[11] Manna represented God's mastery over the primordial forces of chaos. The manna could not be hoarded by the wealthy and used to exploit the impoverished members of society. There were no class distinctions; nobody had to qualify for sustenance. Each person was provided with exactly what s/he needed, not more or less (even Marx would have been impressed). Most importantly, the manna taught ancient Israel that sustenance came to the Jews in marvelous and unexpected ways. From hunger to fullness, from scarcity to abundance, Israel learned that her destiny was not dependent upon natural forces. The manna taught the Israelites that all food is God's gift of manna, from the most extravagant banquet to the smallest morsel of bread.[12]

The idea of being led by God is a notion with which many people today feel uncomfortable. People tend to think of themselves as being in control of their own destinies and that nobody is beholden to anyone greater than oneself. We often think of being powerful as a good thing; it is a prize we covet and strive for. Yet, the spiritual life involves a surrender of the self, the sacrifice of the ego. Like Jacob, the Israelites had to wrestle for their faith in the wilderness, and only then could they discover its meaning on a deeper and more personal level.

Despite the dangers and hazards that characterized the journey into the wilderness, the pilgrimage offered promise and peace. God's Spirit shapes people who are undergoing the wilderness experience. Though it may be a place of death, the wilderness is also a profound symbol of faith, rebirth, purification, and shepherding.[13] The Jews wandered in the wilderness for forty years. An examination of the number forty in the Bible and in rabbinic sources will produce some important insights as to why this number is so important in deciphering the wilderness metaphor.

The Flood lasted for forty days and forty nights. The Flood served as a means of purification. According to the Mishnah, the waters of the *mikveh* must contain

---

11. Being rich allows one to perform acts of mercy and truth. According to Rashi, "manna" is derived from the Hebrew word "appoint" (*manna*) and signifies "food" (cf. "manna" which is the equivalent of the Hebrew *man*); the rich deserve respect because they exercise mercy and provide food for the poor.

12. This could explain why the miracle of the manna is not mentioned anywhere in the traditional *Birchat Hamazon* (Grace after Meals): all food *is* manna. According to ancient Jewish legend, the manna could taste like any type of food one desired. The Talmud (*Yoma* 75a) records the controversy between Rabbi Ammi and Rabbi Assi. One of them said, "They found in the manna the taste of every kind of food, but not the taste of these five" [the cucumbers, melons, leeks, onions, and garlic, which they had enjoyed in Egypt and now hungered for; cf. Numbers 11:5]; the other said, "Of all kinds of food they felt both taste and substance, but of these the taste only without the substance."

13. The number forty signifies the miracle of new life. According to the Talmud, the human form is first developed after the embryo's fortieth day. (T.B. *Bechorot* 21b). For more detailed exposition of the symbolism of the number forty, see Maurice H. Farbridge, *Studies in Biblical and Semitic Symbolism* (reprint New York: Ktav, 1970), pp. 144–156.

forty *se'ah* (measures of water); this is the minimum amount necessary to cover the human body as it undergoes ritual purification. The waters enable a human being to transcend the impediments of impurity. The waters of the *mikveh* cannot be produced by human beings; one may channel purity, but it must come from a natural body of water unperturbed or processed by human beings.[14] The *mikveh* represents a symbolic death. Water dissolves all forms it encompasses and determine new status, hence new creation.[15]

In addition, the number forty is also a symbol of wisdom. Moses studied on Mount Sinai for forty days and forty nights. According to Jewish rabbinic texts, a person begins to appreciate wisdom when s/he turns forty years old.[16] The Book of Proverbs attributed to King Solomon begins with the large Hebrew letter *mem* (signifying forty). Elijah discovered God's voice emanating out of silence after forty days and forty nights (1 Kings 19:8).

Lastly, the number forty also signifies forgiveness and reconciliation. Moses spent the second forty days waiting to obtain God's forgiveness for the Israelites' sin of the Golden Calf. On the fortieth day (Yom Kippur), they were forgiven.

The *midbar* metaphor teaches us that although we may think of ourselves as leaders and disdain being led, it is the Presence of God that always guides and shepherds us. Suffering has the purpose of purifying us; we obtain wisdom and insight as a result of suffering. Spiritual growth demands the journey through the *midbar* at one time or another, for that journey develops our own spiritual growth and maturity. Toward those who undergo the wilderness experience, spiritual leadership, and the covenantal community have a special responsibility to shepherd the suffering person to restoration. In biblical days, the prophet portrayed how spiritual leadership in the past disseminated faith to those living on the ragged edge of life. Each of these leaders provides a vivid example for contemporary Jewish to aspire to.

---

14. The water of the *mikveh* cannot be transferred by a vessel—it must be derived from rainwater—or be the result of human intervention (*Mikvaot* 2:3–5). The Torah specifies that the waters of the *mikveh* must have qualities similar to those of a spring. Just as spring water is on the earth, so too must the water of the *mikveh* be situated in a pit.

15. Christianity borrowed Judaism's concept of the *mikveh* and called it baptism. In the New Testament, Jesus is baptized by John the Baptist in the wilderness (see Matthew 3:13–15). In the case of Jesus, his baptism in the *mikveh* was also for the purpose of theophany. Throughout the Middle Ages, the *mikveh* was used by mystics and hasidim as a means of preparing oneself to receive God's Presence—especially before prayer.

16. See *Pirkei Avot* 5:21. "At forty one attains understanding."

# 9

# MODELS OF SHEPHERDING

*Let the Lord, the God of the spirits of all flesh, appoint someone over the congregation who shall go out before them and come in before them, who shall lead them out and bring them in, so that the congregation of the Lord may not be like sheep without a shepherd.*

Numbers 27:16–17

Lost in a strange and alien land, the Jewish captives of Babylon saw themselves as spiritually homeless people. They felt completely out of place in the metropolitan world of the emperor. This was especially hard, for the community of faith now found itself situated on foreign soil, subjected to Babylonian values, hopes, and wishes. All the elements of the wilderness metaphor existed for the early generations that experienced the landlessness of captivity. The prophet's task was demanding; he had to find a way to nurture the shattered dreams and aspirations of the masses who had mistakenly trusted in political charlatans. The prophet had to help inspire the masses to see beyond the present circumstances by utilizing ancient images of renewal, promise, and hope.

### The Prophet as Shepherd

The prophet restored hope and faith for those who had lost it. He knew the "dark night of the soul," yet he was determined to assure his people that God still loved them and would be ever present. His task was to gather the flock and remind them of their spiritual task and mission. Like the shepherd, whose sweet calm voice drew the flock to him, the prophet's voice provided consolation to a people traumatized by the loss of their homeland and spiritual center.

The real question that concerned the prophet was how to articulate God's Presence among the people. Sometimes, the prophet utilized the language of ritual purity to teach the masses which values defile and diminish life. Violence, jealously, indifference, hatred, and theft remove the Divine Presence from the people. Without God's Presence, there can be only death. God's Presence comes when the covenantal community shows reverence and respect for life. To love God was to affirm life, and respect all of God's creation.

Images of God's relatedness were used by the prophet to stir the collective memories of the people. The prophet used daring poetic speech (in contrast to the discourse of prose) to awaken the sleeping spirit of the people. The prophet's voice pierced the muteness of the people's suffering. Moreover, the prophet helped the people direct their pain and anguish to God. By drawing the people out of the prison of pain, the prophet slowly helped the community move from articulating lamentation to reorienting their lives in a shift from powerlessness to genuine empowerment and eventual reconstitution.

The prophet taught that the word of God that creates the heavens and earth *can initiate a newness in the world.* Prophetic speech was a mighty instrument for evoking social change and reform. In his book *The Hopeful Imagination,* Walter Brueggemann describes the enormous power wielded by the poetic prophet:

> The poet does not only describe a new social reality but wills it. The very art of poetic speech establishes new reality. Public speech, the articulation of alternative scenarios of reality, is one of the key acts of a ministry among exiles . . . Rather, the poetry cuts underneath behavior to begin to transform the self-image, communal image, and image of historical possibility.[1]

Throughout the Bible, the prophet was always reminding the people that God is always present no matter how bad the circumstances may get. The prophet evoked images of the past to awaken the hopeful imagination of the people. The images and metaphors of renewal and rejuvenation gave new hope to the exiled. The prophets inspired them with the hope that they would be restored with honor to their homeland.

> Do not fear, for *I am with you*,
> do not be afraid,
> for I am your God;
> I will strengthen you,
> I will help you,

---

1. Walter Brueggemann, *The Hopeful Imagination* (Philadelphia: Fortress, 1986), pp. 95, 97.

I will uphold you
with my victorious right hand.

Isaiah 41:10

But now thus says the LORD,
he who created you, O Jacob,
he who formed you, O Israel:
Do not fear, for I have redeemed you;
I have called you by name, you are mine.

Isaiah 43:1

Do not fear, *for I am with you*;
   I will bring your offspring
      from the east,
   and from the west I will
      gather you. . . .

Isaiah 43:5

Do not be afraid of them,
   *for I am with you to deliver you,*
says the LORD.

Jeremiah 1:8–9

Do not be afraid of the king of Babylon, as you have been;
   do not be afraid of him, says the LORD,
      for I am with you, to save you
      and to rescue you from his hand.

Jeremiah 42:11

The Midrash observed that the biblical "I am with you" theme is a metaphor of shepherding.[2] The prophet reminded the afflicted that God was present with them as they suffered. Once again, Bruggemann's insightful comments deserve mentioning:

> Jeremiah's vitality comes precisely from his passionate conviction about the power of God to work a newness in the zero hours of loss and exile. Jeremiah does not believe that the world is hopelessly closed so that living is only moving the pieces around. Jeremiah believes that God is able to do an utterly new thing which violates our reason, our control and our despair. Jeremiah bears witness to the work of God, the capacity to bring newness *ex nihilo*. For that reason loss and emptiness are not the last word.[3]

---

2. Rabbi Menachem *Kasher, Torah Shelemah*, vol. 8, p. 146.
3. Brueggemann, *Hopeful Imagination*, pp. 29–30.

All of these passages resonate with words of Psalm 23:4, which states:

> Even though I walk through the darkest valley,
> I fear no evil; *for You are with me.*

This verse teaches us that one of the most important aspects of shepherding, is being *with those who suffer.* A personal anecdote may serve to help illustrate. There was a woman in the hospital who had lost control of many of her bodily functions. She could not talk, and her prognosis was listed as terminal. As this sick woman laid groaning in pain, her sick roommate, who also could not talk, got out of her bed and crawled over to the next woman. She lifted herself, and held her hand, and uttered, "I am here with you." By the end of the week, they were both talking in the solarium, much to the amazement of the doctors. This little anecdote illustrates the power of a healing shepherding presence.

In one place Isaiah (40:11) reminded the people that even in their exile God still looks after them as a shepherd looks after his flock:

> He will feed his flock like a shepherd;
> he will gather the lambs in his arms,
> and carry them in his bosom,
> and gently lead the mother sheep.

People often ask: "Why aren't there any more prophets today?" According to the Talmud, prophecy ended with Zechariah, but moderns find this answer wanting. Though prophecy as a spiritual institution ceased long ago, prophetic speech is still alive. By prophetic speech, we mean invoking the words and images of the Hebrew prophets to stimulate social change and transformation and produce a societal and political spirituality.

Vibrant and alive, prophetic speech calls for a radical restructuring of the community. The prophets evinced an alternative image of how the society and state can and ought to be. They were especially critical of the politicians' determination to maintain the staus quo at all costs. The prophet would not tolerate the leadership to lapse into apathy and numbness. They refused to act as accouterments of the state, nor would they rubber-stamp the state's economic and political policies. The prophets evoked images of a personal God who was personally concerned with all the nation's people—especially the poor, the afflicted, and the marginalized. Their speech was passionate and could not be silenced.

A modern example may be drawn from the life of Martin Luther King, the great civil rights leader of our time. In the fifties, when racial tensions were very high in the South, in Montgomery, Alabama, the home of a peaceful young black family was nearly blown apart by a bomb planted by a white supremacist. Young Martin Luther King gave then what became known as the "Sermon on the Porch," and preached a poetic message of nonviolence and change. The crowds went home peacefully with no incident. Throughout King's distinguished life, he let the word of God transform the South.

To the white supremacists, King was a relentless foe. To Afro-Americans, he was messenger of hope and courage. King illustrated how the word of God can bring radical changes in all segments of society. Like a true shepherd, King gave up his life in order to protect his flock. King personified the shepherd image at its best. When the ancient prophets of Israel utilized the shepherd image, they called upon Jewish leadership to act selflessly in the interests of the people for which they were responsible.

The prophet was intimately familiar with the wilderness experience and all its nuances—especially loneliness. The majority of shepherds since time immemorial have been loners. Nomadic life keeps the shepherd as a homeless wanderer apart from the community of people. Abraham, Isaac, and Jacob often called themselves sojourners (Hebrew *gare*). The prophet risked life and limb to convey the divine words as s/he stood against a leadership that was corrupt and popular. In the case of Jeremiah, all his poetry about the gloom and doom facing his people did not endear him to many people of his generation.

Like the shepherd, the prophet struggled hard to lead his people to a comfortable healing and spiritual space. Like the shepherd of Psalm 23, the prophet found ways to keep the negative spiritual influences that threatened the well-being of the spirit. The prophet had to raise the spiritual consciousness of a people that was either too comfortable with its prosperity or too demoralized by its suffering. In either case, the people were like the sheep turned over on their backs. The prophet as shepherd had *to minister to his people, his "cast sheep,"* and help them get back on their feet. The Babylonian captivity deflated the confidence of the Jewish community. Prior to their captivity, they were convinced that no earthly power could displace them from their ancestral home and Temple.

Like the shepherd, the prophet nudged, directed, and disciplined. He did not cringe in the presence of power. He was unintimidated by the community's religious and political leaders. As a subversive figure, the prophet often challenged the status quo. *He comforted the afflicted while afflicting the comfortable.* The prophets' words often made the ancient kings of Judea fearful and anxious. Despite the kings' behavior, most of the monarchs respected and respected the prophets' words.

The prophet, like the shepherd, shared the fate and the destiny of his people. Being a prophet did not entitle him to any special privileges over the common person. The prophet subordinated his very life to the people he ministered to.

One of the most important aspects of the prophetic ministry was teaching. This idea is alluded to in the Twenty-third Psalm: "He leads me in paths (*magalei*) of righteousness (*tsedek*) for His name's sake." *Tsedek,* as mentioned earlier, could mean deliverance. The prophet (or any leader) acts as a spiritual mentor, whose sole task was to guide the people along the ways of righteousness and deliverance.[4]

Throughout the Bible, the spiritual path is often described as a journey. This is especially true with Psalm 23. There are several words dealing with walking, leading, and providing direction. In the Bible, these terms figure prominently in many passages. A spiritual leader leads, guides, directs, and creates boundaries for the covenantal community.

In Jewish tradition, the laws pertaining to Jewish life are called *halachah*—a word derived from the Hebrew word for walking, *holech.* The rabbi is often called *moreh halachah*—one who shows the way. The ancient rabbis thought of Judaism as a path and a journey leading to God. This attitude is conveyed by the famous verse, "In all your ways acknowledge him, and he will make your paths straight" (Proverbs 3:6). The ancient rabbis developed the *halachah* as a pastoral attempt to guide and shepherd the community along its spiritual journey to God through the "dark valley" of the Diaspora. When the Second Temple was destroyed, Judaism would have disappeared had it not been for Rabbi *Yochanan* and the Torah center he preserved in the city of Yavneh. Throughout Jewish history, the talmudic and halachic insights of the scholars helped keep the spirit of Torah alive. Despite the many crusades, pogroms, and wars of genocide made against her people, the study of *halachah* nurtured the spirit of Israel. God's Presence was to be found within the "four cubits of *halachah.*" As I mentioned earlier, one other responsibility of the shepherd was to keep the flock within certain boundaries. As a metaphor for the halachic process, the sages created healthy boundaries to ensure that Judaism was carefully observed by its people. The rabbinic concept of *seyag la Torah* (fence) may be understood as a yet another pastoral metaphor.

### Shepherding in the Face of
### Despair and Hopelessness

The ancient shepherd often had to risk his life to save the flock from ominous threats such as predatory animals. This was no less true of the prophets. The prophet challenged not only mortal kings but also God Himself to observe his

---

4. For other uses of *tsedek* see Leviticus 19:36, Deuteronomy 25:15, Ezekiel 45:10, Job 31:6. The word may also connote: cleanse; clear oneself; (be, do) justice; justify oneself; (be, turn to) righteous(-ness).

covenant of love with the people (see Exodus 32:11–14). The prophet was a God-wrestler; he was a person of *hutzpa* (nerve).

Abraham challenged God regarding the fate of Sodom and Gomorrah (Genesis 18:23–32). Moses challenged God to erase him from His book if He refused to forgive His people. The prophet stood between the land of the living and the land of the dead (see Numbers 17:13). The biblical examples of Abraham and Moses illustrate that the prophet, like the shepherd, was undaunted when it came to the defense of their people. This motif of challenging God is found in several places in Jeremiah (11:20, 12:1, 18:19–23, 20:12). In all these biblical narratives, the prophet never succumbs to hopelessness and despair. Regardless of how hidden the Divine Presence is, the prophet was determined to reveal God's salvific power. To the prophet, there was nothing deterministic about God's will—it could be altered.

This theme finds poignant expression in the Midrash and Talmud, where it is not uncommon to see famous biblical figures contrasted with one another. The rabbis were not hesitant in critiquing even the most righteous of persons— Moses. The sages were convinced that the Torah is about how human beings became great—often despite themselves. Each biblical figure from Adam to Malachi underwent his/her own spiritual process of individuation. Though the Torah was not given to angels, human beings can become angelic in their behavior through devotion to the Torah in thought, speech, and deed.

### Noah as the Foolish Shepherd

One of the most important critiques of early biblical heroes is found in the Midrashim comparing Abraham and Noah. Each figure represents a type of spiritual leader and shepherd. The rabbis since the time of Philo of Alexandria had ambivalent feelings about Noah's piety—especially when contrasted with the pastoral nature of Abraham.

> These are the generations of Noah: Noah was a just man and perfect in his generations, and Noah walked with God.
>
> Genesis 6:9

> *In his generations.* Some of our Rabbis explain it to his credit; he was righteous even in his generation; it follows that had he lived in a more righteous generation, he would have been even more righteous owing to the force of good example. Others, however, explain it to his discredit: in comparison with his own generation he was considered righteous, but had he lived in a generation of Abraham, he would have paled in comparison.

*And Noah walked with God.* In the case of Abraham, The Scripture says (Genesis 24:40): "He replied, 'The LORD, before whom I have walked.' " Noah needed God's support to strengthen him in righteousness, whereas Abraham drew his own moral strength from himself and walked in his righteousness by dint of his own efforts.[5]

Though Noah deserves credit for saving the world, he nonetheless is criticized for allowing God to destroy the world. When God indicated how corrupt the world was, Noah was eerily silent and indifferent. Noah represents the kind of person who loved God, yet hated much of His creation.

In the Scriptures we read (Genesis 6:9): "These are the generations of Noah: Noah . . ." The great hassidic rebbe Rabbi Menachem Mendel of Kotzk explained this passage:

Why is Noah referred to as a *Tzaddik in peltz*—a righteous man in a fur coat? When one is cold at home, there are two ways to become warm—one can heat the home or get dressed in a fur coat or other warm clothes. The difference between the two is that the first case the entire house is warm and everyone in it feels comfortable, whereas in the second case, only the person wearing the fur coat feels warm, while everyone else freezes!

Noah looked after his own family's welfare but did not concern himself with the community. Though he worked on the ark for one hundred and twenty years, never did it occur to him that there might be another way to avert God's decree. Abraham was different, for when God wished to destroy Sodom, Abraham did everything in his power to save that wicked city.

In the Zohar, we find a very moving confrontation between God and Noah:

When Noah came out of the ark, he opened his eyes and saw the whole world completely destroyed. He began crying for the world and said: "Master of the Universe! If You destroyed your world because of human sin or human fools then why did you create them?" Noah said: "Master of the Universe! You are called Compassionate! *Shouldn't You have shown compassion for Your Creation?"*

The Holy One answered him, *"Foolish shepherd!* . . . I lingered with you and spoke to you at length so that you would ask for mercy for the world! But as soon as you heard that you would be safe in the ark, the evil of the world did not touch your heart. You built the ark and saved yourself. *Now that the world has been destroyed, you dare open your mouth to utter questions and pleas?"*

Rabbi Yochanan said:

Come and see the difference between Noah and the righteous heroes of Israel! Noah did not shield his generation and did not pray for them like Abraham. For as soon as the Holy One said to Abraham "The outcry of Sodom and Gommorah is so

---

5. Rashi's commentary.

great," *immediately*, Abraham came forward and said: (Genesis 18:23) "Will you also destroy the righteous with the wicked?"

He countered the Holy One with more and more words until he implored Him to forgive the entire generation if just ten innocent people could be found. Abraham thought there were ten in the city, counting Lot and his wife, sons, and daughters; that was why he did not pray for more.[6]

The Zohar's use of the term *foolish shepherd* is most instructive, for it addresses not only the Noah narratives but the narratives about Abraham and Moses too. As a shepherd, a spiritual leader must be steadfast in soliciting Divine mercy whenever possible. The Midrash and Zohar both condemn passivity on the part of its leaders. Death, destruction, plague, and sickness must not be accepted fatalistically.

### Abraham and Moses as Shepherds

Whenever human suffering unfolds, it becomes a spiritual dilemma that requires bold, fearless pastoral response. To be passive in the face of danger is to be partly morally accountable for the crisis at hand. When the divine face of God is obscured and hidden (*hester paneem*) it is up to the righteous to reveal God's loving countenance. Noah accepted the heavenly decree to destroy the world quietly without a whimper. In contrast, Abraham challenged the Divine to reveal mercy in the place of stern justice. According to Abraham, it was inconceivable that the innocents should not be held accountable because of the wicked. Like a responsible shepherd, the spiritual leader must save the flock from imminent peril.

Yet even Abraham does not exemplify the ideal kind of pastoral leader, for he was prepared to sacrifice the wicked for the sake of the righteous. Abraham thought there was a limit to God's compassion and that it pertained only to those worthy of compassion and mercy. It is for this reason Moses is often called the *Raya Mehemya*, the shepherd of faith, whereas Abraham is not. Moses is an advocate for all Israel. He was the defender of the righteous and the wicked, and, like the faithful shepherd, he was always prepared to give up his life for the sake of the flock.

Moses also shielded his entire generation. As soon as the Holy One blessed be He said, "Israel has sinned, they have quickly turned from the way which I commanded them: they have made them a molten calf, and have worshiped it, and have

---

6. Daniel Matt, *The Zohar: The Book of Enlightenment* (New York: Paulist Press, 1983) pp. 58–59.

sacrificed thereunto, and said, These be your gods, O Israel, which have brought thee up out of the land of Egypt. . . ." (Exodus 32:8)

And Moses besought the LORD his God, and said, "LORD, why doth your wrath wax hot against your people, which you hast brought forth out of the land of Egypt with great power, and with a mighty hand?" (Exodus 32:11)

Our Rabbis have said:

Moses did not leave the Holy Blessed One until he pledged his life for them both in this world and the world to come, as it is written "Yet now, if you wilt forgive their sin—and if not, blot me, I pray thee, out of your book which you hast written." (Exodus 32:32)

Rabbi Yose said:

"Moses' bravery is demonstrated from this verse: 'He would have destroyed them had not Moses, his chosen, confronted Him in the breach.'" (Psalms 106:23)

So all the righteous heroes shielded their generations and did not allow the attribute of Judgment to have power over them. And Noah? The Holy One Blessed be He lingered with him and spoke many words to him, hoping he might ask for mercy for his generation. But he did not care and did not ask for mercy. He just built an ark and the whole world was destroyed.

In each of the midrashic accounts, human suffering is portrayed as an aspect of divine anger. The central question each of the midrashic stories raises is, how should spiritual leaders respond to the crisis of suffering? The models of Noah, Abraham, and Moses each illustrate different types of responses to the threat of human suffering. Noah was interested only in saving his immediate family and did not care about the community. Abraham was communal yet was reluctant to pray for the outright sinner. If the sinner suffered, then he deserved to suffer. Abraham was concerned with the suffering of innocents. Moses was the ideal shepherd. Each person was worthy of intercession regardless of whether s/he was righteous or wicked. Each Israelite was worthy of divine forgiveness and intercession. Moses' own life had little meaning outside the context of his community.

The narratives about Abraham and Moses serve to instruct that the future spiritual leaders must be fully committed to the betterment of their own people. The role of spiritual leadership is not a right, or an honor. It is a duty that must be tackled with responsibility—even at personal risk, be it physical or spiritual. The last example of Moses serves to show that the spiritual leaders of today must not busy themselves only with the righteous of their flocks; they must do outreach with even the vagabonds and rejects of society.

Throughout Moses' distinguished career, he was constantly providing leadership, nurture, protection, and guidance to the whole Jewish community. Of all the images that Moses used to describe the role of the spiritual leader, he chose the metaphor of the shepherd.

Let the LORD, the God of the spirits of all flesh, appoint someone over the congregation who shall go out before them and come in before them, who shall lead them out and bring them in, so that the congregation of the LORD may not be like sheep without a shepherd.

Numbers 27:16–17

The image of God-wrestling finds poignant expression throughout biblical, talmudic, midrashic, and hasidic traditions. The midrashic imagination often likes to illustrate how true spiritual leadership responds to the drama of evil and suffering. The leader must be a God-wrestler who is prepared to bargain, cajole, and even force God to be forgiving toward His people. In one Midrash, the spiritual leader is portrayed as a gladiator doing battle with God.

> Rabbi Nechemiah said: It is said in regard to *havareem* (scholars), so long as a man is a *haver*, he is not bound to the community (he need not concern himself with its affairs), nor is he punished for its sins. But if he dons the cloak of leadership, he can no longer say, "I live for my own benefit, and I don't care about the welfare of the congregation."
>
> No, the whole burden of the community is on his shoulders. If he sees a man doing wrong to his neighbor and does not prevent him, then he is held responsible. The Holy Spirit cries out, "My child, if you have given your pledge to your neighbor, if you have bound yourself to a stranger," (Proverbs 6:1), "you are responsible for him, because you have struck a bargain with a stranger" [a pun on the Hebrew words for "stranger" (*le-zar*) and arena (*zera*)]. The Holy One, blessed be He, says to him: "Since you [by assuming public office] have placed yourself in the arena (*le-zirah*), and he who enters the arena must be either conquered or conquerer. . . ." The Holy One, blessed be He, says to him: "You and I stand in the arena, either you will conquer or I will conquer You!"[7]

This midrashic theme reverberates thoughout much of hasidic traditions regarding the role of the hasidic rebbe, who acts as the faithful shepherd (*raya mehemya*) prepared to protect his flock from all predators—even God (see Lamentations 3:10–13). In many of the hasidic stories concerning Rabbi Levi Yitzchak of Berditchev, he is often portrayed as taking God to a *Din Torah* (a Jewish court) about the fate of God's people. Elie Wiesel makes use of the same motif in some of his stories about the Holocaust.

It was out of this rich tradition that the Talmud said, "God can decree, but the *tzaddik* (righteous) can annul a Heavenly decree." Jewish tradition does not subscribe to a fatalistic view of the world. Evil must be combated and defeated. Spiritual leadership cannot be passive in the face of tragedy and danger. Thus one of the characteristics of both the prophet and later Jewish leaders was the quality

---

7. *Shemot Rabba Parshat Yitro* 27:9.

of fearlessness evidenced in the life of the faithful shepherd. This model of leadership is found throughout rabbinic literature, and especially in the hasidic profiles of its rebbes.

## Shepherding Souls out of the Depths of Hell

Pits are a part of the wilderness country. Some pits are open and visible, whereas others are concealed from the naked eye, as with pitfalls and traps (as in Psalms 35:7). Like the wilderness metaphor, the pit conjures many images that pertain to suffering, grief, and loss. In the Scriptures, the pit was often associated with the place of the dead (Sheol).[8] When a person is stuck in the pit, he is virtually trapped and cannot get out. Enemies were often left in the pits to die. Walter Brueggemann describes this image as follows:

> There is a great deal of talk about the pit. First, we know that the pit has concrete reality as a place in which to put people to render them null and void. In the pit, people are effectively removed from life. Historically, this is the device used for Joseph by his brothers (Genesis 37:22, 28). The pit is used against enemies. It means to deny the person all resources necessary for life. It is, therefore, not difficult to see how the specific reference became an embracive symbol for death. The pit reduces one to powerlessness . . . the contemporary use of the Psalms should take the image of pit and locate those experiences and dimensions of one's own life which are "the pits." This may include *powerlessness, being abandoned, forgotten, lonely, helpless, cheated.*[9] (Emphasis added.)

The pit metaphor also includes the feelings of being unloved, hated, punished, disconnected from life, and of emptiness and darkness. The pit is where one is lost from the world. It is a place of corruption and decay. Lastly the pit is also the place of despair and hopelessness. According to Dante, on the gates of Hell was written: "Abandon all hope ye who enter here" (*Inferno*, Canto 3). To be in the pit is to be deprived of having a relationship with those who are living.

If a lamb fell in the pit, only the shepherd's staff could extricate it. This image of rescue is pregnant with meaning. How we respond to those situated in the pit is exactly what the imagery of shepherding addresses. When looked at from this perspective, rescuing people from the "pit" and restoring them to life (as in "He restores my soul") is another metaphor of the Jewish belief in resurrection.

It may well be that the most important affirmation in Psalm 23 is that we are not prey to an impersonal force called fate or chance or scientific determinism.

---

8. Hell in the Scriptures is termed Sheol; it is a place of darkness and gloom. See Anchor Bible Dictionary for a complete summary of the biblical citations regarding Hell.

9. Walter Brueggemann, *Praying the Psalms* (Winona, MN: St. Mary's Press, 1993), p. 35.

The world is not bereft of God's concern and Presence; faith and trust must be affirmed even as we face death in our lives. As a metaphor for shepherding, the belief in resurrection teaches us that the community of faith has a duty to enter the portals of Hell itself, to bring back to life those souls who are languishing and yearning for deliverance. The Jewish belief in resurrection conveys infinitely more than is commonly assumed. Resurrection is a Divine imperative to affirm and embrace life in the face of death and hopelessness. Here is a famous hasidic story to illustrate:

Rabbi Levi Yiztchak, one of the most beloved rebbes of the hasidic tradition, relates the story of how the soul of Reb Moshe Yehudah Leib once rescued souls that were lingering in Hell. This was not so unusual, for when Reb Moshe Yehudah Leib was alive, he rescued thousands of Jews who were languishing in prison. Reb Levi Yitzchak recounts that, after he died, the soul of Reb Moshe Yehudah Leib went to Paradise. As he greeted, he heard a distant moaning. He followed the cry, until he came to the entrance of *Gehinnom* (hell). He refused to leave; after all, *he had come to ransom and rescue souls.* The angel at the gate did not know what to do. The rebbe made the following plea to the Heavenly Court:

All my days in the World of Vanity, I have tried to fulfill one *mitzvah* with all my heart and all my might, no matter what the sacrifice. Now that I have come to the World of Truth, should I do less? I shall not move from this place until I have done that *mitzvah*. If the Heavenly Court wishes to hear my complaint, then I am prepared to tell them, but only here, in this place.

The messenger brought his words before the Throne of Glory, and it was decided to grant him his request. He began:

Master of the Universe, You know how great is the mitzvah of *pidyon shevuyeem*— redeeming those who have been taken captive. Because of its primacy, You yourself have fulfilled it, and not by means of an angel or by any messenger. For when the Children of Israel were captive in Egypt, and Pharaoh hardened his heart and would not let them out of the house of slavery, You Yourself, in all of Your glory, went down to redeem them. *And I have sought to hold fast to Your qualities, as our rabbis, of blessed memory, have taught in explaining the verse: "This is my God and I shall glorify Him"* [Exodus 15:12]. "How shall a man glorify God?" they asked. "By following His ways: As He is merciful, so should we be merciful; as He redeems captives, so should we do likewise" [*Shabbat* 133b].

I have labored hard in this *mitzvah* all my days. I have never distinguished between the wicked captives and the righteous ones, between those who obeyed the Lord's commandments and those who didn't. All of them were equally beloved to me, and whenever I learned where they were and who held them captive, I tried to redeem them, for there was no peace in my heart until I succeeded in freeing them. Such is our lot in the World of Vanity. But lo! I entered the World of Truth, and here too, I found many captives. Therefore, I wish to fulfill this *mitzvah*, which depends upon neither place nor time.

And if You say that the *mitzvot* are given to us only in the World of Vanity so that we might purify our lives and the lives of those around us, but in the World of Truth those who are righteous return to the original state of man's perfection and we are no longer required to fulfill the *mitzvot*, then by life I say NO! I will not stir from this place until I shall fulfill this *mitzvah* here, for, behold, it was well known to You that I was never like the servants who served their master only in order to receive a reward. To the contrary, so dear are Your commandments to me that I have done them no matter what the place or time or penalty might be. If it is possible for me to bring these miserable captives out into freedom, let me do so; if not, it were better to remain with them in the fires of Gehinnom [Hell] and suffer with them than with the *Tzaddikim* [saints] and bask in the light of the *Shechina*![10]

Rabbi Levi Yitzchak concludes the story by telling his listeners that Rabbi Moshe Yehudah Leib won his case, and was allowed to redeem the same number of people he had redeemed while he was alive in this world. He concludes his story:

Happy are the righteous who bear blessings and work kindness (*hesed*) in this world and in the World to Come, who turn Heaven's decrees of justice to mercy, and redeem not only themselves but others, too, not only in their lifetime but even in their death. May their merits be a protecting shield for us and all Israel forever. Amen.[11]

### The Holocaust Rebbe as Shepherd

The above story about the rebbe who descended into Hell to redeem lost souls situated in the "pit" is by no means an apocryphal tale. Hasidic leadership often made it a point to reach out and bring the straying soul back to the "fold" of faith. The shepherd imagery of Psalm 23 found concrete expression in the lives of many of the hasidic rebbes of the Holocaust. The historian Pinchas Schindler enumerates eight qualities describing the special bond between the rebbe and his *hasidim*. I will mention only those categories that pertain directly to the pastoral imagery of Psalm 23.

---

10. Samuel Dresner, *The World of a Hasidic Master: Levi Yitzchak of Berditchev* (Northvale, NJ: Jason Aronson Inc., 1994), pp. 56–58.

11. Ibid.

1. Encouragement and consolation. The rebbes during the Holocaust years had to counter the feeling of hopelessness and despair that confronted the *hasidim*. The rebbes strove to encourage and remind their *hasidim* that they should and must resist the Nazi efforts to dehumanize them. Here is one example from the Piazesner Rebbe:

> It is within the power of every Jew to fortify himself in this period of terrible sufferings. Torment [of this dimension, as experienced during the Holocaust] and *Din* [judgment, retribution] are not within the realm of nature [that is, they are beyond human comprehension]. *Hithazkut*, as well, is an extraordinary phenomenon. Common sense would deny that *Hithazkut* [under present circumstances] is at all possible. [Precisely] Therefore, *Hithazkut* will succeed in transforming *Din* into *Rahameem* [compassion]. . . . *Hithazkut*, on its own merit, will convert bad into good and "to bless your people Israel."[12]

Like the shepherd of Psalm 23, the rebbe sought to help relieve his flock from the discomfort of the Holocaust. The rebbe tried hard to keep away the noxiousness of the environment, always seeking to promote the welfare of his flock whenever possible; he was resourceful in reducing the depressive atmosphere of the concentration camps.

2. Refusal of the rebbe to abandon his community. The *hasidim* were often resourceful in finding ways to smuggle their rebbes out of Europe; yet numerous rebbes refused to leave their flock behind. As one rebbe typically remarked: "I am not permitted to leave my flock in time of crisis."[13] Other rebbes would often quote the verse, "I will be with him in his time of trouble." (Psalms 91:15.)

The rebbes shared God's role in the suffering of God's flock. The rebbes mirrored the pathos of God. The rebbes knew that the mystical exile of the *Shechinah* was a call for radical action. The only way to redeem the *Shechinah* from exile, was to shepherd God's people and help them face their ordeals with faith and strength. The role of the rebbe was to channel God's blessing into the world. These rebbes understood that the essence of shepherding is to be present to those who need them the most; they knew that their fate and destiny was with their people.

3. Assistance and rescue. Dr. Schindler notes that the presence of the rebbe served to not only calm down and console the *hasidim*; it also enabled the rebbes

---

12. Pinchas Schindler, *Hasidic Responses to the Holocaust in the Light of Hasidic Thought* (Hoboken, NJ: Ktav, 1990), p. 73.

13. Ibid., p. 74.

to use their clout and influence to help rescue their *hasidim*. The rebbes were proactive and felt that they could not just passively stand by. One rebbe noted:

> As is well known, at a time when, God forbid, we are aware of brethren in trouble, and, in a position to rescue them, we are clearly bound by the biblical injunction: "You shall not stand upon the blood of your neighbor." However, in our times the suffering exceeds by far that which has befallen us in the past and the punishment for assisting rescue is terribly severe. . . . Should this prevent us from rendering assistance? God forbid, no! God tests our strength in these critical times.[14]

The rebbes used their influence to help bring food supplies to the Warsaw Ghetto.

4. *Ahavat Yisrael*—love and compassion for people. The rebbes taught that the sacrifice for a fellow Jew was even greater than personally dying for God. The Piazesner Rebbe maintained that one could not fulfill the will of God unless one fulfills one's obligations to the community as a whole.[15]

5. The hasidic meal. The image of the table in Psalm 23 finds special significance in the "*tisch*" (table) for the *hasidim*. The *hasidim* and the rebbe would often share a special meal in an atmosphere of love, song and dance. The *tisch* was often the place the rebbe would give an inspiring esoteric talk. During the meal, the rebbe would share his own personal food with his Hasidim. Even in the face of certain death, the rebbes never gave up this holy tradition. Like the shepherd of Psalm 23 who spreads his blanket out and feeds the sickly lambs, so too did the rebbes provide both spiritual and physical nourishment to their *hasidim*.

6. The written petition (*kvittel*). A *kvittel* was a *hasid*'s written petition to the rebbe. Under difficult circumstances, the *hasid* would seek the rebbe's advice and blessing. In the Holocaust, the *kvittel* was used by the *hasid* to ask the rebbe to personally intervene on his behalf with God. The *kvittel* enabled the Rebbe to see into the soul of the *hasid*, and focus directly on his individual problems. The rebbe in the hasidic world was a mender of souls. As was to be expected, the rebbe was a figure who played a major part in helping the individual *hasid* relate to God.

7. The *niggun* (melody). The shepherds of old would play the flute to calm the flock. The rebbes too, often used melodies (*niggunim*) as a means of showing

---

14. Ibid., p. 76.
15. Ibid., p. 80.

their trust in God even as they faced certain death. Their melodies helped raise the broken spirits of the *hasidim*, giving them a feeling of transcendence so that they could face even their deaths with dignity and poise. The hasidic melody also enabled Jews to defy their tormentors with dignity and grace.

There were many heroes among the Orthodox Jewish community who made it a point to search out, rescue, feed, and redeem their brethren in Europe against enormous odds. They were the true heroes and shepherds of the Holocaust. One of the most outstanding heroes of that period was Rabbi Michoel Weissmandl of Czechoslovakia, my father's country. Throughout the war, Rabbi Weissmandl devised numerous plans to halt at least twelve thousand deaths at Auschwitz. It was Rabbi Weissmandl who urged the Allies to bomb the military lines leading to the death camps. The Nazis used the same railroad lines to transport their military hardware. Any massive attempt, Rabbi Weissmandl argued, would shorten the war, forcing Germany to capitulate!

Single-handed, Rabbi Weissmandl was able to ransom twenty-five thousand Jews in Slovakia. Kranzler notes how Rabbi Weismendl negotiated with Gestapo agents to rescue Jewish lives. It mattered nothing to Rabbi Weissmandl what religious or political denomination these Jews were. With genuine determination and faith, he let nothing (even sickness and jail could not deter him) get in the way of rescue.

The shepherding archetype was not always embodied by all the hassidic rebbes; there were those who chose to leave their flock for personal safety (though no one can judge to blame them). Among the non-Orthodox, one of the outstanding examples of shepherding was Rabbi Leo Baeck. Baeck's saintly conduct was an inspiration to all who were with him in the camp. In the years prior to the war, Baeck did his utmost to encourage the Jews of Germany to leave the hostile climate of Germany. Baeck refused offers from the Jewish communities in England and the United States. He was determined to remain in Germany until he was the last remaining Jew. Like the shepherd, he was determined to look after the flock regardless of personal danger. Baeck succeeded in getting out one-third of the German Jewish population. He used his pulpit to challenge the atrocities of Hitler and the Gestapo. When he was summoned to appear before the Gestapo on *Shabbat*, he openly refused and defied them.

In 1941, Baeck was deported to the Theresienstadt concentration camp. Theresienstadt was considered by the Nazis to be a model camp where the Jews were supposedly treated well. Prior to his 70th birthday, Baeck volunteered to be responsible for the camp's welfare program. He was determined to keep up the morale of his fellow inmates. Baeck taught Torah and philosophy in the camp while arranging for theatrical performances for the camp's children. Rabbi Baeck recalled after the war:

It was dangerous for us to meet at night. There was an additional danger as well. During the day these men were involved in terrible, back-breaking work. And after such work, when they needed rest, they came together at night to listen to lessons and lectures, which could have weakened their bodies further.

I shall never forget those meetings. We would assemble in darkness. To light a candle there, or even a match, would have brought immediate disaster upon us. We spoke about matters of the spirit and eternal questions, about God, about Jews in the world, about the eternity of Israel. In the midst of darkness, I sensed light in the dark room, the light of Torah. . . . More than once I could not see their faces, but I did see great spiritual light.[16]

When the Church attempted to work out a prisoner swap for Baeck, the Church official replied: Your mission is in vain; if the man is such as you have described him, he will never desert his flock."

---

16. Cited in *Siddur Sim Shalom* (New York: The Rabbinical Assembly and the United Synagogue of America, 1985), p. 832.

# 10

# PARADIGMS FOR A POLITICAL
# SPIRITUALITY

*Mar Ukba said: When the shepherd is lame and the goats are fleet, there will be an accounting at the gate of the fold.*

*Shabbat* 32a

*The verse then says, in effect, "I chose no city until I had observed David to be fitting shepherd of Israel." For the welfare of a city with all its inhabitants depends for its existence on the care of the people's shepherd and leader. If the latter be a good shepherd, it is well with him, well with the city, and well with the people; but if he be an evil shepherd, woe to him, woe to the city, and woe to the people!*

*Zohar* Vol. II 198a

*He should always conduct himself with great humility for there was none greater than Moses, our master of whom it is written, "What are we? Your complaining is not against us . . ." He should bear his people's difficulties, burdens complaints and anger as a nursing mother cares for a suckling. For this reason Scriptures calls him [the king] a shepherd. It is regarding this concept, the Bible teaches: [78:71] from tending the nursing ewes he brought him to be the shepherd of his people Jacob . . .", The prophets have described the behavior of [a king] to that of a shepherd . . . He shall feed his flock like a shepherd: he shall gather the lambs with his arm, and carry them in his bosom, and shall gently lead those that are with young. (Isaiah 40:11)*

*Maimonides Laws of Kings 2:6*

147

Sacred symbols such as the shepherd imagery of Psalm 23 not only contain a deep metaphysical message about the nature of reality; they also contain formulations of the character, tone, and quality of the lifestyle society is enjoined to live. The social anthropologist Clifford Geertz notes:

> [A people's] world-view is their picture of the way things in sheer actuality are, a concept of nature, of self, of society. It contains their most comprehensive idea of order. Religious belief and ritual confront and mutually confirm one another; the ethos is made intellectually reasonable by being shown to represent a way of life implied by the actual state of affairs which the world-view describes. The world-view is made emotionally acceptable by being presented as an image of an actual state of affairs of which such a way of life is an authentic expression.[1]

Symbols serve to synthesize and integrate the "world as lived and the world imagined." The way of life and worldview complement one another. *The metaphysical ideal is inseparably linked to the culture of a people.* Geertz proposes that a religious object, act, or ceremonial event serves as a vehicle for the conception it embodies and that this conception is the symbol's meaning.[2]

Sacred symbols contain a metaphysical ethos that integrates the society's character and quality of lifestyle. Symbols for a society are intimately related to social transformation and social cohesion. Most ancient religious traditions utilized the shepherd image as a model for leadership.[3] In the ancient world, pastoral language came to symbolize the spiritual principles that governed both the universe and the covenantal community and its leadership.[4]

## The Shepherd King in Antiquity

In the ancient world, the king was a symbol and *reflection* of the cosmic order. The king's task was not only to provide order and promote life for the kingdom; he also had the task of defending the kingdom against the forces of chaos and death. His personal behavior had to be impeccable, since he represented the cosmic order. He upheld justice by living justly. For these reasons and more, the

---

1. Clifford Geertz, "Ethos, World-View and the Analysis of Sacred Symbols," *Antioch Review*, 17 (December 1957), p. 424. See also Geertz, *The Interpretation of Cultures* (New York: Basic Books and Harper Torchbooks, 1973), p. 90.

2. Two examples from Jewish tradition illustrate Geertz's theory: *Shabbat* (Sabbath) and *tefillin*. *Shabbat* has a cosmic as well as social dimension. Each Shabbat ritual reinforces the overall theme of rest (*menucha*) in all its various expressions. Another well-known precept is the *mitzvah* of *tefillin*, which symbolizes the outstretched "arm" of God that took us out of Egypt. The *tefillin* serve as reminders that God's Presence is always with us, guiding us at all times.

3. The shepherd metaphor is also a part the Eastern religious traditions. In Hinduism, Krishna was sometimes portrayed as a shepherd. In Buddhism, the Bodhisattva is often depicted as the good shepherd.

4. See Numbers 27:16–17.

ancients regarded the king as a shepherd, for his primary task was to provide nurture and life for his kingdom. In Mesopotamia, the shepherd image was used to designate gods and kings. Many of the ancient epics described their heroes as "shepherd" (cf. Gudea ca. 2144–2124 B.C.E.) or as the "humble shepherd of Nippur" (cf. Lipit Ishtar 1934–1924 B.C.E.). The title "shepherd" was the term for Assyrian kings; many of the Sumerian deities were known as shepherds. In the ancient Babylonian creation myth, Marduk was called "the faithful shepherd." Hammurabi called himself "shepherd of the oppressed and of the slaves." In one place Hammurabi stated:

> I am the salvation-bearing shepherd, whose staff is straight, the good shadow that is spread over my city; on my breast I cherish the inhabitants of the land of Sumer and Akkad; in my shelter I have let them repose in peace; in my deep wisdom have I enclosed them. That the strong might not injure the weak, in order to protect the widows and orphans, I have in Babylon the city where Anu and Bel raise high their head, in E-Sagil, the Temple, whose foundations stand firm as heaven and earth, in order to bespeak justice in the land, to settle all disputes, and heal all injuries, set up these my precious words, written upon my memorialstone, before the image of me, as king of righteousness.[5]

In Hammurabi's Code, the shepherd was held accountable for the flock and was responsible for their care. If a lamb or a cow were lost, he had to restore ox for ox, sheep for sheep. The shepherd had to breed the sheep properly. Any dishonest use of the flock had to be repaid tenfold. The shepherd was not responsible for any loss due to disease or beasts of prey. The shepherd made good all loss due to his neglect. If he let the flock feed on a field of corn he had to pay damages fourfold; if he turned them into standing corn when they ought to have been folded he paid twelvefold. Thus we see in the ancient texts of Babylon a model that later influenced the biblical prophets.

In ancient Egypt also, Osiris was sometimes called a shepherd. The Pharaohs were also compared to the shepherd. The shepherd's crook was part of the royal regalia. As shepherds, the Pharaohs were supposed to embody the orderly processes that kept the universe running.

If a Pharaoh wished to legitimize his rule, he had to exercise a pastoral role in carrying out justice. He also had to comfort those who grieved, be careful not to steal property from landowners, nor oppress the widow. The failure to act pastorally with his people would unleash the primordial forces of chaos and would endanger the kingdom.

Both the ancient Egyptian document *The Admonitions of Ippuwar* and the biblical narrative of the Exodus show how the forces of chaos attacked a kingdom for oppressing the poor and marginalized of society. This imagery had a profound effect on how the Hebrew prophets eventually conceived of the role of the king as shepherd.

---

5. G. R. Driver and J. C. Miles, *The Babylonian Laws*, vol. 1–2 (Oxford, England: Oxford University Press, Claredon Press, 1952–1955), paragraph 260.

Among the Greeks, the heroes of their poetry were shepherds. The Greek dramatist Euripides spoke of the Athenian ruler Theseus as a "young and valiant shepherd." Homer praised Pirithous and Dyras as "shepherds of their people." In Plato's *Republic* the definition of justice finds an analogy in the shepherd–flock relationship. According to Plato, the ideal ruler is one who is like a shepherd toward his subjects, looking out *only* for their good. Plato, like Ezekiel, also mentioned the negative aspects of shepherding. Despite Thrasymachus' arguments to the contrary, Socrates viewed the shepherd as the ideal model for what political leadership should aspire to be.

> Thrasymachus, if you will recall what was previously said, that although you began by defining the true physician in an exact sense, you did not observe a like exactness when speaking of the shepherd; you thought that the shepherd as a shepherd tends the sheep not with a view to their own good, but like a mere diner or banqueter with a view to the pleasures of the table; or, again, as a trader for sale in the market, and not as a shepherd. Yet surely the art of the shepherd is concerned only with the good of his subjects; he has only to provide the best for them, since the perfection of the art is already ensured whenever all the requirements of it are satisfied. And that was what I was saying just now about the ruler. I conceived that the art of the ruler, considered as ruler, whether in a state or in private life, could only regard the good of his flock or subjects; whereas you seem to think that the rulers in states, that is to say, the true rulers, like being in authority.[6]

When the Bible made use of the shepherd metaphor, it was a familiar image that had already been established since time immemorial. It is no coincidence that leadership and shepherding figure importantly in many of its stories, psalms, and history. Many of the early biblical leaders, including Abraham, Isaac, Jacob, Joseph, Moses, Saul, Amos and David, were shepherds.

The leader had the responsibility of looking after the welfare of his subjects and protecting the kingdom from all the outside foreign powers that sought to undermine it. It was the king's responsibility to guard the kingdom from any internal problem threatening the good and welfare of the populace. He could not treat them with utter disdain and contempt. Power in the ancient world had to be wedded to nourishing. The confrontation of Nathan and David concerning the Bathsheba affair illustrates how even righteous leadership must never lose sight

---

6. Plato, *Republic*, 1.342–345.

Aristotle considered the shepherd the ideal model of the king: "Each of the constitutions may be seen to involve friendship just in so far as involves justice. The friendship between a king and his subjects depends on an excess of benefits conferred, for he confers benefits on his subjects if like a good man *he cares for them with a view to their well-being, as a shepherd does for his sheep* (whence Homer called Agamemnon 'shepherd of the peoples'). Such too is the friendship of a father, though this exceeds the other in the greatness of the benefits conferred; for he is responsible for the existence of his children, which is thought the greatest good, and for their nurture and upbringing." (*Nicomachean Ethics*, Book 8, chap. 11.)

of its role and responsibility to the people. Though David had been a faithful shepherd all his life, in this one instance he became a shepherd who molested his flock. The prophet challenged David to remember his own pastoral role toward the governed by reminding him of his own pastoral roots.

> And the LORD sent Nathan to David. He came to him, and said to him, "There were two men in a certain city, the one rich and the other poor. The rich man had very many flocks and herds; *But the poor man had nothing but one little ewe lamb,* which he had bought. And he brought it up, and it grew up with him and with his children; it used to eat of his morsel, and drink from his cup, and lie in his bosom, and it was like a daughter to him.
>
> Now there came a traveler to the rich man, and he was loath to take one of his own *flock or herd* to prepare for the wayfarer who had come to him, but he took the poor man's lamb, and prepared that for the guest who had come to him." Then David's anger was greatly kindled against the man. He said to Nathan, "As the LORD lives, the man who has done this deserves to die; he shall restore the *lamb* fourfold, because he did this thing, and because *he had no pity*." Nathan said to David, *"You are the man!* Thus says the LORD, the God of Israel: I anointed you king over Israel, *and I rescued you from the hand of Saul; . . ."*
>
> 2 Samuel 12:1–7

If political and spiritual leadership embodies the principles of justice and compassion, the Heavenly Kingdom is magnified. Whenever a king failed to live up to the standards and spiritual expectations of the Torah, the king desecrated the Heavenly Kingdom. Jewish tradition calls this sin *hillul Hashem*, the *desecration* of God's name. The Hebrew word *hillul* is derived from the Hebrew word *hol* and is related to a family of words that suggest: "secular," "ordinary," "weak," "sick," "to be empty," "unfit," "tired," "diseased," "unhealthy," "an affliction." The sin of *hillul Hashem* empties God's name of His holiness and importance. When this occurs, the message of faith becomes perverted and diseased.

When spiritual and political leadership is corrupt and unethical, this can spell disaster for the governed. In Sigmund Freud's theory of group relations, Freud noted how the ego of the leader leaves a lasting impression on the rest of the group's members. As their leader, s/he is the personification of what they regard as the ideal. When the leader is corrupt, this sets the standard that the rest of the group will emulate.[7] The danger of *hillul Hashem* lies in its potential to spread like a contagion.

---

7. For an example, in Nazi Germany Hitler was seen as the father symbol of each German family. The German people often referred to Germany as the "Fatherland." Hitler illustrates how, once a leader is twisted and evil, his persona has a destructive effect on the morality of a society. The reverse is also true. If the leader is noble and acts in a kindly, benevolent, and pastoral manner, this becomes the ideal of his followers. A modern illustration is the king of Denmark, who, during World War II, also wore the Star of David out of defiance to the Nazis. The Danish people all identified with the Jews, as they defied Nazi oppression.

Freud's theory well explains why David's behavior was considered a *hillul Hashem*—a desecration of God's name. If the leader could be corrupt and above the law, why should the populace be any different? Faith becomes a mockery when its spiritual leaders act in ways that are contrary to the ethical principles they publicly endorse. If the leadership has an amoral attitude toward matters such as virtue, truth, and fairness, the populace will also adopt a similiar disregard for these important social and ethical values. Morality must be more than an abstraction that is ineffectual in bettering people. When the king embodied the archetype of the faithful shepherd, God's own name became great and sanctified. The parable of Nathan served as a reminder for all political and spiritual leaders to be concerned with the needs of the people, who were in a sense the flock with whom God has entrusted them. Political power had to be nurturing, life-affirming, guiding, and concerned with the powerless and oppressed. Each of these characteristics are personified by the way the shepherd interacts with the flock. When leadership forgot about their role, the prophet was always there to challenge the leaders' use of excessive power.

### The False Shepherd of Ezekiel 34— ### The Antithesis of Psalm 23

In Ezekiel 34, the blame for the homelessness of the Jewish people and their subsequent exile was placed squarely on the shoulders of its leaders, who failed to conduct themselves as "shepherds" toward their people. Far from being a pastoral force, the monarchy degenerated into a self-serving business and brought ruination to its people.

> The word of the LORD came to me: "Son of man, prophesy against the shepherds of Israel; prophesy and say to them: 'This is what the Sovereign LORD says: Woe to the shepherds of Israel who only take care of themselves! Should not shepherds take care of the flock? You eat the curds, clothe yourselves with the wool, and slaughter the choice animals, but you do not take care of the flock. *You have not strengthened the weak or healed the sick or bound up the injured. You have not brought back the strays or searched for the lost. You have ruled them harshly and brutally. So they were scattered because there was no shepherd, and when they were scattered they became food for all the wild animals. . . .'"*
>
> Ezekiel 34:1–6

Ezekiel's ideal model of government seeks to (1) strengthen the weak; (2) heal the sick and injured; (3) search and restore the lost individual members to the community; (4) make sure that the weak are not exploited by predatory people. This, unfortunately, was not the case. Ezekiel compared the leaders to the selfish shepherd who exploited the sheep, taking everything the sheep could give while offering nothing in return.[8] The monarchy had a pastoral responsibility to care for the weak and protect the rights of the oppressed. The Hebrew word for stray, *shogeg*, denotes a wrong turn in thinking. Ezekiel castigates the Jewish leaders for allowing the populace to stray from their faith.

Ezekiel's depiction of the evil shepherd clashes with the good shepherd imagery of Psalm 23. Instead of shepherding the flock, these leaders "shepherded" only themselves. The good shepherd of Psalm 23 was gentle and kind with the flock; he provided for the flock from his own cup. The evil shepherd of Ezekiel 34 was harsh and forceful with the flock of God. Instead of giving the flock direction and helping the flock to lie down restfully in green pastures, and leading them to still waters, the evil shepherd allowed the flock to scatter.

The good shepherd of Psalm 23 was a healer who nourished the body and the soul of his animals.[9] He revived the soul and restored the flock to perfect health and vigor. As a model for leadership, the government has the responsibility to heal and nourish its weak and helpless members. In contrast, the evil shepherd was indifferent to the well-being of his flock; he did not heal the sick or take care of the injured and oppressed. Instead of protecting the flock from its enemies, the bad shepherd allowed his flock to become prey for wild animals.

The pastoral imagery used by Ezekiel was used by other prophets that followed. The shepherd had a responsibility to give an exact reckoning for the animals entrusted to him.[10] The shepherd had to pay for any sheep that were lost or killed.[11] In an age in which monarchs and emperors were considered divine, the Torah saw the king as a servant of the people; his primary duty was to minister the needs of the people.

In the next sequence of verses, the key word used to describe the monarchy's pastoral responsibility is *doresh*, which means "to hold liable"; yet it also means "to search out." The monarchy has a duty to "look out" for the welfare of all its citizens. Government is liable and responsible for the flock's well-being.

Since the monarchy was remiss in this area, God announced that He would take their place as Shepherd. Verses 11–16 allude indirectly to Psalm 23:4, in which God announced that He would go Himself in search of the lost sheep of Israel, which were scattered on a dark cloudy day. The Prophet compared the Babylonian redemption to the redemption of the Israelites out of Egypt. He evoked the images and language of the Exodus,[12] and reminded the people to hope for God's eventual restoration.

---

8. The Hebrew wording in Ezekiel suggests that the shepherds "shepherded only themselves." Cf. the medieval Jewish commentators Kimchi and Rashi on Ezekiel 34:3.

9. Animals have souls, according to the Bible.

10. See Leviticus 27:32; Jeremiah 33:13; Ezekiel 20:37.

11. See Exodus 22:13, Amos 3:12.

12. Verses 13 and 14 are similar to the language found regarding the original Exodus—for

This is what the Sovereign Lord says: "I am against the shepherds and will hold them accountable for my flock. I will remove them from tending the flock so that the shepherds can no longer feed themselves. *I will rescue my flock* from their mouths, and it will no longer be food for them. For this is what the Sovereign Lord says: I myself will *search for my sheep* and look after them. As a *shepherd looks after his scattered flock* when he is with them, so will I look after my sheep. *I will rescue them* from all the places where they were scattered on a day of clouds and darkness. *I will bring them out from the nations and gather them from the countries,* and I will bring them into their own land. I will pasture them on the mountains of Israel, in the ravines and in all the settlements in the land. *I will tend them in a good pasture,* and the mountain heights of Israel will be their grazing land. *There they will lie down in good grazing land, and there they will feed in a rich pasture on the mountains of Israel. I myself will tend my sheep and have them lie down,* declares the Sovereign Lord. *I will search for the lost and bring back the strays. I will bind up the injured and strengthen the weak, but the sleek and the strong I will destroy. I will shepherd the flock with justice."*

Ezekiel 34:10–15

Note the similarities to the five pastoral expressions of redemption found in the Exodus narratives:

"Say therefore to the Israelites, 'I am the Lord, and *I will free* you from the burdens of the Egyptians and *deliver you* from slavery to them. *I will redeem you with an outstretched arm* and with mighty acts of judgment. *I will take you as my people,* and I will be your God. You shall know that I am the Lord your God, who has freed you from the burdens of the Egyptians. *I will bring you into the land* that I swore to give to Abraham, Isaac, and Jacob; I will give it to you for a possession. I am the LORD.'"

Exodus 6:6–8

It is possible Ezekiel addressed the leaders of the postexilic community who fleeced the Jewish community. The exile did not end the internal oppression the people felt. When the leadership continued their old oppressive ways, the prophet announced that God would not tolerate such an exploitation of power. Ezekiel placed the blame of Israel's woes squarely upon the selfish politicians who saw their positions as a privilege rather than a duty. Corruption begins at the top and affects leadership in the lower levels of government. These lower-level politicians were described as "goats and rams."

As for you, my flock, this is what the Sovereign Lord says: I will judge between one sheep and another, and between rams and goats. Is it not enough for you to feed on the good pasture? Must you also trample the rest of your pasture with your feet?

---

example, Exodus 6:6–7: "I will bring out," "I shall rescue," "I shall redeem," and "I shall take unto Me," and so on.

Is it not enough for you to drink clear water? Must you also muddy the rest with your feet? Must my flock feed on what you have trampled and drink what you have muddied with your feet? Therefore this is what the Sovereign LORD says to them: See, I myself will judge between the fat sheep and the lean sheep. Because you shove with flank and shoulder, butting all the weak sheep with your horns until you have driven them away. . . .

Ezekiel 34:17–21

In summary, the prophet Ezekiel contrasted the two types of shepherds and informed us that the same distinction that exists between the two embodiments of the shepherd archetype exists also in government and religious leadership. The selfish shepherd saw political (or religious) power as a divine right for furthering himself. Such leadership ruled harshly and brutally. Instead of uniting the flock, they created division among the populace, while keeping the best for themselves at the expense of the people.

Good leadership was custodial and pastoral. Such leaders strengthened the weak and sick of society; they searched for the lost and indigent. Their government was characterized by love and gentleness. They always gave their best to the people while taking little for themselves. The model for all of this is Psalm 23. The prophet also stressed (verses 22–31) that future generations of spiritual and political leaders must never forget their pastoral responsibility to the people and that God would hold these leaders responsible for the welfare of the flock.

In view of the levels of political consciousness brought about by the Vietnam War, Watergate, and various political scams in the United States, the prophet's admonition to all leaders to be more "pastoral" is no less true today than it ever was. The ancient prophets reminded future generations that political and spiritual leadership will ultimately be held accountable for its excesses and that the road for societal healing must begin with the kindly craft of shepherding.

### Cyrus—The Gentile Shepherd

When Jerusalem fell and the Temple was destroyed, Israel's faith in a nationalistic God who would unconditionally protect them no matter what they did also disintegrated. The Jews had what could be described as a nervous breakdown. Their spiritual identity was inseparably linked to the Temple. Many lost their faith entirely during this traumatic period of time. For many survivors, the "victorious" Babylonian gods seemed more appealing than the vanquished God of the Jews. Others became enamored of the new opportunities to become prosperous in a new land, and they forgot about their spiritual heritage. There were others who expected a new king who would apocalyptically restore the Temple and its sacrifices. Others felt helpless and sad that the Jewish people were doomed to disappear like other nations of history.

Just as the wandering in the wilderness served to restructure the spiritual development of the people, so too did the Babylonian captivity. What emerged from the Babylonian captivity was a restatement of an old paradigm: God can work a newness out of the chaos and nothingness of destruction. The exile could serve to purge the people of their misconceptions and help them renew their faith in God. Israel had to lose its parochial view of the universe and allow itself to become an instrument of God's plan of salvation. Norman Cohn, in his recent book on the origin of ancient eschatology, points out:

> The collapse of the kingdom of Judah, the capture of Jerusalem, the exile itself—these things represented a victory of chaos over cosmos. Only a god who in the beginning had converted primordial chaos into the ordered world could reestablish such a world.
>
> But in that case Yahweh could certainly do more than merely restore Israel to its former status. Second Isaiah was positive: the love which Yahweh bore to his chosen people was about to be manifested in the most impressive manner conceivable. By an act as wondrous as its original creation, the world was about to be transformed—and the people of Israel were about to be given a glorious position in the transformed world.[13]

Second Isaiah taught that redemption occurs in mysteriously hidden and paradoxical ways and can create new possibilities and hopefulness for the covenantal community. Divine Providence always carries surprise and wonder.

In chapter 44 of the book of Isaiah, the shepherd metaphor was redefined. Whereas in Ezekiel 34, the prophet speaks of the kings of Israel as God's shepherds, Isaiah taught that even a gentile could serve as a shepherd of God. Isaiah describes Cyrus's ascent to power as being initiated by God. Historically, Cyrus benefited from many fortuitous circumstances other than his military strength. Two Median armies were sent to fight against him but joined forces with him instead. Babylon's fortified cities opened their gates to him without resistance (Isaiah 45:1). Second Isaiah saw the rapid rise of Cyrus as God's shepherd to the Jewish people.

> Who says to the deep, "Be dry—
> I will dry up your rivers";
> who says of Cyrus, *"He is my shepherd,*
> and he shall carry out all my purpose";
> and who says of Jerusalem,

---

13. Norman Cohn, *Cosmos, Chaos, and the World to Come: The Ancient Roots of Apocalyptic Faith* (New Haven: Yale University Press, 1993), p. 153.

"It shall be rebuilt,"
and of the temple,
"Your foundation shall be laid."
                                    Isaiah 44:24–28

Isaiah's language was provocative and shocked the exilic community. How could Cyrus of Persia be God's anointed *moshiach* (messiah) of the Lord? This passage (Isaiah 45:1) is the only time in the entire Bible that a non-Israelite is called God's "anointed one." This term is usually reserved for the kings of Israel (see 1 Samuel 24, 26:1) and the High Priests (Leviticus 4 and 6). This is not to say that Isaiah envisioned Cyrus as the ultimate Messianic king, but rather that Cyrus was the "designated one" and "the shepherd" God would use to restore His people to Judea. The fact that Isaiah described Cyrus as a shepherd and a Messiah is instructive, for the narrative reveals how even a gentile emperor can be a instrument of Messianic redemption.

The people responded to Isaiah's bold proclamation with utter disbelief and skepticism. Here was a king who did not even know the name of Yahweh! How could an uncircumcised gentile serve as God's anointed one? Many of the Jews believed that God would orchestrate a new apocalyptic "exodus" led by a new Moses who would lead the Jews out of Babylon, dazzling the world with a theophany of supernatural miracles. Others pragmatically argued that accepting Cyrus as the "anointed of God" would mean that Cyrus would have political control over the land and Jerusalem. Undeterred, God would have Cyrus begin the changes He desired to initiate. In every generation God has been responsive to the needs of His people, providing them with rescuers who were always poised to come to the aid of their people. This idea reverberates through much of the Bible,[14] and has always been a profound indication that God has never abandoned His people.

### Shepherding and the God of History

The prophet wished to convey the idea that as God redeemed His people from the Egyptians, so too will God redeem His people from Babylon. The acquiescing of the deep to be dry at the behest of the Divine served as an allusion to the splitting of the Sea of Reeds (see Exodus 14:21). Water was the ancient symbol of the forces of chaos and disorder. The prophet asserted that just as God controlled the primordial forces of chaos at the Sea of Reeds, so too God could initiate a new exodus out of Babylon that could be just as great and miraculous as the original

---

14. See Judges 2:11–20, 1 Samuel 12:6–11, 2 Kings 13:5, Nehemiah 9:27 for numerous examples of how God provides leaders for each generation.

Exodus was when they went out of Egypt. Isaiah taught his generation that redemption does not need supernatural wonders and miracles. An old but forgotten paradigm was reintroduced into Jewish spirituality—that the Divine works through subtlety and mystery. The prophet responds to his critics:

> Woe to anyone who argues with His Maker,
> one earthenware pot among many!
> Does the clay say to its potter,
> "What are you doing?"
> Your work has no hands!
>
> Isaiah 45:9

> I myself have raised him in saving justice
> and I shall make all paths level for him.
> He will rebuild my city
> and bring my exiles home without ransom
> or indemnity says the LORD of Hosts.
>
> Isaiah 45:13

Isaiah's use of the earthenware metaphor as a description of how God shapes and makes history is significant. The clay metaphor is not new. In the Genesis narratives, God formed humanity out of the clay. In the Book of Jeremiah we find:

> The word that came to Jeremiah from the LORD: "Come, go down to the potter's house, and there I will let you hear my words." So I went down to the potter's house, and there he was working at his wheel. The vessel he was making of clay was spoiled in the potter's hand, and he reworked it into another vessel, as seemed good to him. Then the word of the LORD came to me: Can I not do with you, O house of Israel, just as this potter has done? says the LORD. Just like the clay in the potter's hand, so are you in my hand, O house of Israel.
>
> Jeremiah 18:1–11

In both passages, in Isaiah and Jeremiah, we find a similar theological theme. God is likened to a craftsman[15] who is attempting to give shape to His creation. This is symbolized by the difficult piece of clay. The quality of the clay will determine what the potter can do with it. If the clay will not cooperate in one way, the potter is determined to make it work in another way until he completes his art.

The theme of *assiyat hakeli* (the making of a vessel) is popular in the hasidic writings of *Habad*. Blessings require the making of a vessel to receive God's abundance. Without a proper fitted receptacle the blessings of the Divine do not

---

15. The Hebrew word for potter, *yotser*, denotes "to form, shape, fashion." An artist is sometimes called a *Yotser* (see Isaiah 44:9). It may also mean "to devise" (see 2 Kings 19:25).

materialize.[16] Thus whatever we pray for requires us to make a vessel for that particular blessing. For instance, if we wish to receive God's blessing of peace, then we must make the vessel of peace in our own lives and avoid conflict as much as possible. If we wish God's blessing of prosperity to become manifest in the world, then, we must be generous to those less fortunate than ourselves, and so on.

This kabbalistic concept is one of the most important expositions of the pottery imagery. Without such a belief, God becomes what Tillich describes as the "cosmic bellboy" who is nothing more than a slave to our selfish needs. The Kabbalist stressed that the purpose of the soul's descent into the material world is to form a vessel that is strong enough to contain God's effulgence and blessing. When the vessel for God's light is impure or weak, the light shatters the vessel, and all that remains are the shards. Such is the drama of human history. The task of Israel is to rebuild the broken vessel from the debris of the breakage.

The story about Jeremiah and the potter served to show that there is nothing deterministic about human history. Divine justice does not exclude the possibility of repentance (as the story of Jonah also indicates). The Divine demands that we as His creation give positive shape to our own future and destiny. Human beings are not helpless spectators in the unfolding of the divine drama, but are capable of giving a new shape to their own future and destiny.

In the above-cited passage of Isaiah, the people are reminded that the universe is not a place controlled by chaos or the forces of evil. The prophet assured the people that God, the Ever-Present, is in charge. History is open-ended and breathes with new possibilities. Everything that Nebuchadnazar had tried to destroy, Cyrus would in turn restore. Isaiah reminded the people that the ways of God are completely unpredictable, "what man proposes, God disposes." God is a Maker and Shaper of history but works in paradoxical and unexpected ways.

> Truly, You are a God who hides himself,
> God of Israel, Rescuer. . . .
> Isaiah 45:15

The hiddenness of God that Isaiah referred to was not due to punishment; rather, Isaiah is stating that the hiddenness of God is due to God's mysterious nature and power. Maimonides' concept of the *via negativa* draws inspiration from this passage of Isaiah. Clearly, this is not a God any theologian can ever help to "logically" pin down, for He is the God of paradox and hiddenness.[17] This

---

16. Cf. Menachem Mendel *Schneersohn, Derech Mitzvotecha* (Brooklyn, NY: Kehot, 1991), p. 162.

17. Carl Jung's concept of the *conjunctio oppositorum,* the "union of opposites," may well serve as an illustration of how God blends good and evil together. The conjunctio is a term derived from the medieval alchemists, who sought to bring about a union of unlike substances *in order to produce the birth of a new, transformed substance.* The *conjunctio* metaphor is found in many places in the

theme of paradoxical redemption in Isaiah 45 is similar to the theological themes of the Joseph narratives. The entire Joseph story served to illustrate the mysterious and paradoxical ways the Divine operates through history.

> God sent me before you to preserve for you a remnant on earth, and to keep alive for you many survivors. *So it was not you who sent me here, but God;* he has made me a father to Pharaoh, and lord of all his house and ruler over all the land of Egypt.
>
> Genesis 45:7–8

In Psalm 80:1, this theme is even more explicit:

> Give ear, O Shepherd of Israel, you who lead Joseph like a flock! You who are enthroned upon the cherubim, shine forth!

All the events that shaped Joseph's life—from the hatred of his brothers, through the debacle with Potiphar's wife, the dreams of the baker and the butler, to his appointment as viceroy over Egypt and, finally, his administration of food during the years of famine—reveal a God who shepherds history in ways that are not always apparent until we look back in retrospect. Although Joseph is the "provider," the real "provider" is *Ado-nai*—God, whose ways are always mysterious and hidden. The belief in a God who is a Shepherd and a Provider does not mean that Joseph was convinced God's designs would come to fruition with or without human help. Joseph understood that the divine plan requires human participation and resolute implementation.

When speaking of Divine power, we would be wise to remember that God's power is limited because of human freedom. God's power is infinite only *in relational terms—not in coercive terms.* Divine power does not violate human freedom (olam k'minhag noheg). Nor does God's salvific power stand detached from the world's processes. God's power is relational and works with human participation (though humanity may be unaware of God's permeating Presence). Human participation must serve as the locus of God's healing power. God's power has the ability to create a newness that nullifies the spiritual obliqueness of the past.

> The human mind may devise
> many plans,
> but it is the purpose of the LORD
> that will be established.
> Proverbs 19:21

---

Scriptures that portray light/dark, death/rebirth, male/female, infinite/finite. Here, the prophet teaches the communitiy of faith that the power of God is paradoxical and can mysteriously bring about a new union of opposites in ways that the logical mind would never consider possible.

Like Isaiah's proclamation concerning Cyrus, the Joseph narrative teaches that God's redemption not only can but must occur through human participation. Redemption is and must be initiated by human beings. God honors human decisions and the structures of creation. In the case of Joseph, the former shepherd of his family's flock ultimately became the shepherd of all Egypt. Joseph's kind pastoral approach to government came out of his immense capacity to nurture and provide to those who were in need. Joseph in turn revealed how it is God who is the supreme Shepherd of all.

The mystery and subtlety of God's Presence and absence is also the dominant concern of the Book of Esther. The ancient rabbis noted long ago that God's name is not even mentioned once in the entire book. The human intervention of Mordechai and Esther made it possible for the Jews of Persia to avoid the fate of genocide. One Midrash went so far as to suggest that Esther was for her generation a Messiah.[18] The Book of Esther led the early rabbinic sages to redefine the meaning of miracles. Miracles are more than God's calling card; the miraculous unfolds when we allow it to happen.

This same theological message found in the Book of Esther, is also the theme of the books of Nehemiah and Ezra. In 445 B.C.E., within a century after Cyrus gave permission for the Jews to rebuild their homeland (538 B.C.E.), the Persian court named Nehemiah as governor and sent him to rebuild and fortify the city of Jerusalem. With the help of the Diaspora Jewish community, Nehemiah was able to rebuild Jerusalem, fortify its walls, and repopulate it by transferring people from the countryside. What is important about the Nehemiah narrative is that human beings initiated the process leading to redemption out of captivity. In the beginning of the Book of Ezra, Ezra refers to Cyrus' gracious announcement that not only were the Jews permitted to return to their homeland, but that they could take with them their gold and silver and other gifts (Ezra 1:4). The return of the Temple vessels represented a vindication of the God of Israel for, when the Babylonians sacked the Temple, they proclaimed that their gods had triumphed over the God of Israel (cf. Daniel 5:1–4). The parallels to Exodus 12:35 are unmistakably clear. Yet despite the similarities to the original Exodus, the Jewish community was still bound to Persia as a vassal state—a "people of the province" (Ezra 2:1)—and there was no complete political liberation as the Israelites had experienced in the days of Moses. In summary, the Jews of the Babylonian captivity did not wait for an apocalyptic redemption to occur. However, the Jewish leaders regarded the return to Isreal as no less miraculous than the original Exodus out of Egypt.

One last note concerning Cyrus: According to talmudic tradition, had Cyrus fulfilled the divine mandate in its entirety, and rebuilt the Temple and sent back

---

18. See Raphael Patai, *The Messiah Texts* (Detroit: Wayne State University Press, 1979), p. 28.

all the captives to Judea, Cyrus would have been instrumental in bringing about the final messianic redemption.[19] Thus Second Isaiah teaches that the unfolding of divine redemption can occur with a human participant willing to serve as a conduit for God's gift of deliverance. The spiritual implications of the Cyrus narrative are immensely profound and deserve to be seriously considered by moderns—especially in light of the Holocaust and the emergence of the State of Israel.

The theological implications of shepherding are inextricably related to the messianic redemption. The Messiah will come when people least expect him. God's miracles do not violate the laws of nature but *converge with nature to bring about the desired end.* The Talmud points out that miracles are often hidden and unnoticed. Miracles do not occur *ex nihilo*; human effort is required. The Zohar puts it very succinctly:

> Blessings from above descend only
> where there is some substance,
> not just emptiness, below.[20]

Just as nature abhors a vacuum, so does the spiritual realm abhor a place of emptiness. Blessings from Above must descend into hands ready to receive the Divine outflow. This insight of Jewish mysticism is psychologically rooted in the biblical ethos that requires human participation to allow God's blessing to become manifest in the world—especially when the forces of evil seem pervasively strong. Shepherding is a mandate for resolute action.

---

19. According to Amos Chacham's commentary on Isaiah 45:1, the term *Moshiach* does not necessarily mean "One who was annointed with oil," (as the Davidic kings were), but rather "One who was designated and set apart for a lofty purpose and mission." Thus, even a gentile king like Cyrus could play a very important role in God's salvific plan of redemption for His people. (Cf. Kimchi's commentary.)

Cf. T.B. *Megilla* 12a: Rabbi Nahman, son of Rabbi Hisda, gave the following exposition, "What is the meaning of the verse, 'Thus says the LORD to his anointed, to Cyrus, whose right hand I have grasped,' (Isaiah 45:1). Now was Cyrus the Messiah? Rather what it means is: The Holy One, blessed be He, said to the Messiah: 'I have a complaint on your behalf against Cyrus. I said, "He shall build My city and let My exiles go free," and he just said, "Any of those among you who are of his people—may their God be with them!—are now permitted to go up,"' (Ezra 1:3). We may ask what would happen if Cyrus had indeed met all the criteria that God had wanted him to do, would he have then been God's *Moshiach*? This question is discussed in the novella of *Rabbi Solomon (Shlomo) ben Aderet* (1235–1310 c.e.). According to Aderet, Cyrus could never have been God's *Moshiach* for, even if Cyrus would have acted with enough gusto in (1), restoring the exiled Israelites back to their homeland, and (2), supervising the rebuilding of the Temple, King Hezekiah would have been declared the Messiah.

20. *Zohar*, Genesis, 88a. The seventeenth-century halachic scholar, Rabbi David Segal (known as the TAZ), quotes this passage in conjunction with the miracle of *Hanukkah* and explains why the miracle of the Menorah lasted eight days (cf. *Orah Hayyim* 670:1).

# 11

# JOB'S DESCENT INTO DARKNESS—
# A TALE ABOUT SHEPHERDING

*All the ideological arguments among people and all the inner conflicts that every individual suffers in his world outlook are caused by a confused conception of God. . . . One must always cleanse one's thoughts about God to make sure they are free of the dross of deceptive fantasies, of groundless fear, of evil inclinations, of wants and inadequacies.* Faith in God must enhance human happiness. . . . *When the duty to honor God is conceived of in an enlightened manner, it raises human worth and the worth of all creatures, filling them with largeness of spirit, combined with genuine humility. But a crude conception of God tends toward the idolatrous, and degrades the dignity of man and of other beings. . . .*

Abraham Isaac Kook

*Religion is the transition from God the Void to God the Enemy, and from God the Enemy to God the Companion.*

Alfred North Whitehead

The responsibility of shepherding is not only for the people's spiritual and political leaders. Every member of society must be trained in how to embody the shepherd archetype. Shepherding creates community. It involves creating a partnership of a people who are committed to the care, nurture, growth, and well-being of each other's body, soul, and mind. For those who suffer from the perennial problems of hopelessness, wandering, and despair, shepherding represents a theology of hope, care, and compassion. Shepherding is one of the ways God's love becomes manifest in the world.

The various theories concerning the origin of Psalm 23 accentuate this vital theological theme. Each of the proposed theories points to the theme of wandering through the wilderness (for example, the Sinai wilderness, David's personal exodus, and the first experience the Jews had in the Diaspora of Babylon). The psalm's message is one of hope, and it proposes that the community of faith visualize its role as shepherds to those who are lost in life's wilderness. In every instance, the psalm's imagery alludes to God's hidden Presence and His surrogate shepherds. The human shepherd (Abraham, Joseph, Moses, Barzillai, Abigail, leaders, kings, Cyrus, and so on) reveals the Heavenly shepherd. Psalm 23 is a blueprint for the good society, stretching from the highest echelons of government to the common person.

In this section, we will attempt to weave the imagery of Psalm 23 with that of another book of the Bible—Job. Let us propose that Psalm 23 is a response to the problems raised by trauma and human suffering. If this analysis is correct, then the shepherd imagery of Psalm 23 may help us decipher the nature and source of much of Job's suffering. In many respects the Jobian narrative is emblematic of much of Jewish history and especially the experiences of post-Holocaust Jews. Indeed, the Jobian story bears many resemblances to that of the Holocaust Jew.

- Just as Job struggled with traditional answers, the post-Holocaust Jew struggles with the traditional answers offered by well-meaning teachers, rabbis, and theologians.
- Just as Job was accused of sinful behavior that caused his "karma" to catch up with him, so the same was true of the Holocaust Jew. The story of Job serves to illustrate how callousness and apathy exacerbate suffering. Many Christian leaders across all denominations held that the Jews were being paid back for "killing" Jesus. During the Holocaust, the Jewish people were treated and regarded much as Job was treated by his community and friends. Fueled by centuries of virulent anti-Semitism in the form of inquisitions, accusations of spreading disease, conspiring to "rule the world," pogroms, and so on, many simple and sophisticated Christians viewed the Holocaust as God's way of punishing the Jews for being responsible for the sin of killing Jesus. At the opposite end of the spectrum, some Orthodox rabbis have blamed Jews for the Holocaust because of the sins of assimilation and Zionism.
- Like Job, the post-Holocaust Jew has experienced a profound absence of God's Presence. This predicament has caused much spiritual agitation, for the modern Jew finds it hard to see how skepticism, questioning, and doubts are part of the spiritual journey.

- Like Job, post-Holocaust Jews are used to hearing the voices of others (the professional theologians of our times) rather than developing their own spiritual voices.
- Like Job, post-Holocaust Jews yearn for a spiritual experience that will help them be able to put their lives and the Holocaust in clearer perspective. Job reflects the Holocaust survivor's desire to settle the records with God.
- The Job story is also being re-enacted in the lives of those suffering today from the AIDS epidemic. Like Job, those suffering have been told by many that their "sinful" behavior has made them sick.
- In a broader and more generally practical sense, Job is every person who experiences loneliness, acute loss, and suffering.

### Job as a Parable about Pastoral Care

The Book of Job must not be approached as an abstraction but as a model of how the principles of shepherding can be applied in a community. In the modern setting, a surprisingly large number of people feel that pastoral care is the task of the professional minister or rabbi. Most congregants I have served do not see themselves as shepherds to one another. Most people do not see pastoral care as part of the important biblical imperative—"Love your neighbor as yourself." Many fail to see that pastoral care is the way God's own love is transmitted and communicated. In times of crisis, we are taught that it is a lot easier to dial 911 than get directly involved. Society has special agencies to help those in need. The average person feels that it is not his/her duty to be concerned—especially when caring can be delegated to others instead.

My travel agent told me about a recent incident in which her daughter was involved in a serious accident and knocked on somebody's door. She begged that person to call the emergency road service for help. The man ignored her plea for help. It seems as though we live in such a frightened and paranoid society that people are afraid to act in a caring and neighborly way. One of the major tragedies of our postmodern society is the severe individualism that has unraveled our marriages, families, neighborhoods, and communities. Loneliness and a sense of isolation are rampant. In earlier times, neighbors would help raise each other's children; every family took care of its aged and sick. Today's institutional and bureaucratic agencies are filling these responsibilities and roles, once performed by families.

The isolation people experience in suffering (especially after they had a fall from grace, or some other form of loss) becomes inflated and exacerbated by a community that refuses to come out and show concern or compassion. All the imagery associated with the wilderness certainly applies to the Jobian narrative.

The pastoral implications of Job are especially relevant for today's times, in which we are seeing thousands affected with the HIV virus.

Beneath the veneer of apathy, there exists for most people a real horror that what they are looking at could be, under different circumstances, a snapshot of themselves. In his book *Denial of Death,* Ernest Becker describes the mechanism that exists in contemporary society to deny our own sense of human mortality and frailty. The sufferer often becomes a faceless person whom people refuse to see or help. Many of the issues raised by Becker were also intimated in the Book of Job. All the images associated with the wilderness experience are delineated in Job. It is for this reason that the book of Job speaks to all sufferers and would-be consolers. The Jobian saga is still as controversial as it ever was.

Many of the commentators, both Christian and Jewish, have attributed Job's suffering to all sorts of divine,[1] satanic, karmic, and physical causes. Most modern commentaries have seldom attributed Job's suffering to a *human* origin. An examination of his complaints will show that much of Job's pain was directed at a community that did not show compassion to him when he most needed it. On the basis of how we define the term "community," we could say that Job did not have a community. He lived in a city in which all the citizens lived by the ethic of rugged individualism; every person was out for him/herself. The people who inhabited Job's world measured spirituality in terms of wealth and property.

This approach was first expressed by the most famous of medieval Jewish exegetes—Rashi (twelfth century).[2] A computerized search conducted on the text seemed to confirm Rashi's observation. The word *hesed* (loving-kindness) appears only three times in the Jobian narrative, and only when Job implores his friends for help. Likewise, the Hebrew word for comfort, *nechama,* appears only seven times in the entire book. Only twice does Job ever receive *nechama* from his friends. The first time was at the very beginning of the book of Job (2:11). At this stage, Job's friends were uncritical of him. The second instance is at the very end of the Jobian narrative (42:11)—after Job had been vindicated. Strangely,

---

1. According to some rabbinic legends, Job lived during the time the Jews were originally enslaved by the Egyptians. At that time, he served as an advisor to Pharaoh.

2. ". . . so that we may learn from it a response to those who condemn God's attribute of justice; furthermore, Job also serves to instruct us that no person ought to be blamed for words that he utters because of personal pain" (Rashi's commentary to *Bava Batra* 15a). Rashi writes on the verse in Job 42:7:

For you did not comfort me with your "verbal defense" as did my servant, Job. His only sin consisted of saying "He destroys both the innocent with the wicked . . ." (Job 9:23). And whatever else Job said came from his suffering, which weighed heavily upon him and forced him to speak thusly. But you [the friends], on the other hand, were wrongful to accuse him of being wicked. In the end, it was you who were silent and defeated before him. Instead of attacking him, you should have comforted him as Elihu did. *As if Job didn't have enough suffering, you added guilt to your sins by angering him.*

the entire book seems to be empty of metaphors depicting human and divine compassion. This would seem to substantiate Rashi's view that the entire book is a parable about pastoral care.

Rashi's interpretation of the Book of Job as a parable about pastoral care stresses how empathy and tenderness are essential ingredients in healing the sufferer. Conversely, the story of Job shows how religious-minded people will sometimes see the sufferer as a pariah, a person to avoid at all cost. Job's community thought that whatever happened to Job might also affect them. The general attitude espoused by Job's friends was "Woe to the wicked, woe to his neighbors," and "Stay away from an evil person, otherwise you will end up like him." This is precisely what happened to Job. Job's life became full of loneliness and felt disconnected from God and those around him. Why does Job put up with such friends? The Talmud notes that human beings need friendship in order to live. Death itself is preferable to not having any friends at all—even if they are like the friends of Job.[3]

### Encountering the Diabolic

In the beginning of the Jobian saga, Job was described as a person who did everything right when it came to his religious duties, who played by the rules without deviating one iota. In one early passage we are told:

> And when the feast days had run their course, Job would send and sanctify them, and he would rise early in the morning and offer burnt offerings according to the number of them all; for Job said, "It may be that my children have sinned, and cursed God in their hearts." This is what Job always did.
>
> Job 1:5

Prior to Job's religious experience, his spiritual worldview was narrow. He believed that God was to be feared, placated, and pacified. The consequences of not doing so were dangerous. Job, in the beginning of the story, did not worship out of love. He assumed that righteousness is rewarded by God in material terms, while poverty and suffering are the lot of the wicked.

Although Job's prosperity was accepted by his community as a sign that he was a holy man, Job did have one adversary—Satan. Satan questioned Job's integrity and accused Job of being pious and obedient only because it profited him to be so. A challenge developed between God and Satan. Satan was allowed to do everything but destroy Job, while God sat back and observed. As the story

---

3. T.B. *Taanit* 23a; *Bava Batra* 16a.

continues, one can see a striking similarity between the questions raised by Satan and the accusations made by Job's friends.

The cynicism of Satan and Job's friends is instructive. Though Satan withdraws from the prologue, his cynical voice can be heard through the voices of Job's friends. The entire Jobian story suggests that all self-righteous responses to suffering bear a satanic quality. The Hebrew word *satan* means "adversary." Job's friends became his satanic adversaries who refused to acknowledge Job's integrity and innocence. The Greek word for Satan is *diabolos* (διαβόλος). By examining the Greek word, we may construct a Greek Midrash that may shed light on the role of Satan in the Jobian story.

The Jobian story is about a man of faith who experiences the diabolic. Jung and others have pointed out that the science of etymology deals with the unconscious side of language and often provides valuable psychological insights. The word *diabolic* is from the Greek word "to cast asunder," or "to divide."[4] According to the *Theological Dictionary of the New Testament, diabolos* also conveys:

> "to separate from," "to be set in opposition," "to be hated," (passive) "to accuse," "to repudiate," "to give false information."

Diabolic faith throws things apart; it sets the Divine and human in opposition with one another. The diabolic causes estrangement from the Divine as well as from the interpersonal relationships each of us have with each other. Part of the journey of faith is the experience of the diabolic. There are many points in our lives when we feel estranged and abandoned by God. Many of the greatest *tzadikkim* (righteous people) have often felt this way. To experience the diabolic is to feel disconnected and estranged from God's Presence.

The close association between Psalm 23 and Psalm 22 may be more than merely coincidental. In Psalm 22, the psalmist speaks of Divine abandonment.

> My God, my God! Why have you forsaken me?
> Why are you so far from helping me,
> from the words of my groaning?
>                                    Psalms 22:1

In contrast to Psalms 22:1, Psalm 23 comes to reaffirm that we have not been abandoned by God: "The Lord is my Shepherd / Even though I walk through the darkest valley, I fear no evil," (Psalms 23:4).

As a spiritual and psychological metaphor, the diabolic cuts through the bond

---

4. The word "diabolic" is derived from the Greek *diabolos* (which is derived from *dia*, through, and *ballein*—thrown apart).

that links humanity with her Maker and focuses on the polarity and tension that exists between God and the creation. Diabolic faith emphasizes how human beings are fallen creatures, sinful to the core and worthy of Divine retribution. This faith often depicts God as a capricious and alienating force that is "out to get us" if we do something wrong. Diabolic imagery reduces the stature of humanity and sees human beings and their existence in the worst possible light. The diabolic utilizes imagery that isolates the individual from experiencing the Divine as a loving Presence. In a practical sense, once people accept the concept of the diabolic, society becomes God's avenging angel and seeks to uproot "evil" people (such as Job) out of its midst. If our images of God are loving and healing, then our interaction with other people is calibrated morally to regard all beings with compassion and concern.

Job's friends portrayed the Divine as a Deity who was out to avenge His honor. When people experience the diabolic, their spiritual world is shattered, and they are left to pick up the pieces. Buber once phrased this phenomenon as "the eclipse of God." The community can either aspire to reveal God's Presence, or else it can further obscure the Divine Presence.

In the prologue, Job was no different from his friends. Job, at this point, would never think of holding God responsible for what had happened to him. Job was convinced that his God was a God of retribution. Every person got what s/he deserved. From ancient times to modern times, people afflicted with a disease or some other form of suffering were often portrayed as responsible for their own suffering. Centuries before the book of Job was written, there was a mighty biblical tradition that taught that the righteous ought to prosper, whereas the evildoer ought to suffer. Unfortunately, there are a plethora of verses in the Scriptures that are superficially interpreted to support this point of view. In one place we find:

> But if you will not obey me, and do not observe all these commandments, if you spurn my statutes, and abhor my ordinances, so that you will not observe all my commandments, and you break my covenant, I in turn will do this to you: I will bring terror on you; consumption and fever that waste the eyes and cause life to pine away. You shall sow your seed in vain, for your enemies shall eat it. I will set my face against you, and you shall be struck down by your enemies; your foes shall rule over you, and you shall flee though no one pursues you. And if in spite of this you will not obey me, I will continue to punish you sevenfold for your sins. I will break your proud glory, and I will make your sky like iron and your earth like copper. Your strength shall be spent to no purpose: your land shall not yield its produce, and the trees of the land shall not yield their fruit.
>
> Leviticus 26:14–30

One cannot help suspecting the anger and pain stewing inside Job. When he proclaimed piously, "The LORD has given, the LORD has taken; blesseth be the

LORD for ever and ever!" we wonder how sincere he really was. Perhaps Job said those words out of fear that if he didn't, God would strike him with even more pain. Job suppressed his pain and offered the platitudes and clichés that one would expect a righteous man like Job to say. But inside, Job was imploding with silent rage. This teaches that the colloquial way people speak of God and faith is often superficial. Shortly afterward, Job lost all his children and all his livestock, and he was stricken with ulcers.

His initial silence was perceived by his friends as a humble submission. It is when Job struggled to dare ask "Why?" that his friends, one after another, began chastising him. Each friend of Job felt threatened by the religious "apostasy" of Job. Job's questioning threatened to undermine conventional wisdom and beliefs. Perhaps the friends were not secure in their own faith, for they, too, could end up like Job.

When a person experiences loss, the sufferer must find a way to express and identify his suffering. If the sufferer cannot talk about his affliction, he will be destroyed by it, or else he will be consumed by apathy. To become speechless is to be totally without relationship; death is a state of silence (see Psalms 115:17). The deeper the relationship we share with parents, friends, pets, the deeper the pain we feel when we experience loss. Job's losses left him in immense pain. He had to experience a catharsis, for his stress was consuming him. Alone and silent, Job began to verbalize his pain. From this moment on, Job's life changes and is never the same again. A new Job begins to be born.

For centuries people have been told that suffering should be carried alone in isolation. According to the the book of Ben Sira we find:

> Let your weeping be bitter and your wailing fervent; make your mourning worthy
> of the departed, for one day, or two, to avoid criticism; then be comforted for your
> grief. . . . Do not give your heart to grief; drive it away, and remember your own
> end. . . .
>
> Ben Sira 38:17, 20

Perennial wisdom taught that those who grieve over loved ones should avoid dealing with their feelings of anger, abandonment, and pain. Grief had to be expressed in the initial mourning period, but afterward, it was considered impolite and excessive to talk about it to others. How much more was it inappropriate to question God on these matters. The friends of Job expected him to behave as was expected of a man of his stature. Job's community expected him to swallow his grief with stoic silence. Perhaps they expected Job to react as Aaron did when he lost his two sons Nadav and Avihu, who died in the prime of their youth: "And Aaron was silent (*Vyedam Aharon*)" (Leviticus 10:1–3).

The death of Aaron's sons, Nadav and Avihu, is shrouded in silence. Nowhere does the Torah provide us with a sense of what Aaron must have been feeling.

Did he blame himself? Was this God's payback for his making the Golden Calf? To decipher Aaron's response, we must read between the lines and look for clues.

Among the Hebrew words for silence, *dumah* stands out as a term associated with grief and loss. In both the narratives of Job and the death of Aaron's two sons Nadav and Avihu, there are a number of nuances that define the shape and pathos of a grieving silence. *Dumah* denotes astonishment, numbness with grief, lifelessness, being stonelike, a feeling of being cut off, the sensation of terror, and lastly, the silent yearning for hope. Job could not accept his loss in stoic silence. He had to confront his torment and anger. Whereas Aaron's silence was pierced with a Divine visitation by God, Job was not as fortunate as Aaron. Job's own silence, and the silence of God, threatened to destroy him.

It is an experience known well by anyone who has ever suffered: restlessness; disorientation; incoherence; dumbfoundedness; terror. Suffering often reduces us to silence. Extreme suffering often destroys our ability to communicate. The weight of suffering leaves us feeling incapacitated. We feel stonelike and lifeless. Trauma makes us feel overwhelmed, terrified, and distressed. When we suffer, we must find a language that will lead us out of our bondage of muteness and through the wilderness of silence. We seek a language of redemption. We have felt wronged; we have cried, and we have felt outraged.

All the subtle nuances of Aaron's and Job's silence are familiar experiences to most Holocaust survivors and to a lesser extent to their children, who grew up in the captivity of silence. Many survivors like my father, whose family was murdered in Auschwitz, lost their capacity to speak about the horror of the camps. Many second-generation children such as myself grew up never hearing our parents speak about the atrocities that they experienced. Frightened and confused, we never encouraged our parents to tell us their stories. Many of our parents and relatives lost their capacity to pray. Many expressed their doubts and a loss of faith in a God who did not answer them as He did for generations of the past. Their feelings of disbelief must not be misconstrued as an act of defiance; they are the natural response of those who suffered. Yet, this phenomenon is not unique to the survivors of the Holocaust; it is an experience common to all who have experienced severe trauma, to all who have suffered deeply at one time or another. Any close brush with the diabolical makes it exceedingly difficult even to talk about faith. Martin Buber asked poignantly:

In this our time, one asks again and again: how is a Jewish life still possible after Auschwitz? I would like to frame this question more correctly: how is a life with God still possible in a time in which there is an Auschwitz? The estrangement has become too cruel, the hiddenness too deep. One can still "believe" in a God who allowed those things to happen, but *how can one still speak to Him? Can one still hear His word?* Can one still, as an individual and a people, enter at all in a dialogical relationship with Him? Can one still call on Him? Dare we recommend to the survivors of Auschwitz, the Jobs of the gas chambers: "Call on Him, for He is kind, for His mercy endureth forever?"[5]

When we suffer, we hunger for a restoration of God's Presence (theophany), and a settling of the records. Like Aaron and Job, *not only do we wait for consolation—we expect it.*

> *For God alone my soul waits in silence;*
> from Him comes my salvation.
>                                                    Psalms 62:1

Victims of severe trauma often feel trapped in a prison of silence. Their healing must begin with speech. The language of lament and crying has always allowed healing to begin. Lament has traditionally been one of the primal forms of Jewish prayer. Feeling negativity, asking uncomfortable questions, are all part and parcel of the spiritual journey back to health. The verbalization of pain is extremely important, not just for individuals but, especially, for the community that suffers. The alternative is far more serious. If silence and speechlessness are comparable to death, then speech may also serve as a metaphor for resurrection. To give verbal expression to our deepest yearnings is to allow ourselves to receive a new theophany, a new revelation, a deepening of our personal faith. For those who suffer, the capacity to verbally express pain represents the beginning stages of healing and personal resurrection. Job's own resurrection will not begin until he verbalizes his pain to both his God and his friends; only then will Job find release from his suffering.

> God damn the day I was born!
>     and the night that forced me from the womb
> On that day—let there be darkness;
>     let it never have been created;
>     let it sink back into the void.
> Let chaos overpower it;
>     let black clouds overwhelm it;
>     let the sun be plucked from the sky. . . .
>         Job 3:3–5 (Stephen Mitchell's translation)[6]

The first step of Job's liberation from silence was his verbalization of pain. Although Job's anger was directed at God, he was either afraid or unwilling to blame God directly. He appeared to direct his anger at himself but was really directing his anger at God. As Job learned to get in touch with his real feelings,

---

5. Martin Buber, *On Judaism*, ed. Nachum Glazer (New York: Shocken, 1967), p. 224.
6. Stephen Mitchell, *The Book of Job* (London: Kyle Cathie Limited, 1989), p. 13.

he discovered that it was important to be truthful about his pain. Eventually, he learned to direct his rage at God and his ambassadors of faith, as well as his uncaring community, who were the main sources of his anguish and torment, as we shall see in the next section.

### The Miserable Friends of Job

Intimidated by this emerging dissident who freely spoke his mind, the friends were frustrated with Job's reaction to suffering. Job's friends felt threatened by Job's words, since they endangered the social system of the wealthy and the powerful. The wealthy were blessed by God, while the poor were cursed. The social realities reflected God's justice and maintenance of the social order. Job's fearless words could create a social upheaval among the poorer classes. Representing the status quo, the friends were determined to keep Job silent and make him wallow in self-remorse. Job had to beg God for forgiveness; he spoke heresy! The friends tried to intimidate Job with homilies about philosophy, morality, and theological discourses about the carrot and the stick. They tried to "force-feed" Job with the perennial wisdom of the day. The friends knew that if Job could be silenced, then life would continue to be good for the wealthy and the powerful. Job's friends found scriptural support in the older doctrine of retribution. Cleverly, the friends masked their true intentions by speaking in the name of God's righteousness. Eliphaz, the first of Job's "friends," attempted to persuade Job:

> Think now, who that was innocent ever perished? Or where were the upright cut off? As I have seen, those who plow iniquity and sow trouble reap the same. By the breath of God they perish, and by the blast of his anger they are consumed.
>
> Job 4:7–9

According to Eliphaz, everything that happens to human beings is determined by their own deeds. Eliphaz is convinced that Job can experience a complete reversal of fortune if he sincerely repents. Another friend, Bildad, echoed the same view as Eliphaz:

> See, God will not reject a blameless person, nor take the hand of evildoers.
>
> Job 8:20

To Bildad, there could be no such thing as innocent suffering, nor was there anything such as divine injustice. Bildad extols God's justice so much (see chapter 25) that he seems to ignore Job's suffering. According to Bildad's view, Job's fall from grace could mean only that Job was not as perfect as everybody thought he was. Had Job been righteous, how could God have allowed Job to suffer so intensely? Job's children deserved to die, since they were hopelessly wicked (Job 8:4). Today, we hear the same self-righteous rhetoric against those who suffer from AIDS; during the Holocaust we heard this response from sincere Christians who were convinced the Jews were being paid back their "karmic debt" for killing Jesus.

Job could not accept such a simplistic view of God. Job regarded Bildad's belief as a misrepresentation of God's justice. He refused to believe in a God that was vindictive and insecure. Such a sinister deity was incompatible with the God of mercy in the Bible. The God of retribution portrayed by his friends was to Job an idol fashioned after the depths of human depravity.

> What you know, I also know;
> I am not inferior to you.
> But I would speak to the Almighty,
> and I desire to argue my case with God.
>
> As for you, you whitewash with lies;
> all of you are worthless physicians.
> If you would only keep silent,
> that would be your wisdom!
>
> Hear now my reasoning,
> and listen to the pleadings
>     of my lips.
> Will you speak falsely for God,
> and speak deceitfully for him?
>                                        Job 13:2–8

Job will have no part of thoughtless clichés and rhetoric. Job yearns for healing. The Hebrew word for healing is *rofay*, which is also an expression used for mending. A true friend must be a healer, and mender of torn spirits. Job's friends did not allow him to heal and mend but exacerbated his wounds by instilling guilt and alienation. They kept Job's wounds open, keeping his pain ever fresh. Job could not accept such an idolatrous depiction of God; their *imago Dei* was so distorted that they misconstrued their role as friends and healers. They would have been far wiser to remain quiet. Outraged by such a capricious image of God, Job yearned for his friends to reveal a God who delights in compassion and mercy.

Zophar, a third friend of Job, expressed the same argument against Job that the others had expressed, albeit somewhat differently. The wages of sin *is suffering;* there can be no other explanation. He insisted that Job acknowledge that he was a sinner, and only then would his suffering cease. All Job had to do was to admit that he was a sinner and put his spiritual house in order. Remarkably, in the first round of the friends' discussion with Job, Zofar did not even acknowledge the depth of Job's pain;

> Do you not know this from of old, ever since mortals were placed on earth, that the exulting of the wicked is short, and the joy of the godless is but for a moment?
>
> Job 20:4–5

Refusing to accept his circumstances, Job was perceived by the community as a hypocrite and a scoffer. His so-called piety was seen as pretentious: Job had to suffer because the justice of the Lord had finally caught up with him. Elihu, the youngest of Job's friends, attempted to put the entire debate in perspective. He lashed out at the friends for trying to find fault in Job instead of trying to see Job's innocence. He accused the friends of pretending to know what was in God's mind. Elihu attempted to get Job and the friends away from viewing the justice of God from an anthropocentric perspective. It was not what Elihu said that was different; it was *how* he said it. Elihu spoke out of love and a genuine concern for Job, in contrast to the other friends, who saw Job as an adversary to be conquered in verbal battle.

> Therefore, hear me, you who have sense, far be it from God that he should do wickedness, and from the Almighty that he should do wrong. For according to their deeds he will repay them, and according to their ways he will make it befall them.
>
> Job 34:10–11

Sarcastically, Job tells his friends, "Miserable comforters are you all" (Job 16:2), and says of their words, "You comfort me with empty nothings" (Job 21:34). He urged them to comfort by listening instead of speaking (Job 21:2).

Job refused to be cornered into silence and submission. He would not acquiesce in the charges that he was a sinner who brought on his own suffering by previous misdeeds (*karma*). Job presents a very different picture of how he was perceived and treated in society prior to his afflictions:

> Oh, that I were as in the months of old, as in the days when God watched over me; when his lamp shone over my head, and by his light I walked through darkness; when I was in my prime, when the friendship of God was upon my tent; when the Almighty was still with me, when my children were around me; when my steps were washed with milk, and the rock poured out for me streams of oil! When I went out to the gate of the city, when I took my seat in the square, the young men saw me and withdrew, and the aged rose up and stood; the nobles refrained from talking, and laid their hands on their mouths; the voices of princes were hushed, and their tongues stuck to the roof of their mouths. When the ear heard, it commended me, and when the eye saw, it approved; because I delivered the poor who cried, and the

orphan who had no helper. The blessing of the wretched came upon me, and I caused the widow's heart to sing for joy. I put on righteousness, and it clothed me; my justice was like a robe and a turban. I was eyes to the blind, and feet to the lame.

Job 29:2–25

Subsequently, however, at Job's home, his own family did not want to have anything to do with him. He had become alienated from everybody—even his own wife. He had become a social outcast; people gossiped against him. Job's former friends did not want to know of him. Following their parents' example, the community's children treated Job with utter scorn and contempt.

Job's suffering reached new depths as he was ostracized from a community that once venerated him as a holy man. Job was seen as a man who had fallen from grace; he became the recipient of taunts and torments and insults. Those who saw Job as the embodiment of evil, as one who was condemned by God, may even have physically harassed him. Job's call for justice (19:7) went unheeded; he was victimized by a society that treated him as though he did not exist. Job's suffering meant nothing to those around him. He felt cut off, isolated, and "fenced in." It was as though he had no self-worth whatsoever as a human being.

> He walled up my way so that I cannot pass,
> and he has set darkness upon my paths.
>
> Job 19:8

Anyone who has suffered loss of any kind can easily relate to the apathy and callousness Job experienced from his community. There are many types of loss in our lives, such as the loss of a spouse, a family member, a child; a relationship that has ended in divorce; the loss of a job; illness; the loss of a home or a limb; or incarceration for a crime. Job's reaction is well known to all who have suffered and received little or no support from the community. Those who experience the pain, and the shame, often feel that they are hated by God and their community for their sins. In our own day, this is what happened to the Vietnam War veteran who came back to a country that was ashamed of him. The Vietnam War veteran became like Job—an outcast who was despised by all. Walt Davis, in his new book *Shattered Dream: America's Search for Its Soul*, writes:

> Finally, the deepest feeling of shame is that sense of abandonment that comes when one has nothing left to trust—no person, no group, no belief system, not even God. One vet expressed his rage at God for such abandonment: "God," he shouted, "you mother———! Where were you in Vietnam?" This is true homelessness, when cynicism and skepticism slide on down into the pit of isolation and despair. *"Loss of trust, exposure, failure, the feeling of homelessness—these experiences of shame—become still more unbearable if they lead to the feeling that there is no*

*home for anyone, anywhere.* . . . . Experience of shame may call into question not only one's own adequacy, and the validity of the codes of one's immediate society, but the meaning of the universe itself.[7] (Emphasis added.)

The Jobian experience has often been described in the mystical writings as the Dark Night of the Soul. When we enter the Dark Night, we feel as though our last link of hope—our relationship with God—has been lost or severed; we long and ache for God's loving Presence. Whenever we enter the Dark Night, we often feel as though God is an enemy who is out to punish us for wrongdoing.

### Job as Public Enemy Number One

There is no doubt that when we suffer, it is easy to feel that God is like an enemy and adversary instead of a shepherd and a friend. The name "Job" is derived from the Hebrew word *oyev*, signifying "enemy," "hated," and "hostility." Who was the enemy? Was it Job? Was it God? Or, was it Job's community? His friends and community all regarded Job as God's enemy. Since Job was God's "enemy" he had to be their "enemy" too, so they treated him with hostility. From Job's point of view, God seemed like his enemy (Job 33:10) who was out to "get him." The metaphor of God as enemy is expressed elsewhere in the Scriptures. Jacob's battle with the angel is one example. The Book of Lamentations portrays the image of God as enemy in very radical terms:

The Lord has become like an enemy; He has destroyed Israel; He has destroyed all its palaces, laid in ruins its strongholds, and multiplied in daughter Judah mourning and lamentation.

Lamentations 2:5

He is a bear lying in wait for me, a lion in hiding; he led me off my way and tore me to pieces; he has made me desolate; he bent his bow and set me as a mark for his arrow. He shot into my vitals the arrows of his quiver.

Lamentations 3:10–13

What is true of the suffering of an individual is equally true with the suffering of a nation. The metaphor of God as an enemy gives vivid expression to the collective pain and suffering we feel when God's Presence is hidden.

When people experience pain and suffering alone, they risk future emotional problems resulting from not channeling their bitterness through interacting with the community. Often people are told not to express anger toward God, and this

---

7. Walter Davis, *Shattered Dream: America's Search for Its Soul* (Valley Forge, PA: Trinity Press International, 1995), p. 88.

causes people to exile God and religion from their lives. The prayers of lament have always provided ways for people to emerge from their suffering. The community can help greatly *by being there* and validating their feelings of anger, hostility, and loss.

Job's suffering was compounded by what appeared to be a divorce and break-up of his own family life. Job discovered that he had many fair-weather friends who abandoned him rather than help him heal:

> He has put my family far from me, and my acquaintances are wholly estranged from me. My relatives and my close friends have failed me; the guests in my house have forgotten me; my serving girls count me as a stranger; I have become an alien in their eyes. I call to my servant, but he gives me no answer; I must myself plead with him. My breath is repulsive to my wife; I am loathsome to my own family. Even young children despise me; when I rise, they talk against me. All my intimate friends abhor me, and those whom I loved have turned against me.
>
> Job 19:13–19

Job's wife wanted Job to shrivel up and die. In effect she told her husband to curse God and drop dead. His breath was so disgusting that she kept a distance from her husband. The absence of family support is often the case today, particularly when a parent or an older relative becomes seriously ill. When a crisis immediately takes place in a young healthy family, often the strain gets to be too rough for the spouse—especially if there are other problems threatening the marriage.

The friends of Job felt a false sense of superiority and condescension over him. They regarded Job as a moral inferior to themselves. Most of Job's "friends" acted in a very pompous self-serving manner toward him. The one exception was Elihu, who always phrased his statements with gentleness and sensitivity. Even though much of his speech was critical of Job's attitude, he never criticized Job as a person.

### God's Response to Job

The great twelfth-century Jewish philosopher Maimonides noted that although Job was a very upright and decent individual, the one characteristic he lacked was the quality of insight.[8] In the beginning, Job feared God and did not act out of love. Despite Job's devoted religious behavior, he did not have a personal religious experience. Maimonides suggests that much of Job's own suffering was due to wrongful notions and beliefs he had regarding the ways of Providence.

---

8. Maimonides, *Guide to the Perplexed*, 3:22.

Much (but certainly not all) human suffering is often attributed to the dysfunctional images people have inherited concerning God. Ignorance conditioned Job into thinking that he was a separate entity, apart from God, pitted against a hostile world. Job's ordeal represents the painful journey of all sufferers; for this reason Job's transformation is most instructive.

The journey to God requires a purging of our preconceived images, sensory perceptions, and affective attachments concerning that which is not God. As we enter the Dark Night of the Soul, we are emptied of all preconceived "graven" images of faith to which we have held fast. In the Dark Night, we experience loneliness and separateness. Darkness fills our intellects; our hearts yearn for God's love. We yearn for friendship and companionship. We feel spiritually impotent, tired, and discouraged. We feel as though the soul is caught within a maze that it will never get out of. Worse still, we experience the bitterness and pain of feeling utterly abandoned by God and humanity. We cry out that God should illumine our lives with the radiance of the *Shechinah* (Psalms 146:2). But through these sufferings we must grow, and develop a new response to faith, hope, and love. This journey is not one on which we deliberately embark; rather, we are thrust by God into the darkness. In kabbalistic terms, we enter into the mysterious realm of *ayin*, of Nothingness, to be reborn as a new creation (*yesh m'ayin*).[9]

Job's journey through the Dark Night changed him and his relationship with God, his family, and his community forever. Using today's terms, we could say that Job had a profound religious experience. By the end of the story, Job exclaims:

> I had heard of you by the
> hearing of the ear,
> but now my eye sees you;
> Job 42:5

What did Job discover? According to Rashi, Job received a revelation of God's *Shechinah* (immanence). The *Shechinah* represents the maternal, nurturing Presence of God. Yet the *Shechinah*'s appearance is not an unconditional thing. Human behavior determines to what degree God's feminine Presence is revealed in the world. Every action of compassion and justice reveals God's immanence in the world. The *Shechinah*'s appearance is not coincidental, for all Job's friends

---

9. The imagery of night is a major topic in much of the Habad hasidic literature, as it is for Christian mysticism (cf. Saint John of the Cross) as well. See Menachem Mendel Schneersohn, *Ohr HaTorah Parshat Lech Licha*, 146–148. Yosef Yitzchak Schneersohn's discourse on Psalms 146:2 in *Sefer Maamareem 5700* (reprint, Brooklyn, NY: Kehot, 1986). *Levi Yitzchak*'s comments on the *Bereishit Rabbah 3:10 Kedushat Halevy Parshat Berashit*. *Levi Yitzchak* notes that the goal of darkness is to help the soul come to a genuine love of God that is brought about by repentance of the past.

portrayed God in solely masculine terms (and dysfunctional masculinity at best!). Experiencing God's immanence filled Job with love; he became reconciled with his human mortality. Whereas others spoke about God, Job in the end experienced God's majestic Presence. He came to see that all God-talk pales before the actual experience of God's *Shechinah*. Job discovered an interconnectedness that weaves all aspects of creation together. It is the *Shechinah*'s love that keeps the world intact despite itself. Job came to the realization that at the core of human suffering is the delusion that one is separate from God. It is humanity's grandest illusion that situates God against His creation.

### *Job and Plato's Allegory of the Cave*

For the greater part of Job's spiritual journey, he sought a cognitive knowledge of God that would explain away all his difficulties. In the end, God shows Job that He cannot be reduced to an object of contemplation. The universe and all of its fullness has mystery. God's very Being is veiled in paradox and cannot be reduced to a theological axiom. God helped Job move away from his anthropocentric view of the universe. Not everything needs the intellectual assent of humanity to be valid.

Rav Kook observed long ago:

> The nature of the spiritual reality cannot be discerned through scientific probing. Objective knowledge, rational analysis, philosophy—these disclose only the external phenomena of life. Even they deal with the inner aspects of existence, they are focusing only on the shadows cast upon life's essence, but not on its inner content. The true achievement of rational demonstration is only to prepare a path for the spirit to reach the outer chamber of the spiritual domain. But as long as man is immersed in his senses and their narrow confinements, he will not be able to know fully the spiritual dimension of life, only faint shadows thereof will be discernible through them. And if he should relate to these shadows as though they were the true reality, then these shadows will turn for him into a heavy burden and they will diminish both his physical and his spiritual vigor, so that he will seek to flee from them as something detrimental.[10]

God showed Job that human intelligence can fathom only a small fragment of the processes that exist in the cosmos. If this is true of the physical order, how much more difficult will it be for humanity to ever understand the spiritual workings of Providence?

God's answer to Job bears some similarities to Plato's Allegory of the Cave. In this famous tale, Plato describes a deep subterranean cave in which people

---

10. *Abraham Isaac Kook*, trans. Ben Zion Bosker (New York: Paulist Press, 1978), p. 287.

were imprisoned since childhood. Enchained from the neck down to their legs, all they could see was the back of the cave and the shadows that were cast upon it. These prisoners could not see even the source of the shadows that were on the wall, much less believe that there was an outside reality beyond anything they had ever known. One prisoner was set free and led out to see the outside world for the first time. The sun's light blinded and irritated the prisoner's eyes; he couldn't bear to look at it. Finally, he realized that everything that he had seen in the cavern had been only shadows on a wall—and nothing more. By gradually training his eyes to recognize the shadows and the reflections, eventually

> He will require to grow accustomed to the sight of the upper world. And first he will see the shadows best, next the reflections of men and other objects in the water, and then the objects themselves; then he will gaze upon the light of the moon and the stars and the spangled heaven; and he will see the sky and the stars by night better than the sun or the light of the sun by day.
>
> Last of he will be able to see the sun, and not mere reflections of him in the water, but he will see him in his own proper place, and not in another; and he will contemplate him as he is. He will then proceed to argue that this is he who gives the season and to endure anything, rather than think as they do and live after their manner?[11]

God's answer to Job taught him that the universe is full of mystery and beauty. There are processes in the universe that humanity will never understand, manipulate, or control. God told Job that his perception of reality was profoundly and woefully limited by his mind and senses; it is the height of arrogance to think that God can be understood and controlled like the other elemental forces of nature. Many of Job's problems came as the result of his cognitive distortions of God. Job was like Plato's prisoner, who could not see beyond the shadows cast upon the wall. God's answer must be seen as a repudiation of the enterprise of theodicy. God's anger was aimed, not at Job, but at the friends who brazenly claimed to know the workings of God.

Job's way of viewing the world also changed. The old Job was kind and considerate to the poor because he felt it was his legal obligation to be so. His worship was not motivated by a sense of love and empathy but, rather, by fear of punishment. It is for this reason the Talmud contrasts Job's worship with that of Abraham. In one place Job was considered greater than Abraham, whereas in another place Job was considered inferior, since his actions were not for the sake of Heaven but for the sake of reward. The Talmud thus asserts that Job's suffering was in part designed to help him develop sensitivity to those who suffer. God

---

11. Plato, *Republic*, 8.515–517.

wanted Job's faith to be enhancing and life-affirming. He did not want Job to be a fearful servant cringing with fear.

God's response to Job was also instructive as a model for pastoral care. Job was not criticized for what he said to God out of pain and anguish. Furthermore, Job's friends were criticized for not being helpful. These friends did not speak to honor God but for their own honor. God was offended by their self-serving arguments. The friends of Job neglected Job's plea to feel love and compassion; instead they tormented his soul with man-made illusions about God's retributional power.

In Job's vision, God showed him that there are processes in nature far beyond human control. Being righteous does not mean one is impervious to the woes that are common to all. Being righteous did not mean Job would be blessed with earthly rewards, nor did it mean that he would not have to suffer. Instead of worrying about processes that are beyond his control, Job is instructed to look at what lies within his power to change and alter.

Though God created the world and all its life-forms, it was humanity's task to look after the world as its protector and caretaker. Because human life is so fragile, Job was instructed to handle life with love and treat it with respect and sentience. Instead of pointing fingers to Heaven when evil strikes, wondering "Why?", God encouraged Job to take a pro-activist stand to eradicate evil and suffering. Most of the evil that we see in the world comes from human cruelty or indifference. Evil is a recalcitrant and determined force, and never voluntarily relinquishes its short hold on power, even at the expense of its own well-being.

Questions raised concerning the nature of God's justice (theodicy) cannot be asked without considering how justice is administered in the social process. Theology *per se* can legitimize human suffering only by silencing the sufferer's endless cry from the dust and ashes of the world. God encouraged Job to open up to the suffering of others and to make their suffering his concern. Job discovered that without his participation, the world remains a place of irredeemable suffering; this world is as Keats once poetically described the soul's purpose on earth as "a vale of soul-making." By eliminating suffering, our souls become truly human.

As God showed Job the order of creation, Job came to realize that the human vocation is higher than those of the other creatures and life-forms that preceded him. Creation requires active human stewardship and participation. Creation finds its completion through tenderness and care. Job, like Adam, had a pastoral duty to look after the Master's flock. The new Job now realized that the only viable theology of God was one that reveals God's justice, compassion, and love to those who suffer and are in need. Like the shepherd's rod and staff, justice and compassion are the only ways God's Presence can be realized in society.

Job discovered that God's power is not coercive; it is limited by human freedom and choice. God's love gives humanity the space to develop its own spiritual potential. Human suffering can end only when human beings decide to eradicate it from the face of the planet. Cognitive faith and retributional theology kept Job suffering and entrenched in his misery. The popular belief in a retributional theology could not solve Job's problems; it could only exacerbate them.

Hasidai Creacas, the great arch-critic of Aristotelian philosophy, was convinced that all theological discussions about the nature of God were of little value unless they inspired love and compassion. God's love is the Power that is behind the creative processes of the universe.

> It is the joy of *giving*, it is the joy of the good that is *lavished unto His creatures*. He makes them act by His will and intention. He makes them persist by the emanation of His good. God loves to spread Goodness and Perfection. The joy He feels is due to this constant gift of being that spreads throughout creation, in the most perfect manner possible. *The joy that God experiences in an infinite and an essential way is through the act of giving.*[12] (Emphasis added.)

We become Godlike only when we share and disperse love. By spreading this gift, we participate in unfolding God's own love to the world. This alone is where human salvation can be found. Our concern for justice must emanate from the desire to promote God's goodness in the world. The withholding of this gift is what creates evil and suffering. For human beings, Creacas maintained, the mere possession of cognitive knowledge does not in itself represent the highest good attainable by humankind. Nor is the love of God measured by paying lip service to dogmas, creeds, and other forms of mindless orthodoxies as the friends of Job erroneously and arrogantly thought. The love of God is engendered by our capacity to experience communion with our fellow human beings—especially those who suffer. The stronger our sense of communion, the stronger our love for God will become. Once Job discovers this, his life will be changed forever. Though he has not found a simplistic answer to all his penetrating questions, he has received that one revelation that could enable him to countervail his pain and suffering. In Job's vision he discovered that it is not pain which has meaning. It is what Job would bring to his that gives pain its redemptive meaning. It was this discovery that, paradoxically, allowed Job to begin his life anew.

### Job as a Wounded Healer

God simultaneously taught the friends a lesson; *they* now became the victims hated by society. Each of the friends had a Jobian experience. The real test for

---

12. Cited from Colette Strat, *Philosophy in the Middle Ages* (Cambridge and New York: Cambridge University Press, 1993), pp. 363–364.

Job now surfaced. Would he sit by and adhere to a retributional theology—especially in light of the shabby way his friends tormented him? Would Job, perhaps, bask in the euphoria of his newly gained spiritual consciousness while being oblivious to the rest of the world? Would Job forget about his new religious experience and act as he did previously? Would he still remain emotionally aloof from those who suffer?

Job's new theology found its realization in showing compassion for those who grieved and suffered. Job thus became a shepherd of hope. Job redeemed his own suffering by reaching out to those who had oppressed him. Whereas the old Job acted in a "holier-than-thou" manner and was personally indifferent to the pain of others, the new Job brought comfort, mercy, compassion, prayer, and healing. He did not offer any pious platitudes as his friends did with him. Job became a wounded healer who was sensitive and responsive to the pain of others. The suffering Job had experienced made it impossible for Job to go back to the way things once were. Like Jacob's after the encounter with the angel, Job's life, too, was altered forever. Job's woundedness became his own source of inner strength. Any person who has experienced suffering knows the Jobian odyssey all too well.

Job was determined to reveal a God that is loving in a world brushed by tragedy. The new Job was a man of hope, a *hasid,* a bearer of Divine compassion. He continued on with living; he brought hope, comfort, and prayer to the sick and the oppressed. Job was transformed by his illness and afflictions; he could not look at the suffering of any sentient being without feeling sympathy and compassion.

Healing came to Job once he forgave his friends for the painful ordeal they had put him through. It would have been easy for Job to watch his friends stew in their suffering. Hate is the natural response when one feels the wound of an adversary for no just cause or reason. There are degrees of hatred. Lewis Smedes describes two kinds of hatred that are similar to each other.[13] There is aggressive hatred that leads to fury and violence. This feeling often comes when the person we hate causes us harm and suffering. Aggressive hatred seeks to punish and inflict pain, whereas passive hatred withholds showing feelings of mercy and tenderness.

Here is an example of passive hatred: Clarence Darrow, the famous criminal lawyer, once said, "Everyone is a potential murderer. I have not killed anyone, but I frequently get satisfaction out of obituary notices." Most moral people would refrain from showing hatred to another but would feel a smug satisfaction seeing their adversaries suffer. Passive hatred occurs when we do not wish the other person the same good we would wish upon ourselves.

---

13. Louis Smedes, *Forgive and Forget* (New York: Harper and Row, 1984), pp. 20–21.

Smedes' concept of passive and aggressive hatred will help us understand the last test God put Job through when he saw his "friends" suffer. Job's moral sense dictated that he could not show open animosity toward his friends, as they had shown unto him. As a man of integrity, he would not lower himself to hate—but could he sincerely pray and beseech mercy for those who hurt him? Who could blame Job if he did not act as a healer for his "friends"?

The author of Job wanted to underscore the importance of letting go of hatred in all of its forms. Moreover, Job's own healing was contingent upon his letting go of passive hatred. Once Job prayed on behalf of those who had harassed him, he found healing for his own pain and suffering. By forgiving his friends, Job allowed himself to be liberated from the cancerous anger that was eating him inside. Smedes later points out the reason people hurt others is often their own weakness and fragility.[14] If the righteous Job could undergo such pain and torment, how much more so could they! They responded to Job out of fear that a similar fate could await them. The friends tried to justify their own righteousness by castigating Job.

In Job 42:10, "he prayed for his friend (re'ehu)"—he acted like a compassionate shepherd, and only then did he find restoration with God. He prayed for each of his friends individually; he did not lump them all together. Job reacted with understanding and kindness to each of the persons involved.

The Talmud concurs on this point. The ancient sages taught, "Any person who prays for the welfare of another (rather than for himself); will be answered first."[15] The Talmud deduces this teaching from the life of Job.[16] Ultimately, Job found healing through shepherding his adversarial friends. How did his friends respond when they got better?

> Then there came to him all his brothers and sisters and all who had known him before, and they ate bread with him in his house; they showed him sympathy and comforted him for all the evil that the LORD had brought upon him; and each of them gave him a *kesitah* and a gold ring.
>
> Job 42:11

Most translations render the word *kesitah* as "piece of money" or "a coin."[17] The Aramaic Targum and the New English Bible (NEB) render *kesita* as *churfah*—a young lamb. According to the distinguished biblical scholar Amos

---

14. Ibid., p. 21.

15. T.B. *Bava Kamma* 92b.

16. According to one old midrashic tradition, the attribute of God's justice was situated against Job during the entire time Job opposed his friends and his friends opposed him. Only when he was appeased by them and they prayed for him did the Holy One, Blessed be He, return to Job (*Pesikta Rabbatai* 38).

17. As in Genesis 33:19.

Hacham, the friends gave Job a lamb, which served as barter.[18] Perhaps the author of Job is telling us something deeper. The friends of Job learned a valuable lesson about the importance of shepherding one another. By giving a lamb, they had obtained true wisdom and insight about shepherding. This explanation accords with the midrashic view, which stated that Job's friends asked him what they could bring, and he requested a lamb, so that he would be able to provide clothes and food for the poor. It is possible that even the gift of the golden ring may also contain symbolic significance, for gold in ancient times represented sun-glory, majestic power, freedom from decay, self-generating radiance, immortality, and spiritual luminosity. These qualities emerged from Job as the result of his ordeal with God and his friends.[19]

Job's spiritual transformation continued even after his confrontation with God. It would appear that the Job of the debates never made as much as one reference to his children or their names. Until the time of Job's vision, he was preoccupied with himself; as a result of his spiritual awakening, he felt and became more connected with all life around him. He seemed estranged and distant from them. The new Job became involved in his children's lives—especially, those of his daughters. Each name he gave his daughters reflected God's gift of light, spice, and beauty.[20] The new Job also sees to it that they inherit equally with their

---

18. *Da'at Mikrah*, Amos Hacham's commentary on Job.

19. Carl Jung has written extensively in his *Collected Writings* about the psychological significance of the fifteenth–sixteenth century study of alchemy (of which Isaac Newton himself was an excited devotee and exponent!). Jung never believed in the actual physical transformation of lead into gold but was fascinated by the psychological and *philosophical* meaning of the alchemists' symbols of spirit and matter. The alchemists were not concerned only with the creation of common gold (*aurum vulgi*) but with the pure gold (*aurum nostrum*) of the illuminated and enlightened soul. The quest to form gold was as much an internal spiritual/psychological process as it was an external process. Jung saw the whole process of alchemy as a metaphor for the soul and its spiritual odyssey. Courage, honor, love, faith, compassion—these are the "golden" attributes the alchemists sought to transform from the base materials found in every human being. The alchemist would carefully choose elements that were fundamentally opposed to one another. It was hoped that the attraction of opposites would produce a new substance that did not exist in nature. If we apply Jung's concept of alchemy, perhaps we can *speculate* that the Book of Job may be better understood if we see it from a perspective of God's alchemy. Job went from being a pious but unenlightened believer (symbolized by base metal) to becoming a true healer of God (as symbolized by the gold). The golden ring, used in ancient times, represented eternity. Being circular, the ring represented the cycle of life—birth, marriage, and death. The ring also represented a change in status (as symbolized by marriage rituals). According to one sixteenth-century Kabbalist, the empty space of the ring represents the empty space that God used to create the universe. All the forces of creation surrounded this empty space like a ring, so that creation would eventually take place. Thus, the ring may also have represented both Job's feelings of emptiness and his personal spiritual rebirth.

20. Rashi observes that *Yamimah* comes from *Yom* (light), since *Yamimah*'s beauty was like the glow of the sun. *Kitziah* was named after spice, since she had a pleasant aroma; *Keren Hafuch* denotes coloration—she was especially beautiful.

brothers. Job lived to be one hundred forty years old (twice seventy), a number that symbolizes a life of extra fullness and abundance.

As a wounded healer, Job now ministered to the suffering and woes of other people. When the narrator describes how Job was restored, one notices he had no slaves, as he did previously. Perhaps Job became more aware of the horrors of slavery and did his part to eradicate this institution of human suffering. Job became a shepherd of faith; he used the experience of his own pain and suffering to help others who were afflicted. We must remember that the real question the book of Job raises is not, "Why do bad things happen to good people?"—but, "How do good people respond when bad things happen?" Real faith must be relational, nurturing, ultimately healing—in short, shepherding. Job's friends came to discover that all philosophical claims to wisdom without compassion were meaningless and cruel. Kindness, compassion, and mercy alone constitute the greatest theophany of God's Presence in the world. By being a healer, Job affirmed that we must choose to make this world a place of blessing and a world of abundance.

### Psalm 23 and Job

How the community of faith responds to the shatteredness produced by suffering is of vital concern. It is for this reason that the imagery of Psalm 23 offers a realistic and inspiring response to help shepherd people who encounter the diabolic dimension of suffering. The close sequential relation between Psalm 22, which speaks of Divine abandonment:

> My God, my God, why have you forsaken me? Why are you so far from helping me, from the words of my groaning?
> O my God, I cry by day, but you do not answer; and by night, but find no rest.
> 
> Psalms 22:1–2

It would appear that the composer of Psalm 23 may have had a Jobian type of experience. Contrast the first two verses of Psalm 22 with the message of Psalm 23:

> The LORD is my shepherd, I shall not want.
> He makes me lie down in green pastures; he leads me beside still waters; he restores my soul. He leads me in right paths for his name's sake.
> 
> Psalms 23:1–3

While Psalm 23 speaks of the feeling of abandonment, Psalm 23 affirms that, despite God's hiddenness, He is still "my shepherd." Is it a coincidence that the two psalms are placed next to one another? Were the editors of the psalms unconsciously or consciously aware of a purposeful relationship between the two psalms? Would it be inconceivable that the redactors of the psalms wished to convey that the way we respond to abandonment is through the act of shepherding?

Earlier, it was pointed out that the Hebrew word for shepherd, *ro'eh*, is a cognate cousin to the Hebrew word for friend, *re'ah*. This would imply that the model of friendship is portrayed through the way the shepherd nurtures and cares for the flock.

The qualities of Psalm 23 were conspicuously absent in the way Job's friends responded to his crisis. Job felt abandoned and depressed. His God seemed capricious and indifferent. Job felt the same way about his community. The vast majority of Job's former friends and the people he had assisted walked away from him in his moment of need. Except for a small handful of critical and judgmental friends, Job found himself all alone and vulnerable.

The friends of Job did not offer unconditional love for him as a person. If Job's friends had affirmed his value as a human being and as an upright decent member of the community, perhaps some of his suffering might have abated. Job needed some undiminished appreciation affirming the love they felt for him and, most important, to know God had not forsaken him. Job's friends all portrayed an excellent example of the things a person should not do when dealing with a person who suffers: listen poorly, judge, accuse, rationalize, theologize, moralize, oversimplify, argue, and project one's own personal insecurities to the sufferer.

In terms of providing care that is pastoral, the story about Job's suffering (or that of any human being), represents a spiritual challenge to the family, friends, and community. The Bible does not subscribe to a belief in fatalism. The existence of the poor and needy is a spiritual problem for any just community. The way we respond to suffering defines and reveals the depth of our own spirituality and faith. The imagery of Psalm 23 provides a spiritual way good people can respond to the problem of suffering in their communities.

Here are several ways the pastoral imagery of Psalm 23 might serve as a praxis to help caregivers become shepherds to those who are experiencing loss and a sense of abandonment. In the Jobian story, the pastoral imagery of Psalm 23 was absent in the way Job's caregivers related to him.

1. *The Lord is my Shepherd.* First, the friends of Job should have helped him realize that God has not forsaken him; that the sufferer is still beloved and worthy of God's love. Illness and pain have a demoralizing effect upon the sufferer's ability to feel God's love and concern. The sick person often feels abandoned as indicated by the psalmist (Psalm 22): "My God, why have You forsaken me?" Questions like, "If God loves me, how can He allow me to be sick?" or, "If God cares about me, why is my child sick?" or, "What have I done to deserve this?"

are all common questions asked by those who suffer. For those who feel that they are being "punished" by God, the caregiver must be careful not to give flippant responses. Ministering to the ill is one potent way of helping sufferers feel that they are being shepherded through the love of the caregiver. Slowly and patiently, shepherding unties the knots that bind, and provides the way for the self to find healing and reintegration.

The caregiver must realize that he or she is reflecting the image of God to the sufferer; the visitor mirrors God's Presence. The Human face and the Divine face are said to resemble one another. In William Blake's etchings of the book of Job, one of the characteristics that appears in all the etchings is the resemblance of the face of God and that of Job. Job's pain was also God's pain; like a mirror, one reflected the other. Blake's pictures suggest that the redemption of Job's suffering is also a redemption of God's own suffering—the suffering of the *Shechinah*. Blake's insights were anticipated centuries ago by the ancient rabbis of the Midrash and Talmud. (See Excursus I at the end of this chapter.)

2. *He maketh me lie down in green pastures*. The second insight Psalm 23 offers is the importance of providing rest and respite to the one going through the spiritual wilderness experience. The goal of pastoral care is to tend to and fulfill the needs of the sufferer, both physical and spiritual.

3. *He restoreth my soul*. Restoration of the body is an essential requisite for providing care for the soul. To take care of a person's body is to nurture and restore the soul. Job's friends were more concerned with saving his eternal soul than they were in providing care for his body as well. The friends could have assisted in pulling Job out of the hellish pit he felt himself situated in; instead, they kept him in a state of hopelessness and despair.

Later, at the end of the Jobian odyssey, God restored to Job everything that had been taken from him. Job's own restoration came only after he forgave his friends and prayed on their behalf.

4. *For His name's sake*. Caregiving requires humility. Human beings are at best agents for divine healing—not originators. The more egocentric we are in providing caring, the less effective we will be in healing our loved ones and friends. Caregiving must never be reduced to something mechanical, perfunctory, or heartless; there must be a conscious effort to allow the spirit of God to heal. The friends of Job appeared to have been concerned with self-adulation when they visited Job. Their egos got in the way of Job's healing. Treating the sick with respect and dignity helps them considerably. The story of Job teaches, among other things, the importance of nurturing of the care-receiver for the sake of Heaven.

5. *Even though I walk through the valley of the shadow of death, I fear no evil; for You are with me. . . .* The Jobian experience is a journey through the valley of darkness; it is easy to give up hope and feel a sense of abandonment. The sick and needy often feel the way sheep walking on the edge of a cliff feel—just a step away from death. The caregiver must help the sufferer realize that his/her suffering can have meaning and purpose. The caregiver would be wise to remember the words of Victor Frankl, who once said, "Suffering ceases to be suffering at the moment it finds a meaning." On the other hand, the lack of meaning increases and intensifies suffering. Though its presence does not necessarily end suffering, even the awareness that meaning exists can help the sufferer better cope with life. Suffering can help us reevaluate our lives and help redirect us toward a new way of being and becoming.

6. *Your rod and staff, they comfort me.* Shepherding must involve giving protection (rod) and support (symbolized by the staff). The person who is sick feels violated in the most personal way imaginable. The individual's physical health has been compromised. Protection and support are necessary to help the sick make it through. The words that are used can serve as instruments of healing and hope.

Throughout his ordeal, Job's coping abilities were reaching their limit. Job did not know what new peril was going to come next. How was he ever going to recuperate from his deteriorating physical condition? Job's life was full of stress and uncertainty; it is no coincidence that the image of the wilderness is evoked repeatedly by Job. How a suffering person perceives and interprets his/her situation will influence how s/he reacts emotionally and physiologically.

Job needed soothing words, words of hope to help him through his pain. Instead of kindly words, Job received harsh rebukes for questioning the orthodox thinking of his time. When the griever is asking questions, s/he is not interested in answers. The questions stem from a deep desire to give expression to the depth of pain s/he is feeling. The book of Job underscores the importance of allowing the sufferer to explain and tell his/her "story" of lament. Anguish needs to be expressed in words and externalized. If the griever cannot externalize his/her pain, s/he will internalize it and implode. We show support to those we love by allowing them to tell their stories and give expression to their pain and anger.

In today's culture, society admires the quiet stoic temperament. The secular community expects the grieving person to have a "stiff upper lip." Mourners are to make little or no reference to their loss. Many feel uncomfortable around a mourner; they feel embarrassed by the mourner's inability to relate meaningfully to the loss of the mourned. Quite often, the mourner acts and works as if nothing happened and is admired by his coworkers for showing such "courage" and "strength of character."

The comforter would do well to remember that sometimes the best way to comfort a grieving person is by simply saying nothing. One can acknowledge the sufferer's questioning with sympathy and understanding. What the griever is experiencing is the loss of a relationship, the anxiety that comes with separation. The language of touch, the language of caring eyes, the effectiveness of a listening ear provide a salve for the griever's wounds.

At first, the mere sight of Job produces a sense of intense sadness in his friends. Each "wept aloud, and tore their cloaks and tossed dust into the air over their heads." For seven full days they sat next to him; they were stunned into silence. At this point, Job's friends truly acted in a kindly, sympathetic, and supportive manner. Their body language and silence probably meant more to Job than his friends could have imagined. The language of tears might have sufficed. It is only when they open their mouths and speak as "professional theologians" that they lash out at Job with one insensitive comment after another.

7. *You prepare a table before me in the presence of my enemies.* The tragedies that befell Job illustrate how the sick and needy require care in the most elementary manner; they need somebody to look after their material welfare and help maintain their living quarters and take care of their bills in the face of illness. The critically sick person often feels resignation toward death and will often refuse even to eat food. Providing a table for the ill and taking care of their basic physical needs help that person realize that life is worth living, and give the person the hope to go on. Job's bleeding ulcers, his general disfigurement, and his body odor had a powerful effect on the way Job's friends regarded him. Their loss of composure certainly was of no help to Job and his condition.

The friends of Job did not tend to Job's physical or spiritual needs. Like Job, many who experience grief neglect their bills, homes, children, or business. Nowhere in the book of Job do any of the friends offer Job practical help in reordering his broken and shattered life.

The covenantal community must help the sufferer muster his/her resources to face his/her situation one step, one day, at a time. The loss of independence is one of the hardest problems people who undergo sudden illness experience.

8. Even after the person recovers from his/her sickness or sorrow, the good pastoral caregiver stays in contact with the sufferer. Goodness and mercy must follow the sufferer, enabling him/her to realize what it means to dwell in the loving Presence of God all one's days.

### The Practical Guide to Shepherding— Creating Ties That Bind

*The Practical Guide to Shepherding* originated in the classes I had with the synagogue on the pastoral themes of Psalm 23 and the Book of Job. The points covered here are the highlights the community felt were the important practical measures to be implemented in developing a lay guide to pastoral care. We thought that it would be useful first to define the common problems lay people have in shepherding others.

One of the difficult areas ordinary people have regarding pastoral care is the question, "What can I do to help?" People often remain at a distance rather than make themselves available, out of fear that they might say something inappropriate. This section will focus mostly on one small area that will greatly enhance their shepherding skills—the sphere of listening and being present to the person you are shepherding.

When you hear somebody is ill or going through a very stressful time because of death of a loved one, loss of job, divorce, loneliness, and so on, make it a point to *get involved*. Absence speaks volumes, but so does ministering others with one's loving presence. Remember that the Torah states that we should not stand idly by the suffering of our neighbor. There is an imperative to act and to provide nurturing (be it material, emotional, or spiritual). The following guidelines may be gleaned from Psalm 23 and its relationship to the Book of Job.

1. You can't listen and do something else at the same time. Giving the patient all your attention enables you to be present to what s/he has to say.
2. Don't try to anticipate what the next phase of the conversation will be. Learn to shut out distracting thoughts.
3. Don't visit the sick unless your stress level is low. Worrying about one's own problems makes it hard to listen effectively to the sick person.
4. Visit the sick out of the joy of being a healer and not out of a desire to receive praise and compliments.
5. Acknowledge how the care-receiver feels. People convey more than just information; there is a flow of feeling that is also conveyed. Learn to listen inwardly to what isn't being said in words. Respond to feelings and not to information.
6. Do not try to control the conversation. Allow for the care-receiver to express his/her own feelings.
7. The eyes are often regarded as the "windows of the soul." Communicate with your eyes and an occasional thoughtful nod. Mouths shouldn't be the only thing communicating; the eyes can express far more than the lips at times. Be aware of nonverbal rejection, looking at one's watch, or gazing away from the sick; tapping one's finger gives the subtle message that you are not being present to the care-receiver.
8. Allow your face to express love and caring. The face in Hebrew is called *panim*, which also means inward. The face reveals what is

inward, what is inside a person. Be sure to allow yourself to show caring in your face when you are visiting somebody who is feeling distressed.

9. Speak in a gentle, soft tone. Language is evocative, like produces like. Angry words produce angry feelings; loving words produce loving feelings.

10. Acknowledge with pithy remarks that reflect how the other feels.

11. Encourage disclosure by asking the care-receiver, "Please tell me more." Be prepared to disclose a little bit about yourself, but keep it simple and to the point.

12. When the other person says something that isn't clear, ask the care-receiver for clarification. This is especially important if the care-receiver is upset. Allow the person to express what s/he may be feeling.

13. Validate feelings, when the care-receiver expresses them. By affirming feelings, you let the other person know that s/he is being listened to.

14. Don't be judgmental, and avoid using negative words. Negative words can hurt the care-receiver and frustrate further communication and self-expression.

15. When another person is relating the pain s/he is undergoing, ask yourself, "How have I felt in similar situations?"

16. If the person is experiencing the loss of a loved one, be careful not to say, "I know how you feel." Unless you have experienced a similar kind of loss, don't be glib. A more sensitive approach might be, "I know you're hurting; I'll be thinking of you in my prayers." Likewise, never suggest the replacement of a loved one. The feelings a mourner is feeling come from the loss of that special relationship that can never be replaced. Avoid comments like this:

"You'll get over it."
"Time will heal."
"Are you going to try to have another baby?"
"You'll get married again."
"You're such a nice-looking person; you'll have no trouble marrying again."

17. Don't offer advice or homilies. The care-receiver may not be interested in receiving wise advice. Unless he asks for it, don't volunteer it. Don't fight with the other person's pain and anguish. Avoid pat answers such as, "Count your blessings," or "Don't take it to heart."

18. Don't attack or deny what the patient is feeling. Words can add anguish or awkwardness to the situation. Validate what the patient may be feeling. View the other person with compassion.

19. Hold his/her hand, or embrace the sufferer. The power of touch can be very soothing and healing. Touching is a way to break the communication barriers that may exist. Human beings long for touching as a way of showing affection and concern. In the Torah, the laying on of hands has always conveyed blessing.

20. Do not gossip about the person who is sick or suffering loss. This is especially important because of the clannish way synagogues and churches alike often function. Gossiping can hurt not just the sick but also their families as well. A respect for privacy is a must in developing sharp pastoral skills.

21. Avoid telling the sick any scary stories about other people they know who were in similar circumstances. Not only does this not help the sick; it can frighten them. Try not to show disgust and revulsion when visiting somebody who is disfigured or has a foul odor from his/her sickness. Try being relaxed.

22. Write a note expressing briefly that you are thinking of the sick person in his/her time of trouble. An inspirational poem often raises the spirit. Similarly, getting a gift can raise the morale of the care-receiver. This gift may be flowers, a stuffed bear, anything that can help you touch and heal the person's inner child. Bringing food that the sufferer likes (when permitted by hospital regulations), notes from relatives or friends, or reading materials may help the sufferer feel good because other people are taking a sincere interest in his/her situation.

23. Let the person and his/her family and friends know that they are not alone, and that you truly care for them. Offer words of hope and prayer. Let them know that they are still beloved by God.

### *Ecursus I: The Shepherding of God*

One of the most radical concepts expressed in Jewish ethical writings is the idea that *human beings have the power to shepherd God!* The Midrash to Song of Songs comments on the verse "Behold you are beautiful, *my* love!" (Song of Songs 2:10). The word *rayatee* (my love) also means "shepherd Me," that is, *When you feed the poor, it is as though you have fed Me* [says God].[21] Rabbi Eliahu HaCohen, the great nineteenth-century moralist, explains this Midrash in detail; his comments provide yet a new insight regarding shepherding.

One could inquire: how can feeding the poor be considered as though one sustained

---

21. *Yalkut Shir HaShireem* on Song of Songs 1:15; *Shir HaShireem Midrash Zuta* 1:13.

God? An earthly response solicits a Heavenly response which in turn produces a flow [of blessing unto below]. . . .

The poor person has an eternal complaint with the Holy One, blessed be He. *Why should his fate be so different from his friends? Why should he be impoverished while his friend be wealthy?* After all, one God created both of them; both souls emanated out of the same Heavenly Throne to enter this lowly world. The Jerusalem Talmud states, "Whoever eats from others cannot face his benefactor. *How could God bring the soul into this world without adequate means provided by people? What of his abundant shame?* . . .

It is for this reason the Blessed Holy One says, "Anyone who provides charity establishes peace between Me and the poor." When the poor are provided they do not come to me with their complaint. That is why the Midrash says, "When you feed the poor it is as though you have fed Me too." This is also the meaning in the verse, "Whoever is kind to the poor lends to the LORD, and will be repaid in full." (Proverbs 19:17). This teaches us that when we are gracious unto the poor, it is as though we made a loan to Him and He will pay back His loan, for the poor will not come to Him with their complaint about being poor. There is more to be said on this topic: When the poor are not provided and they suffer from the pangs of hunger, God too suffers [as it were] with them.[22]

## *Excursus II: Job as a Symbol of AIDS-Victims*

The retributional thinking that was expressed by all Job's "friends" can be heard today as well. One of the most important teachings of the Eastern religions is the belief in *karma*. Many of the apostles of the "New Age" subscribe to a belief that everything that happens to a person is due directly to some karmic debt that must be paid for by the individual through his/her disease. This approach invariably implies that cancer, AIDS, or any disease has occurred because of some spiritual imperfection in the patient's life. Every person is thus responsible for "creating their own reality."

Years ago, I debated the issue of karma with a Religious Science minister from Central California. This "New Age" religion believes that if a young child is raped and mutilated it is in order that the child may "clear" his/her karmic debt. Religious Science is one of the new religions that blend Christian teachings with the metaphysical and theosophical teachings of the East. One of its most popular apostles, the well-known minister Louise Hay, author of *You Can Heal Your Life*, maintains that all human beings are responsible for creating every circumstance in life.

According to Hay, all disease comes from a lack of self-love and unwilling-

---

22. Eliyahu HaCohen, *Mi'eel Tsedakka*, ed. Hillel Kooperman (Jerusalem: Jersulem Press, reprinted 5752 [1992]), pp. 110–111.

ness to forgive others. This is true regardless of whether one has headaches or hemorrhoids: all disease comes from a lack of loving oneself. The fact that some of the world's greatest saints, mystics, and healers often suffer from common diseases like the rest of humanity does not seem to affect Hay's theological worldview. The reverse is also true. If a person is blessed with riches and "abundance," it must mean that the "Universe" is pleased with him/her. Despite being termed "New Age," Hay's theology reflects the same good, old-fashioned retributional thinking espoused by the friends of Job. It explains handily why certain people are blessed with all the goods, while others are not.

The journalist Michael Da'Antonio relates a conversation he had with Louise Hay. Her views on Third World nations and AIDS victims are very revealing:

> People starve amid the "abundance of the universe" because of low self-esteem, said Hay. A poor self-image is more damaging than one might imagine. The soul projects a person's self-image, said Hay, and attracts the kind of experience that seems appropriate. That's why, she said, women who are raped are responsible for what happens to them. They attract the rapist because they expect and fear an attack. Similarly, she told me, the poor of the world are responsible for their plight, as are those afflicted with AIDS. With the right spiritual approach, she said, any poor person can raise himself up, any sick person can make himself well.[23]

In one conversation, Hay boldly speculated that the AIDS victims were the reincarnated souls of the Nazis, who were being paid back for their crimes against the Jews! According to this way of thinking, the six million Jews exterminated by Hitler, somehow deserved their "karmic" fate. This view is not much different from the view espoused by many Christians, who maintained the Holocaust was because of the crime of deicide. What is true of the story of Job is equally true of the superficial way Westerners have convoluted the Hindu concept of karma. Such a portrayal of God resembles Shakespeare's of the Merchant of Venice, who is determined to demand a pound of flesh in order to exact payment for debts owed.

Job's story is told by every person stricken with the dreadful disease AIDS. Unlike other diseases, the victim, like Job in the Bible, is made to feel like a pariah. Society has yet to learn that the AIDS epidemic represents a profound spiritual dilemma forcing us to learn how to shepherd the unwanted and unloved people who have been ostracized by a self-righteous "religious" society. Like the friends of Job, many of the religious voices used their power to inflict more pain and suffering.

Sadly, the people who ought to be most supportive are conspicuously absent.

---

23. Michael Da'Antonio, *Heaven and Earth: Dispatches from America's Frontier* (New York: Crown Books, 1992), pp. 94–95.

Within the Orthodox and Conservative Jewish communities, scholars debate whether one is even duty-bound to save the AIDS-infected homosexual's or drug-user's life since such persons lead a "provocative sinner's life." There is even a view that one is *not* obliged to save the life of such a sinner.[24] At no time,

---

24. In the Talmud *Avodah Zara* 26b, the question of the fate of an apostate, an informer (one who informs against the Jewish community), and a habitual sinner is raised. If any of these individuals happens to be in a pit, according to one view, one may scrape the steps away (thus condemning the apostate to death in the pit); according to another view, one may cover the pit's opening with a large stone. Lastly, there is a view that one may take the ladder away, thus leaving the apostate with no means of escaping. For a modern example of retributional theology, see David Novak's article "AIDS: The Contemporary Jewish Perspective," reprinted in *Frontiers of Jewish Thought*, ed. Steven Katz (Washington, DC: Bnai Brith, 1992), pp. 141–156. In this article, Novak definitely sees a direct correlation between the disease and the sinful behavior that has led to it. For Novak, the fundamental halachic question boils down to this: Should the community get involved in the care of such a wanton sinner? Novak writes: "Indeed, one need no longer argue for the immorality of these acts based on abstract philosophical or theological definitions, one can point to concrete and seemingly inevitable consequences. Arguments on behalf of AIDS sufferers which ignore these indisputable facts can only be regarded as rationalizations motivated by pathological denials of empirical reality" (p. 143). As a counterexample to Novak's empirical theology, it would seem that the lesbian population is probably the safest group—the group least likely to get the deadly AIDS virus. This, of course, is hardly a group Novak would endorse as "moral." A much broader question ought to be asked here: *Must we regard every human plague as a visitation from God for not observing the rules He has ordained, and if so, why couldn't God pick on a more deserving group such as adulterers or incest perpetrators, whose atrocities dwarf the homosexual community?* Novak opposes showing sympathy to all aspects of the homosexual's life and compares the homosexual's affliction of AIDS to that of smokers who are suffering from lung cancer. Novak also subscribes to a literal belief that the children will suffer for the sins of the parents. Certainly, this response was articulated to Job by his well-meaning friends.

Surprisingly, Novak neglects to explain what precisely is meant by the talmudic dictum *moredim ve'lo' maa'lin*. He writes on p. 143: "one is *not* only not to help such a person, but one is *actually not to save his life.*" The real meaning as the phrase *moredim ve'lo' maa'lin* is, as the Gemara and Maimonides state explicitly, "a person (or persons) *may actually assist* in abandoning the sinner to his death." Novak is, no doubt, well aware of the true meaning; he knows fully well how insensitive and intolerant this extreme view actually is. Nonetheless, if a scholar is going to cite such a provocative source, s/he might as well be candid about it. For Novak, the question of the AIDS victim boils down to this: What is the role of the Jewish community with regard to the AIDS victim? What are its halachic obligations? Could one justifiably *be exempt* from assisting the so-called deviant? According to the *Bach*, the removal of a ladder is considered as if one actively killed the person with his hands. The *Taz* disagrees, stating that the removal of the ladder does not make one legally culpable for murder. The *Taz* stresses that this interpretation applies only if there is no animosity between the sinner and the individual for abandoning him (*Yoreh Deah* 158, *Taz*).

This writer takes issue with Dr. Novak's interpretation of the Gemara. *Never was the law ever designed to affect person(s) who were afflicted with a contagious disease.* Even to suggest such an interpretation is to subvert the fundamental ethos of the *Halachah* that speaks of reaching out with compassion toward the ill—regardless of their sinful behavior. Cf. *Midrash Temurah*, ed. J. D. Eisentein, *Otzar Midrashim* (New York, 1915, II, 580–581). Though many of the rabbis did believe that sickness was sometimes attributed to sinful behavior, nowhere does the Talmud ever suggest that sinful behavior should ever abrogate the community's responsibility to visit, pray for, and take care

however, was the community allowed to directly hurt the sinner, nor could their animosity be directed at Job because of personal animosity.

Such thinking may help us understand why Job was perceived by his community and friends as an "enemy." Perceiving him as a provocative sinner, the faith community would be duty-bound to let him wallow in his misery. At

---

of the sick. In fact, the Gemara in T. B. *Nedarim* 40a suggests the very opposite. Here is what the Gemara says:

> Rav Helbo was once sick. But nobody came and visited him. Rav Kahana reprimanded the scholars, saying, "Didn't a similar incident occur when once one of the disciples of Rabbi Akiba's became ill, and the Sages did not visit him?" So Rabbi Akiba himself entered this man's house to visit him, and instructed his disciples to clean his sick student's home. After they swept and sprinkled the ground before him, the sick student recovered and said to Akiva: 'My master,' said he, 'you have brought me back to life!' Immediately, Rabbi Akiba went forth and lectured: *He who does not visit the sick is like a shedder of blood.* When Rav Dimi came from the Land of Israel, he said: "He who visits the sick causes him to live, whilst he who doesn't visit the sick, causes him to die. How does he *cause death*? Shall we say that he who visits the sick prays that he may live, whilst he who does not prays that he should die, — 'that he should die!' How could you think that he would really die? But say thusly: He who does not visit the sick prays neither that he may live nor die."

According to the *Rosh*'s commentary, if someone withholds prayer from the ill, it is considered as if s/he has withheld the gift of life, for prayer has a healing effect on the sufferer. According to the *Ran*'s commentary, there are times when praying for somebody's demise *is* a valid prayer—for example, when a person is so moribund that death would be indeed a release from bodily torment. Withholding prayer and kindness from a sufferer is to deprive that person of compassion; to withhold compassion is to condemn the sufferer to more anguish and suffering. Adin Steinzaltz explains that the difference between Akiba's teaching and Rav Dimi's is significant—Akiba speaks of a visitation in which the visitor takes care of the sick, whereas Rav Dimi speaks of a visitation in which the visitor prays on behalf of the sick. Both teachings are necessary and can make a considerable difference in the recovery of the ill. According to Moshe Feinstein's *Igeret Moshe* (Responsum 223), prayer can be offered only by the person who is visiting, in contrast to taking bodily care of the sick, which is a *mitzvah* that can be delegated to other people. Though others may pray on behalf of the ill, nonetheless, prayer is more effective when more people participate together. Seeing the sick and praying on his/her behalf affects (1) the way the sick person feels, and (2) the person visiting the sufferer, who is emotionally moved by seeing the severity of the other person's pain. For both of these reasons, this *mitzvah* should not be delegated to somebody else. (Ibid.)

Elsewhere the Gemara, *Sanhedrin* 73a, states: "Whence do we know that if a man sees his fellow drowning, mauled by beasts, or attacked by robbers, he is bound to save him? From the verse, 'Thou shalt not stand by the blood of thy neighbor!'" The Hebrew phrase *La Ta'amode bdam re'eche* literally means, "Don't stand *in* the blood of your neighbor." When somebody's life is endangered, the faith community has a duty to rescue life whenever possible. This interpretation is consistent with the view in *Nedarim* 40a—either the community is a part of the sufferer's healing process, or else they are a part of the sufferer's problem. This entire Talmudic ruling of *moredim ve'lo' maa'lin* was aimed that person who threatened the spiritual or physical safety of the Jewish community.

The question regarding the deviant was a problem in the Christian world also. Aquinas stated more radically than Maimonides in his *Summa Theologica* (II, 11, 3 and 4) that the unbelievers should be "shut off from the world by death." Such a course, he argued, "is justified, since it is a serious matter to corrupt faith, through which comes the soul's life."

worst, the community was permitted to exacerbate his suffering whenever possible through passive-aggressive means. It is as if the community were saying to Job, "Listen, Job, we must abandon you; we hope you understand. It's nothing personal, you know." In the Jobian story, Job was left by the community to stew in his misery.

The AIDS epidemic has all the characteristics of the diseases that afflicted Job. Like Job, the AIDS victims are stricken with shame. Like Job, the AIDS victim often feels abandoned by his/her friends. The person stricken with AIDS, in addition to dealing with the dreaded pain of the disease, also must contend with the anguish of isolation, which can be as painful as rejection. One HIV-positive caregiver poignantly pleads:

> Don't look at people with AIDS and be afraid of them. Just treat them normally. I have this disease that I have lived with for seven years. You liked me before you knew I had it, so don't treat me any different than you treat the next person down the street. Because you are going to die too. Maybe I die of AIDS and you die of cancer or a heart attack. But we are all going to die. So don't treat me any different.[25]

Job's illness and condition left him stigmatized. In ancient Greece, the term *stigma* denoted an actual physical mark that was burned or cut into the victim's skin. Through this bodily sign, the individual became a social pariah to be avoided. Like the ancient "mark of Cain," Job's suffering left him as an outcast from society. All Job's previous social relationships were effectively terminated. What was true of Job is also true of the AIDS victim.

A colleague of mine told me a woeful tale of how one AIDS victim called up five different churches for support. The first two churches hung up their phones; another minister criticized the caller for his homosexual lifestyle; another church did not respond; and only one church offered support. Families also suffer immensely from the cruelty of the stigma. One family I knew in California lived in a state of fear and apprehension. The father (age fifty-seven) had contracted AIDS through blood transfusions. They had no one to turn to for support. Though I was not their rabbi, I became their personal rabbi as I worked to minister to the need of the AIDS patient and his family. This was my first personal encounter with somebody who had reached an advanced stage of AIDS. This experience helped me realize the terrible stigma of sickness and how suffering often comes as a result of human insensitivity.

AIDS victims and their families can easily identify with the Jobian metaphor of the "miserable comforters." Abandoned by much of the religious community, AIDS victims often feel abandoned by the doctors entrusted to heal them. Dr.

---

25. Debra Jarvis, *The Journey through AIDS* (Batavia, IL: Lion Publishing, 1992), pp. 19–20.

Larry Dossey mentions the case of a woman with AIDS who once wrote how she was being treated by a doctor who was cold, detached, dispassionate. Each visit, the doctor would remind her how hopeless her situation was. She complained about her doctor's demoralizing effects on her:

> I began to realize my doctor doesn't *believe* I'm going to live. . . . It takes me two weeks to recover from a visit to him. He leaves me depressed and feeling sick. But after two weeks have passed, I always begin to feel terrific. Then, when it's time to return for an appointment, a feeling of dread overwhelms me. I have to make myself keep my appointment. After the visit, the cycle repeats itself. . . . Why do I feel like my own physician is *killing* me?"[26]

Dossey notes that because of the possibility of litigation, doctors feel they have to be very factual with their patients and are afraid to use the power of belief when working with them. Cartesian medicine that treats the body as though it were a machine will have only limited success because it does not aim to cure the total person. Modern medicine would induce more healing if the physicians saw themselves more as shepherds toward their patients.

The specter of AIDS represents one of the great spiritual challenges of our times. The AIDS crisis requires a spiritual approach that is compassionate and caring. To treat the AIDS victim as a pariah is to subvert the Bible's most important teachings concerning how we as the community of faith respond to the broader questions pertaining to human suffering and pain.

---

26. Dr. Larry Dossey, *Healing Words* (San Francisco: HarperSan Francisco, 1994), pp. 140–141.

# 12

# FROM MUTENESS TO EXPRESSIVITY

*May my teaching drop like the rain, my speech condense like the dew; like gentle rain on grass, like showers on new growth.*

Deuteronomy 32:2

*O Lord, open my lips, and my mouth will declare your praise.*

Psalms 51:15

*"Go, lie down; and if He calls you, you shall say, 'Speak, LORD, for your servant is listening.'"*

1 Samuel 3:9

*For He is our God, and we are the people of his pasture, and the sheep of His hand. O that today you would listen to His voice! Do not harden your hearts. . . .*

Psalms 95:7–8

*I am the LORD your God, who brought you up out of the land of Egypt. Open your mouth wide and I will fill it.*

Psalms 81:10

Moments of doubt, feelings of abandonment, asking uncomfortable questions, are all part of the spiritual journey. The verbalization of pain is extremely

201

important, not just for the individual who suffers but also for the community. In numerous places in the Bible speechlessness (*dumah*) is comparable to a state of death, whereas speech is often used as a metaphor for creation and rebirth.

The language of lament and crying has always allowed healing to begin. Job is not the only book of the Bible dealing with lament. The books of Jeremiah, Isaiah, and Lamentations, as well as the Psalms, all contain themes of lament. Whenever Israel was visited with catastrophe (whether it was a natural or political), prayers of lament were composed to allow the collective pain of the Jewish people to find expression.

## *The* Lectio Divina

Since talmudic times and before, the ancients reflected upon the words of the Scriptures and experienced them as a living reality. The Word of God was never perceived as something static or monolithic. Philo of Alexandria often interpreted the stories of the Bible as allegories of the soul. The ancient Rabbis taught that the Word of God is dynamic and alive; they often quoted to address various problems and issues that concerned the convenantal community. Every life experience and situation found expression in the words of Scripture. Ben Bag-Bag described the Torah as a looking-glass:

> Learn it and learn it [the Torah],
> for everything is contained in it.
> And You shall see through it
> and grow old and gray with it. . . .
> *Avot* 5:21

In the Talmud, we find that the practice of bibliomancy was in vogue. Bibliomancy is the practice of opening the Bible at random while selecting a verse (or a series of verses) for the purpose of personal guidance. In one of his Responsa (number 173), Maimonides himself, though opposed to divination in general, expressed approval of this form of scriptural meditation—especially since the Talmud itself mentions that even the sages engaged in this practice.[1]

In the Middle Ages, the theologians of Judaism, Christianity, and Islam continued to cite the sacred text for support. The quotation of scriptural verses was never random; each verse cited served as a vehicle for meditation, reflection, prayer, and spiritual growth. The Christian sages called this method of encountering God through the Scriptures the *lectio divina*—the Divine Reading. For brevity, we shall refer to it as the *lectio*. Through the *lectio*, any scriptural

---

1. Cf. T.B. *Chullin* 95b and *Teshuvot HaRambam*, ed. J. Blau (Jerusalem, 1957), Responsum 173.

narrative, every word, provides a way and path to release our deepest concerns to God. In some ways the *lectio* is similar to Freud's concept of free association. In the process of free association, the patient is asked to verbalize whatever comes to conscious awareness—for example, thoughts, images, wishes, feelings— setting aside the psyche's internal static. With the help of the patient, the analyst examines the patient's data and tries to enhance the patient's life by helping him/ her become more aware of him- or herself. Like free association, the *lectio* is a fluid process of disclosure. Unlike free association, the *lectio divina* is a spiritual exercise. Its goal is not merely self-knowledge; *the goal of the lectio divina is more holistic.* The *lectio divina* is designed to foster and promote spirituality, healing, and personal growth.

The *lectio* can help us take personal stock of ourselves (*heshbon hanefesh*) and examine our core beliefs. The *lectio* allows for a catharsis of our feelings and enables us to give constructive voice to our pain and to direct our concerns to God, the Master Healer. The *lectio* enables us to become aware of moments in which we have sensed God's Presence or Providence, as well as moments in which we have sensed God's absence.

The *lectio divina* is a personal encounter with the Word of God in which the thoughts, images, feelings, and wishes of the individual are shaped by God's Presence entering and permeating us. It is a deepening of our interpersonal relationship with God. Ideally, when we recite the words of Scripture, whether in study, prayer, or meditation, we are directed by the words. This concept of being directed is what the ancient rabbis termed *kavannah*—*attentiveness* (to borrow Heschel's translation). Yet, in addition to attentiveness, *kavannah* also denotes a specific direction. As we participate in the *lectio divina*, we are led to the message the Divine wishes to disclose to us—all we have to do is listen (*Shema Yisrael*) and respond. When we read the Psalms (or any biblical book or liturgy) in this way, the words of Scripture can once again become a living source of strength and spiritual guidance.

It is no linguistic coincidence that the Hebrew word for the Scriptures, *Mikra*, comes from the root word *qara*, which denotes "prayer," "encounter," "cry out,"[2] "summon,"[3] "meeting," "to meet unexpectedly," "to set in opposition,"[4] "accosting."[5] All these different nuances portray how the reading of the Scriptures *summons* us to *encounter* and *meet* the Eternal You who *calls out* to us. When we study the *Mikra* or engage in prayer, *we do battle with God.*[6] We are *accosted* by His Presence as the Transcendent One is with *ours.*

---

2. Cf. Judges 9:7.

3. Cf. Exodus 34:15.

4. Cf. Isaiah 51:19, Jeremiah 13:22.

5. Cf. 1 Samuel 4:1.

6. "I now give to you one portion more than to your brothers, the portion that I took from the hand of the Amorites with *my sword and with my bow*" (Genesis 48:22). The Targum of Onkelos renders

The term *lectio* refers to a way of listening and communing with the Scriptures. When the reader engages in the *lectio divina*, a sentence or perhaps even a word may stand out in his/her mind. The *lectio divina* allows the empirically minded person to use his/her reasoning processes to expand the biblical text and personalize its meaning. The *lectio divina* suggests that this tradition views the Torah as an aid to the spiritual life; it goes far beyond the limitations of the historical and analytical approaches of the post-Enlightenment epoch. In the simplest sense, the *lectio* is a devotional way of engaging the sacred text. To appreciate the *lectio*, we must believe that all our fundamental convictions are rooted in the narratives of Scripture. In this sense, the *lectio* allows the imagery and metaphors of Scripture to speak to us as they spoke to our ancestors of the past.

The *lectio divina* has much to teach us about the psychic reality of the soul's inner voice. The inner dialogue with the text enables the reader to move from an egocentric way of experiencing the world to a God-centered way of experiencing the world. With the *lectio*, we allow God's voice to summon us to a soulful journey, leading to communion. The internal dialogue enables us to break beyond the walls of the illusory self, the false self that keeps us prisoners. The *lectio* teaches us to surrender to the Spirit that seeks to unfold and enrich life. The *lectio divina* thus represents a personalized Midrash of the biblical text. According to Thomas Keating, it is a way of "savoring the text."

> Lectio Divina was not just a mental or purely spiritual activity. The monks of the Middle Ages used to whisper the words so that their bodies were engaged in the conversation. They would also read very slowly, the whole process of Lectio taking at times a couple of hours. In our day we are almost completely desensitized to sacred reading because we are so used to newspapers, magazines and speed reading. We tend to read the Scriptures as if they were just another book to be consumed. Lectio is just the opposite. It is the savoring of the text, a leisurely lingering in divine revelation.[7]

The *lectio* has many usages, some which are used in Depth Psychology. The Jungian analyst Dr. Ira Progoff calls this process "symbolic unfoldment." He describes a therapy session he once had with a man who was having relationship problems that were interfering with his personal happiness. One night, while out carousing, the man was robbed and seriously beaten by three hoodlums. Eventually, he ended up in a hospital, feeling distraught and depressed over his

---

the last portion of the verse as: *with my prayer and with my entreaty*. Many of the hasidic commentaries point out how prayer can be a form of warfare. According to Rebbe Hayim Meir of Penistov, Jacob's weapon against his brother *Esav* was his power of prayer. Cf. *Maayanot Shel Natzach, Pninima HaHasidut* for several examples.

7. Thomas Keating, *Intimacy With God* (New York: Crossroads, 1994), p. 47.

condition. The man had difficulty making sense of what happened, and he felt that this was his special fate in life. As Dr. Progoff spoke with him, they started talking about the Bible. The name Jacob came up, and together they started reading the story of how Jacob "got mugged" by an angel. The story had special relevance to the man. He felt as though he were Jacob; all the sensations Jacob must have felt, he felt too. Later, Dr. Progoff instructed his patient to enter into Jacob's struggle once more by himself, in the privacy of his room. As he wrote about it, he felt as though he had become one with Jacob. Progoff writes:

> As he was present in the image—and it was now an old/new image, for it was both modern and ancient at the same time—its symbolism became a reality and carried him on. There was a blessing to be given. That had been the outcome and the meaning of Jacob's struggle, for Jacob struggled until the blessing had come. Now he too would continue until a blessing would be given to him. He remained within the experience of the image until a blessing did come to him. . . .

Jacob wrestled with his God until he emerged after his nocturnal struggle with a clearer sense of his own destiny, a better understanding of the world, and a more intimate relationship with his Creator, so too did the man in the above story come to a clearer perspective of who he was, and how he was to relate to other human beings and to his God. Dr. Progoff concludes:

> In the course of the blessing of his inner transformation he would be freed from the compulsive habit [that is, his sexual promiscuity] that was making his life so difficult. Shortly afterwards, when he was going to the hospital to have the doctor take the cast off, a curious punning quality of his mind told him that this would also be the time when he would "cast off" his habit. And so it was.[8]

In hasidic circles, the rebbes encouraged their followers to internalize the imagery of the psalms. The words of the psalms had to be experienced pictorially. The verses of the psalms became a mirror reflecting the feelings of pain and joy of the worshiper's life. Midrashic interpretation is timeless and protean. The Jewish mystics often saw the biblical text as a spiritual allegory of the soul (see the passage from the Zohar cited on page 15). Rather than speaking of their own personal spiritual journey, the rebbes, too, couched their language in an ambiguous tone so that what they wrote could apply to others.

Shneur Zalman of Liadi (eighteenth-nineteenth century) once explained, in his mystical commentary on the name of the Baal Shem Tov, that when Noah was instructed to go into the ark (*teyva*), he was also instructed to enter the word (*teyva*). Thus, the word uplifts the soul to God. The sacred word becomes the

---

8. Ira Progoff, *The Dynamics of Hope*, p. 34.

vehicle for coming into God's Presence. The word picks us up and transports our souls to a higher and more spiritual dimension of existence. We are enveloped by the Word. We are nurtured by the Word. With the *lectio divina*, we wait for a revelation, an insight, an image of how the Divine will reveal Himself to us.[9]

There is mystery and intrigue. The Word takes us on a journey to the unknown. What makes the *lectio divina* so important is that it enables ordinary people to relate to the holy text in the same way the ancients of Judea and their descendants have done since time immemorial. Every meeting with the Word is an invitation to encounter God's Presence. We are invited daily to participate in the Torah's reality while the Torah's reality participates *in* us as well as *through* us.

The *lectio* has many dynamic facets. Some individuals may perceive a call to worship, others may be inspired to behave in a certain way that reveals spirit. To others, the *lectio* may be nothing more than a way of experiencing God's tender embrace and love. To others still, the *lectio* may bring words of criticism and rebuke. The *lectio* is an intimate process and will reveal to the reader aspects of his/her spiritual life that may be hard to accept. The *lectio* enables people to give voice to their deepest yearnings, which seldom find expression in their conscious lives.

The *lectio* was used by one of the most celebrated heroes of modern Jewish time—Natan Sharansky, the famous Soviet "Refusenik." The Refuseniks were Jews who were not allowed to emigrate freely to Israel. In 1978, Natan was sentenced by a Moscow court to thirteen years in a prison camp for his "treasonous" struggle to help Russian Jews emigrate to Israel. While he was in prison, his wife, Avital, sent him a tiny book of psalms. After some effort, he managed to smuggle it into his cell. Natan found the psalms to be especially helpful when he learned of his father's death. For Sharansky, the words of King David became *his* words and reflected *his* suffering also. Of all the psalms, it was Psalm 23 that inspired him most. Natan was so inspired by this psalm, that he called his autobiography, *Fear No Evil,* after Psalm 23. He comments on Psalms 23:4

> Even though I walk through the valley of the shadow of death, I will fear no evil; for you are with me— (Psalms 23:4). Even when you are left all alone, there is still a Force upholding you. . . .
> Whether the soul of King David exists or not, King David, three thousand years

---

9. Elsewhere Shneur Zalman observes that the mere reading of the Torah *reveals the Ain Sof (the Endless One) into the world through the letters of the Torah (Mikra). Sheneir* Zalman, *Torah Ohr* (Brooklyn, NY: Kehot, reprinted 1990) 73:3. According to Nachmanides, the entire Torah is composed of the Names of the Holy One (see Nachmanides, *Introduction to the Torah*). This would suggest that each word in the Torah conveys a truth about the Divine reality, much as the name of a person conveys something about a human personality.

after his death, came to me with his Psalms to my prison cell and gave me lots of strength, and that is what is important to me . . .[10]

Despite the isolation from his family and friends, despite the silence of the Western world, the *lectio* provided Sharansky with an internal spring from which to draw courage and strength. To Sharansky, the message of Psalm 23 was inextricably related to the biblical verse, "man does not live on bread alone" (Deuteronomy 8:3). God's Word enabled Sharansky and other Refuseniks to find the inner strength to sense God's presence even within prison walls. The *lectio* enabled Sharansky's spirit to sense God's Presence despite the adversities he and others were confronted with. His prison experience became, for him and others, a place of spiritual awakening and transformation.

With the *lectio,* each biblical verse will speak differently to each individual based on his life experiences and maturity. Moses, Aaron, Pharaoh, Job each become alive and speak to us about our specific life situation. The image of a hardened heart may well typify the disposition of what I am feeling today—that is, the refusal to listen to God's voice speak to me, especially when I consider doing something wrong. Job's own words may speak volumes and give voice to many who feel rejected by friends and community. The *lectio* allows people to experience a catharsis. It allows for those experiencing life transitions to give verbal expression to their doubts and feelings of ambivalence. The *lectio* allows the participant to engage in a holy dialogue, allowing him/her to have a close encounter of a spiritual kind. The *lectio* helps tune our ears to discerning God's own voice giving expression in our own lives.

### *The Four Parts of the* Lectio Divina

The *lectio divina* consist of four parts: reading, listening, meditation, and prayer. The first step is reverently to read the sacred text in a way that is intimate, quiet, and personal. We wait for the word or words that will stand out and call to us. Once the individual word or passage speaks to us, we then enter the second stage.

The second step involves focusing on the word in the sacred text that stands out and speaks to us. As we hold the word in our memory, its various images will unfold like the petals of a rose. We chew "our cud," so to speak. The same is true with the *lectio*. Out of God's Word, through our review and thoughtful meditation, a message slowly emerges that is specific to our own life situation. Repeating the word or passage will enable us to draw ourselves back when our minds wander.

The third step involves prayer. We take whatever insight or message we have

---

10. Anatoly Sharansky, *Fear No Evil* (New York: Random House, 1988), p. 272.

received and offer it up as a prayer to God in the spirit of thankfulness. This step enables us to sublimate suffering and give it redemptive meaning. Though we are weakened by suffering, we affirm that we are not defeated. There may be times when nothing insightful comes to our minds; nonetheless, even those rare moments may, even if they accomplish nothing else, provide us with quiet for a brief moment. With prayer, our communication with God becomes a dialogue of love, a conscious revelation of ourselves to God.

The fourth step is contemplation. In contemplation we allow ourselves to feel the peacefulness of merely being in the Presence of God's *Shechina*. Since the *Shechina* represents God's maternal Self, we experience a sense of peacefulness and tranquility as we feel loved, nurtured, and guided by God's Presence.

### Entering into the Word

One of the most important aspects of my adult education program with the congregation has been the implementation of the *lectio divina* as a dialogue with Psalm 23. Since my community was not used to the concept of *lectio divina*, I put together a questionnaire designed to help break the ice and facilitate a spiritual dialogue employing the basic principles of Psalm 23.

The purpose of these questions was to help the community dialogue with the psalm, allowing the words (or word) to stand out and speak to them. The psalm was broken up into nine short sections. With each section I asked my congregants to ask themselves three basic questions:

1. What does this verse say to you? In what way is it true? What is God's word calling you to do?
2. In what way isn't this verse true?
3. How would you like to see this verse become true?

Not everybody answered all the questions, nor did they have to. The questions were props designed to facilitate a spiritual dialogue with the imagery of Psalm 23. Consequently, the results recorded in this book are not always symmetrically consistent with the questions. It took a considerable amount of time for the participants to fill out the forms and mail them back to me. I have found by talking to many people, either in person or on the phone, that for many it is much easier to speak about their social, sexual, and economic life than it is to speak about their spiritual life. The divine–human relationship is so private that many Jews have difficulty expressing their vulnerability, doubts, and insecurities in matters of faith. The sharing of one's story of faith cannot be forced. With considerable reverence, the Jewish community slowly opened themselves up to sharing their own faith journeys with each other. I received the exact information

I needed for my research. I also tried using the *lectio divina* on Psalm 23 in groups, as we all shared its meaning together. The responses I have received have been fascinating. This approach has helped many of my congregants see the imagery of Psalm 23 in a way that was spiritually uplifting and inspiring.

Many of the immigrants tearfully recalled how they barely managed to escape the death camps on their way to this country. Other members could relate to times of crisis—for example, illness, when they were restored to good health. Some would reminisce about the loss of their loved ones and how the loss affected their lives at that time. It was as if a ray of light finally penetrated their empiric mist. Morning had finally broken through. Our get-together proved to be special, a close encounter of a spiritual kind. One of the vital characteristics of this exercise was the protean element of change. Psalm 23 became a lens looking at the world. As people's life situations changed, so, too, did their view of the psalm. Thus, there were times when individuals could not feel God's shepherding Presence, whereas, at other times, God's Presence was unmistakably felt.

The insights these students had provided an experiential basis for encountering God as Shepherd. This study taught me that the so-called average person has much to teach the professional theological and the rabbinical world. Here are some insights these students shared with me.

*What does this psalm say to you? In what way is it true?*

**The LORD is my shepherd. . .**

ANTON: This verse brings up the question of acceptance. Do I accept the Lord as my Shepherd? It depicts the existential question of whether my own actions are of my own choosing or whether I am directed, guided, and shepherded by the Lord—if I accept the Lord *is* my shepherd. I don't know in what way this verse is true.

The verse "The Lord is my shepherd" is a declaration of someone who has a relationship with God. It is a statement of acceptance and companionship. The title "Lord" is given to someone of power, knowledge, and ability; it's a status.

SONYA:

A. That is God is my caretaker.
B. For me, God knows my destiny—the universal energy (God) silently watches over me. I feel the presence of this energy constantly—that is, when I ask for it. Also, my conscience lets me know what is right or wrong.

CHARLOTTE: A shepherd guides and protects. "My shepherd" implies that God's concern is for each of us. "Is" individually, currently "is."

As a spiritual shepherd, God guides and protects through moral law. But, as a literal shepherd, God can only *lead us to* the richest pastures. . . .

AARON:

1. It begins with the Lord, and not "me" or "my." This reminds me that God and God's concerns should come first, which means that my desires, my agendas, and my "self-fulfillment" are subordinated to God's plan for me and God's world. That's not to say that God doesn't want me to be happy or "self-actualized"; it's just to say that serving God ought to come before my self-interest. I believe this is also what the first, second, and third commandments of the Ten Commandments are about.

2. It says "is," not "was" or "will be" or "might be." God's shepherding of me is current, and not just a thing of the past or the future. Right now God is my shepherd.

3. This first verse also does not make God's identity as my shepherd contingent on whether I accept it or not. The Lord simply is my shepherd. That's who God *is*.

4. If God is my shepherd, then I must be one of God's sheep. This is a metaphor which I take to mean: (a) that God knows better than I what is good for me; (b) that I need to be led and protected: if left to my own devices, I will get lost or injured; and (c) that God takes responsibility for caring for me as His creature. I trust that God is a good shepherd.

5. If God is a shepherd, and I am created in God's image, I am also supposed to care for others. But my shepherding must always defer to God's shepherding.

6. God is my shepherd. There is a personal dimension to faith; the community of faith is made up of *persons*, or it is not a community.

It is always true, but sometimes I behave more as if it's true by:

1. putting God first and getting out of myself;
2. trusting and following God's guidance in my life through God's Scriptures and the people God puts in my life; and
3. caring for others.

RACHEL: With God in my life I cannot fear because He is with me always and will make all things possible for me. I will lack for nothing. He will provide me with what I need.

MORDECHAI: Often, it is in retrospect I have seen God as my shepherd. When I went through hard times it was hard to be consciously aware of this. After hitting what seemed at the time to be rock bottom, I discovered faith in God I didn't know I even had.

ELEANOR: For me, when my husband was very sick, I was able to make the decision to invoke the living will. We surrendered our will to God's will.

MIRIAM: God watches over me. I believe in *Bashert*—God has a plan for me.

MICHAEL ABRAHAM: The Lord *is* my shepherd *if* I allow Him to be and even despite the times I attempt to *direct* without following His lead. While He expects us to aid His direction, we often declare, "His will to be done *my way, Lord.*" The shepherd maxim is gained, lessened, lost, and regained. To me, this *makes* the Lord *my* shepherd again and again, restored and revitalized; renewed and forever vital.

## I shall not want;

ANTON: This verse brings to mind a number of questions:

What shall I not want?
Why shall I not want?
Where shall I not want?
How should I not want?
When shall I not want?

As I shall not want, I am not tempted. . . .
Life is simpler, less stressful, less strife.
When I have not wanted,
I have less desire,
less energy is spent wanting materially,
emotionally, sensuous exploits.

When energy is less channeled to wants,
there's more energy for other purposes.

Accepting this verse necessitates that I relate to others and myself in a less egocentric focus and manner. "I am interacting with You, not because of something that You have. . . . Our interaction will be of a different meaning."

If we link up verses 1 and 2: The Lord is my Shepherd. I shall not want.

I have another thought enters through me. . . .

Whether I want it or not, The Lord is my Shepherd. It is unconditional and caring. Whether I want it or not, my biological parents are the ones who gave birth to me. The relationship is affirmed. This is a new awareness for me. Whether I accept this or not, it is. Even if I shall not want it to be, the Lord is my Shepherd.

If I accept it as it is, then it brings to mind [the question] how do I relate to Him? And how does He relate to me? Moreover, how do I relate to others?

The many blessings I have received, the many new insights and awareness I have gotten, makes it clear for me that I do have a *relationship* with the Lord, however diffused my present awareness is. The role is a clearly defined role.

SONYA: We have all that we need to fulfill our destiny and our karmic debt in this world. Also, we are not given problems that we cannot handle. With God's help, nothing is insurmountable.

CHARLOTTE: We are offered riches spiritually and physically. This is a beautiful earth, and life has opportunities for each of us—if only we recognize them. I am particularly aware of the gifts of life and earth.

AARON: Nothing that I really need will ever be denied me. It is always true, but I feel more as if it is true when I'm feeling satisfied and when I see others getting enough.

**He makes me lie down in green pastures.**

ANTON: The shepherd cares for me lest I forget [and] I do not keep it in mind. [This line] also directs my attention to what is expected of me and how I should relate with others.

SONYA: Green pastures—means healing, growth, and forgiveness. In meditation, I rest and am healed. I am forgiven as I forgive myself. In this silent communion God speaks to me and guides me, nourishes me, and heals me.

CHARLOTTE: Green suggests growth, fertility, richness, fullness of life, and rebirth.

AARON:

1. Green pastures suggest food. God nourishes me and calls me to be fed physically and spiritually. I am fed through the Scriptures, through relationships with the rest of God's created order, and through a relationship of prayer with God.

2. Lying down suggests rest. God calls me to rest, and sometimes indeed makes me rest by knocking me off my feet if I work too hard. I think about Sabbath re-creation in this verse.

3. God leads me. I follow.

RACHEL: Green, the color of healing and new life will be my continuous pasture of life—my path to Divine wisdom, love, and power. When I lie down and when I rise up, the pasture of God's guidance will remain with me.

MORDECHAI: The verse says something else to me: What one person regards as green, another may view it as barren. Perhaps the words are suggesting that my faith affects whether I will see God's goodness as a green pasture, or as an arid pasture—it's all a matter of perspective. Another image comes to mind: If the pastures are green, then it is not enough that we pass through them, but let us abide in them and find peacefulness.

MICHAEL ABRAHAM: These wants in [verse] 2 (still waters, green pastures) being refined, allow, permit, encourage me to lie down in green pastures alongside the still waters. Pastures are not green nor are waters still when we are not green, receptive, and desirous to the still waters.

**He leads me beside still waters;**

SONYA:

A. Water symbolizes cleansing for me. God is my meditation, cleans me, and bathes me in still (peaceful) waters rather than stormy ones.
B. It is true as long as I believe it and do the work—that is, take the time to communicate with God and thank the Divine constantly.
C. It has always been there for me.

CHARLOTTE: Still waters—suggests life again. Water is giving and sustaining. These two images (green and still waters) add the spiritual feeling and the idea of a nurturing God who helps us to find peace. "Still waters" as opposed to turbulence.

We're not always led to green pastures, and so on, but perhaps we just fail to see them!

AARON: Still waters suggest serenity, peace, calm, quenched thirst. The opposite of turbulence. I can be at peace. It is always true, but seems more so when I feel nourished and rested. I believe God leads me to such places, but I don't always follow.

MORDECHAI: Still, peaceful waters, the waters of *Shabbat* rest. The waters of healing. Waters of sweetness. Waters that are clear. Waters to immerse my heart, soul, and mind. The word "still" reminds me to be silent enough to allow God's word to speak, for too often I can't hear beyond the noise of my own wheels in motion. Another image comes to my mind: To find the waters of stillness, I must surrender my will to God's will. For me, this has always been difficult.

ELEANOR: We can find peace and tranquility if we are ready to accept it.

MIRIAM: Tranquility to me means being satisfied with what one has. I know that God is not too busy to watch over me.

*What does this verse say to you?*

SONYA:

   A. Again, by resting in serenity gained by meditation, God will restore my
      soul.
   B. The Presence is always there; we just have to go to it and ask it for help.

CHARLOTTE:

   1. God offers nourishment for our souls. It is up to us to recognize it and
      accept it.
   2. See previous comment regarding "green pastures" and "still waters."
   3. I believe that there must be an order and meaning in life (though it's
      often hard to hold off when things go wrong). Belief gives one comfort
      and peace.
   4. The word "restores" suggests a continuous process.
   5. It makes me try to define soul! Is it perhaps that touch of God within
      each of us? Is it the deeper and often hidden spirit of love and caring
      which is God?

MORDECHAI: I have taken many wrong turns along the spiritual journey. I
cannot begin to describe all the many ways You brought me back to the land of
the living, and kept me from falling into the abyss. My soul, my life, my integrity
have been restored, and for that I am eternally thankful, for having been given a
new chance at life.

ELEANOR: When things go wrong it is normal to feel sad and depressed: "Why
me?" However, by thanking God for having raised two wonderful children
together, having shared 45 years with ups and downs, but someone always at my
side . . .

MICHAEL ABRAHAM: Restoration of soul is soundly apparent through and after
crisis. Why we cannot know restoration without first being drained, exhausted,
fatigued is the cleansing path of first being disquieted, unserved, or bankrupt.

ANDREA: It makes organized religion and righteousness for his name's sake
more important than any amount of human goodness or acts or kindness.

## He leads me in paths of righteousness
## for His name's sake.

SONYA: God is always with me and the rod keeps away the evil and the staff
guides me. As long as I ask, I shall receive protection.

MIRIAM: My faith was personally deepened as a result of my many experiences with suffering. Being a Holocaust survivor, having lost most of my family

in Europe; the Jewish community helped restore my own connectedness with God and Judaism. My husband, his best friend, my own community helped shepherd me and restored my soul. Whenever I have felt sick, and I begin to start feeling better, I consider myself lucky.

CHARLOTTE: We are shown the paths of righteousness to bring us closer to the spirit of God.

I think my personal righteousness and almost extreme sense of right has always been part of me. Is this from God or is it from my mother?

AARON:

1. Again, as by the still waters, God is leading. It is up to me to follow.

2. *Paths of righteousness.* God leads me on the right path in and to life, not the wrong one. God leads me to be faithful to who God has revealed Godself to be. Again—a life of caring.

3. *For his name's sake.* God doesn't lead me on the right path just for my good. God leads me this way for the sake of God's reputation. My being led on the right path is so that people will know and respect who God is.

4. When I think about the right path, I also think of how God can bring good out of bad. Even when I'm not sure about the life path to take, even when I make a wrong decision, God can bring good out of it.

It is most true when I consciously follow God's ways.

MORDECHAI: Step by step, I walk toward You. The paths of righteousness have been formed long ago, if only I would take the first step forward. I am tired of walking haphazardly in directions in which I don't know where I am going. I wish thistles, briar patches, and unforeseeable pitfalls were not such an important part of my own spiritual journey. Sometimes I feel like Alice in Wonderland.

MICHAEL ABRAHAM: Being led into paths of righteousness "for His name's sake" is that to which we revert—the instinct of natural goodness. Living in the world entices us to constant inquiry. Inquiry is the only path that leads us to a choice of righteousness for His Name's sake.

**Even though I walk through
the valley of the shadow of death,
I fear no evil;
for You are with me;**

SONYA: When God is asked for help—one is answered that help will be received. In many incidents in my life, God has not only protected me but also given me a reason to celebrate the outcome.

When asked, God will provide protection. I know, for I have experienced it. I don't think that the "shadow of death" taken literally is evil. I believe that this evil is ignorance.

CHARLOTTE: Note the switch from third-person "he" to more personal form—"Thou" (for you).

1. This verse asks for a deep faith.
2. It suggests life itself, for we are always in "the shadow" from birth.
3. "You are with me" is not merely God's protection. It is also a realization of all the good in our lives that comes from a caring God.

RACHEL: Each day our shadows haunt us and cause us to do things we know are wrong—not in the best interest of ourselves or our God-selves. But with God guiding me to the right path I will realize my error and will correct it. No evil will influence me for long, and He will protect me when from myself my shadow self—so long as I am committed to Him and my Truth, which comes directly from Him.

CLAIRE: I know all about the valley of the shadow of death. I was there. In the month of August, they took ninety men (including my twin brother) and took them out of town. They had them dig their own graves and shot them. It was *Shabbat* between Rosh Hashanah and Yom Kippur of 1941.

The rest of the Jews of the town were gathered to the town square on *Shabbat Shuva* 1941. They also took eight thousand Jews from the surrounding area, and they were shot and killed. My mother and two sisters were among them. My mother took off her coat and instructed me to go with my father. She said she would join them later. This happened between September and October when the weather was getting cold.

My father and I were hiding in the bathhouses. Later at night, we fled to the forest to hide. After, we were in the forest for two nights without food. My father knew of a farmer that no one knew was Jewish; so we went and stayed at this farmer's home. As more Jews sought refuge with this farmer, my father decided to leave the farm, and so he went and stayed with a gentile farmer he had grown up with whom my father bribed to help save us. This gentile man risked his life and provided us with food and shelter. My father never lost his faith, he continued to *davin* (pray) three times a day.

I was on the farm, and I missed my father. I decided I had to see him. One Sunday morning I got dressed like a Christian woman going to church (so nobody would think I was Jewish) and went to look for my father. I didn't know which farm my father was on. The farmer guessed where my father went, and so I went to see him.

I knew of a Jewish mill, and I tried to go in, but they would not let me in. My father was not there. As it grew dark, I stayed under a haystack, and in the morning I looked through a window, and I saw the farmer's wife making pancakes. The lady was careful not to mix the pancakes with bacon. I knew that she was making these pancakes for my father. I went into the farmhouse, and my father was so excited to see me. I stayed there for a couple of weeks at this poor farmer's home. My father decided to leave the farm, and so he went to the small town of Svir and stayed at the Jewish ghetto. He knew he could not stay with the gentiles for very long.

I continued to stay at the farmer's place for an additional two weeks. Even though they were kind to me, they used me for very hard labor. Later I decided to go to Svir, and I was determined to stay with my father (regardless of what would happen). We were together in Svir for at least a month. Then, one night, the Nazis came to liquidate the ghetto. This was in the middle of February 1942. Svir had a beautiful lake, and many of the young Jews went to the lake to run away from the Nazis. My father broke through the ice and placed me in the water, and he lay on top of me to protect me from the Nazis' bullets. We stayed underwater until the Nazis went.

Afterward, we went to the Jewish ghetto of Mishaleikske, which was twenty kilometers away from nearby Svir. We stayed there till the beginning of April. Then they took us to the Vilna ghetto. We were in the Vilna ghetto till September 1943. We had an acquaintance in the Vilna ghetto who was a very prosperous man. His name was Mr. Buerstein. He promised my father that he would take care of me.

They separated me from my father and took me to Estonia, and I went with his family. Our gentile host received a handsome sum of gold and hid us in a cellar for seven months. One morning we heard lots of noise, I peeped through the hatch of the cellar. The Nazis saw me and they started shooting. The bullets grazed my stomach and instantly killed Mr. Buerstein, my father's friend.

MORDECHAI: At times, the journey of my own faith has been difficult. I have discovered what my faith means to me and what I am in turn made of when I had to plunge deeply . . . deeply . . . into the depths of my own personal soul. The shadow contains the suppressed parts of the personality—the good, the bad, and the ugly—parts of me I do not like. For me, I know part of my life journey is to wrestle with my own dark angel, and hopefully take on a new spiritual identity. My solace is that, as I stuggle with my shadow, I know that You are with me.

Another image comes to mind:

The metaphor of darkness has always been familiar to me. I have experienced the dark valley whenever life seemed empty and void of meaning. Whenever I have felt little desire for the life of the spirit, I encountered darkness. Whenever

I battled with indecision and fear, I encountered darkness. The feelings of having my vitality sucked out of me, for me, has been a journey through darkness. Whenever I have embraced life with scarcity and negativity I have experienced the path of darkness.

When I look back to experiences of my past when I was confronted with a crisis, I always hear the words resonate inside me: *I will fear no evil, for You are with me.* These words helped renew me—especially when things seemed so dismal and bleak. I now know that, no matter what the world does to me, I must rise above my fears and insecurity and surrender to the Power who is beyond my control.

Another thought: The reason we experience the Valley of Darkness is that we feel as if God's Presence is not with us. The psalm affirms that God is always present even when He seems absent. This for me is a source of strength and comfort.

One last reflection: The valley of darkness is also a valley of shadows. As much as I may fear these shadows, I must remember that these fears are only shadows, and shadows cannot harm me, but fear can.

SHEMUEL: As I say these words, "I will fear no evil, for You are with me," I see images of Joseph flow through my mind. Hated by his brothers, he ended up in a pit, left to die. Suddenly he then found himself in Egypt. Joseph knew that God would not leave him. And just when he thought life would be great working for Potiphar—wham! He ended up in the slammer. Once again he found himself in the pit. But God was still with him. After becoming the Pharaoh's analyst, Joseph was content never to see his dysfunctional family again. But the Shepherd had different plans. Joseph came to see God's Presence in a strange and mysterious way. He affirmed God as the Shepherd when he told his brethren, "And now do not be distressed, or angry with yourselves, because you sold me here; for God sent me before you to preserve life." (Genesis 45:5.) God walked with Joseph and He walks with me through my dark valleys and my triumphs.

ELEANOR: We always are in the shadow of death since we never know when it [death] will come. Yet, I fear no evil. I feel I have made my contribution to humanity. God will take me when my work is done.

MIRIAM: I have comfort knowing that God is not too busy to worry about me. I felt lucky escaping Romania alive after the war. Recently, after having a stroke, I was still able to use my right hand.

MICHAEL ABRAHAM: The valley of the shadow of death is that valley in which all that is under my control is no longer under *my* control. When I *know* I can no longer control, I enter the valley and taste death's shadow without fear *because* I have *allowed* Him to be with me. This "death" is experienced in every crisis until we allow Him to be with us.

AARON:

1. It echoes a theme I find in Psalm 139, that there is nowhere I can go that God won't be there with me—even death and the hours and days approaching it for the dying, or the hours and days following death for the grieving. God goes with us into death.

2. I need not despair of God's presence even when my days seem darkest or when I am depressed. God is there.

3. At the same time, evil is real. There are things and events in this world which are contrary to God's plan. But I do not have to be afraid of those things because God goes with me as I face them. The "fear not" of both Hebrew and Christian scriptures echoes in my imagination here. I have nothing finally to fear because God goes with me.

4. I have felt God's presence in some of the darkest hours of my life. There have been things in my life which I do not think God caused, but I have felt God's presence in the healing, reconciliation, and growth which came from them—often expressed through the caring of other people.

## Your rod and Your staff,
## they comfort me.

SONYA: God is with me and the rod keeps away the evil and the staff guides me.

CHARLOTTE: Shall we take the rod and staff further? "Rod" suggests control and even punishment. "Staff" on the other hand, has a more comforting, gentler connotation; we can lean on a staff.

AARON: God eases my pain and brings me solace through the use of two tools, a rod and a staff. I've always heard that the shepherd's rod was used to discipline, and a shepherd's staff was used to pull sheep from harm and to ward off predators. The rod (a disciplinary tool—and I take discipline, from its root, to be teaching and not punishment or abuse), I suppose, might be the scripture, the prophets, and the events that God allows to happen to us as a consequence of our disobedience. God doesn't cause them but doesn't prevent them either. The staff may also be the Scripture—if I follow it and use it, I can keep myself out of a lot of trouble and recognize God's presence in the midst of other trouble. The staff may be the hand of a faithful friend, another follower who reaches out to me in my hour of need.

When I learn from the consequences of my actions or feel consoled in times of sorrow, the Shepherd's rod and staff are bringing me comfort. When I am kept safe when harm could befall me, or when I feel the presence of God through another person when harm has befallen me, the Shepherd's rod and staff are bringing me comfort. When I follow the guidance of Scripture or take solace in its words of consolation, the Shepherd's rod and staff are bringing me comfort.

RACHEL: God is ever with me and never deserts me even though I desert Him at times. His love and comfort never change, no matter what I do, so long as I come back to Him and shelter myself within His loving arms. Many people, situations, temptations—anger, hatred, and confusions— will rise to destroy me. But God's staff is ever steadfast and will be there to support me as I fall and rise up again.

MORDECHAI: There have been times I have felt the rod; there have been many times I have felt Your staff supporting me as my own strength failed me.

ELEANOR: The rod and staff used as guides will lead me to my proper place.

MIRIAM: Touching and helping me in my moments of dire need, your staff helped lift me up out of the pit to safety. There were footprints in the sand and the sensation that God was carrying me when the walk in the desert seemed too difficult to traverse.

MICHAEL ABRAHAM: His rod and staff only become a comfort most deeply as we lose and regain time and again the confidence that as we fail, He restores. We must be hungry before we can be fed; we must be weak to be strengthened; we must be naked to be clothed; we must be bankrupt in order to know our true needs. It is at this juncture that we feel the substance of His rod and staff. It is truly in bankruptcy that comfort knows its fullness.

**You prepare a table before me
in the presence of my enemies;
You anoint my head with oil,
my cup overflows.**

SONYA: This really resonates with me. When I have been consciously wounded by someone I trusted—God creates a miracle that showers me with many gifts. Oil symbolizes purity. The cup signifies the container of good things while the table signifies the lifted platform upon which the truth shines.

CHARLOTTE: Once again, there is an increasingly personal relationship. "You" is repeated. God is close to us and not merely leading or guiding. Instead He is almost our servant and utterly faithful to and offers each of us so much, shouldn't we do the same for others?

MORDECHAI: As I recite this passage, images of my father come alive, for he indeed found the strength and faith to make a new life in this country after the death camps of Europe. Like Job, my father made the choice to start a new life instead of stewing in the painful memories of Europe. In many ways, Psalm 23 is a story about my own father's life, and for that reason I am grateful that he is still alive and well. Were it not for the many miracles he had personally experienced, my earthly existence would be naught.

ELEANOR: Even when we are surrounded by foes, we must look for the way to avoid conflict and soothe the hurt. Sometimes a compromise is necessary to close a business deal, or prevent a conflict. Often compromise does the job.

MICHAEL ABRAHAM: The table is prepared without apprehension to enemy or foe only as we approach a fear no longer of earthly enemy. While we can offer this table to all, even the enemy becomes clay in the presence of love and kindness. Anointment is healing, and in healing upon my head, the cup of goodness forever flows because of healing and restoration. I can only face my enemy without fear when I am confident in healing. When I am confident in the Shepherd, my cup forever overflows.

AARON:

1. *You prepare a table before me:* I think of the Passover meal, the manna and quail in the wilderness, the visit of Melchizedek to Abraham, David eating the Bread of Presence, which for me recalls all those biblical suppers and more—the other times when I personally have been fed in the midst of danger, the other times when I have been extended fellowship and hospitality by people of God. The verse says that God gives me nourishment, hospitality, and fellowship in times of physical and spiritual danger.

2. *You anoint my head with oil:* I think of Psalm 133 here—and the oil of ordination. In some Christian traditions (but not my own) oil is used in baptism as well. This portion of the verse says to me that I (like all other people who claim to be God's people—Jews and Christians alike) am set apart for God's work. Anointed. I also think here of the individual attention a shepherd gives to a sheep, rubbing its head.

3. *My cup overflows.* I think here of gratitude and of Psalm 116. The cup of salvation overflowing. The thanksgiving sacrifice. I am provided for. A life of thanksgiving is the only adequate response to God's goodness and blessing.

1. *Table.* It is always true, but I feel it more so when I share in communion, when I break bread with another, when I feel nourished, when God's people extend a hand of hospitality to me or someone else in need.

2. *Oil.* It is always true. I feel it more so when I can acknowledge that I am set apart with the rest of God's people.

3. *Cup.* It is always true. Sometimes I feel it more than other times. I'm not always materially or even spiritually blessed, but I can be assured of God's steadfast love. That should issue forth in a life of gratitude. My own thanksgiving should be overflowing.

**Surely goodness and mercy shall follow me**
**all the days of my life;**
**and I shall dwell**
**in the house of the LORD**
**forever.**

SONYA: As long as I do the work I am supposed to do, God will always shower me with blessings and I shall never feel isolated. Whatever I do comes back to me immediately. If I follow God's advice and do good deeds then good deeds follow me. Again, the concept of understanding the karmic law is very important.

CHARLOTTE: The words "shall follow me" intrigue me. God's goodness and mercy are no longer leading and directing. Perhaps having been shown the way—we are now on our own.

The "house" of the Lord becomes all of our world—not merely a personal dwelling or a religious institution. The "house" also implies the place where we are all part of God's family–living, loving, protecting, respecting each other and what God has set before us.

ANDREA: I hope that wherever I have been I will have done goodness and shown mercy.

As I move through life, whatever I have done will follow me. If I have done good deeds and shown mercy, then I hope those attributes will follow me. Likewise, if I have inflicted pain and suffering in life, I should expect that too will follow me—wherever I go.

ELEANOR: In the hereafter, the Lord will be there for me, guiding me in the path of righteousness.

MIRIAM: I am a very lucky woman to have had the love and admiration of many people and that Abe is finally learning that we must be open to whatever destiny has assigned me to do in this life and that I cannot just be a wife, mother, and helpmate. There are other things calling me and I cannot ignore them all. I have a God who always watches over me and if I trust in my instinct I will always do the right thing by listening to my inner voice. I feel that I am a very religious person in the true sense of the word without the *shtick* (pretentiousness) often associated with "religious" people.

MICHAEL ABRAHAM: While goodness and mercy are assured throughout my life, my personal assurance may yet falter. In this faltering and distress, we *know* the assurance of goodness and mercy all the days of our lives *each time* we return to the fold of the Shepherd who never withholds His goodness and mercy. Dwelling in the House of the Lord forever makes earthly trials so completely anticipated. The Shepherd's Dwelling is always our abode in each *forever*— especially following the "fiery furnace" in life. Each forever becomes more eternal as each day's journey is fulfilled. To dwell in the House of the Lord forever is always a choice, a choice increasingly more tender with each return.

AARON: God's goodness and mercy will always follow me. God's goodness and mercy toward me and the rest of God's creation won't stop—it will last my whole life long. I may not always be able to see it, but it will be there. And I won't be able to ignore the demands of goodness and mercy on me for long either—those demands will follow me. I am called to be good and merciful.

This does not mean that life will always go well for me. Sometimes my life will seem like it isn't going "good" [sic]. But God's goodness and mercy will never end.

Hopefully [sic], one way it is true is in the actions of the people of God—practicing goodness and mercy, even when their very goodness and mercy are rejected. In that sense, hopefully, no one will be able to get away from goodness and mercy. Their lives won't always go well, but goodness and mercy will follow the worst nonbeliever and the most righteous person of faith through their lives. Neither will be able to escape goodness and mercy—it will be shown to them by God through God's people to the end of their lives. In this way, people will know who the Lord really is. A shepherd who never gives up on his sheep. Of course, I also leave room for God to act outside of how God acts through God's people—God has more hands than just ours—and can act without people, or with people we would never expect God to act through.

### and I shall dwell in the house of the Lord forever.

AARON: I will live in God's house forever. I will have eternal life. I think of John 14:1–6: In my Father's house there are many dwelling places—I go to prepare a place for you. I think of heaven.

It is always true.

MORDECHAI: I know that I am not merely a denizen of just this world. Within me, there is a part of me that is eternal. As a thought of God, how could I ever disappear?

The Talmud teaches that if we are righteous we can be alive even when we are dead, but there are people who are dead, but there are people who are dead but just don't know it! I pray that I should always be a member of Your home—wherever I happen to be.

### In what way isn't this verse true?

### The LORD is my shepherd . . .

ANTON: For me to accept that the Lord is my shepherd, I must experience that the Lord possesses a caring relatedness with me and has the proven ability to shepherd me. Yet, since he's the almighty and can't be defined, I find it hard to accept blindly that notion that the Lord is my Shepherd.

When I hear someone say, "The Lord is my Shepherd," my eyes are cast upon that person, and I want to know who he is and what he has that I don't. What kind of person is he, and how does he relate with God and others? And if I accept that "the Lord is my shepherd," what kind of personal responsibility do I have toward myself, others, and my shepherd?

I don't know in what way this verse is true. I am not ready to accept *in toto* the verse, "The Lord is my Shepherd." It is hard for me to answer in what way this is not true.

If I have no previous experience of relatedness with God, how meaningful is it to be told, "The Lord is your shepherd?" I have to begin relating with God before it becomes meaningful to say, "The Lord is my shepherd."

SONYA: I don't believe that God provides for us without our asking. Through my experience and understanding, I have a strong belief that you have to ask God for help, advice, guidance, and you have to work at it.

CHARLOTTE: God cannot protect us in our daily lives—we have free will and often stray.

AARON: In what way isn't this verse true?

1. It is always true, but I have my doubts when: (a) God doesn't take care of me the way I think God should; (b) When awful things happen in the world, things like the Holocaust or, more recently, the massacres in Rwanda.

2. It is true, but I don't behave as if it's true, when I do things that I know are contrary to God's leading.

ANDREA: Some people need to be led but know better than to look to other people for their leader; instead they elevate the leadership role to Lord.

It is evident through religious participation that the Lord is a shepherd, but this makes me want to rebel. The very words, "Lord" and "Shepherd" imply total domination and therefore negate individual power and human free will.

MORDECHAI: When I close myself off from others and fail to share, I act as if God were not my shepherd. Stinginess, hard-heartedness, have often left me with the illusion that I am my own shepherd—yet I want. When I am so full of myself and my ego, I feel like I am running on empty.

## I shall not want;

ANTON: In what way isn't this verse true?

It does not guarantee no disease, no war, no poverty, or earthquakes, or no murder or theft. It just said, "The Lord is my Shepherd." If I as a sheep decided to drift away and got eaten up by the wolf, there is nothing my shepherd can do about it.

CHARLOTTE: Taken literally, this seems to fail. Millions of people live in poverty and would find it hard to believe that God provides.

AARON:

1. Sometimes I feel like I'm not getting what I want, but more importantly, sometimes I even feel that I'm not getting something I really need.

2. It troubles me even more that there are there are folks in the world who have taken this psalm seriously and yet have not had enough to eat. Others have been killed for what they believe. In those ways, it seems as if their needs aren't being addressed. What does "I shall not want" mean for them? I don't imagine they feel it's true.

ANDREA: What does this verse say to you?

"Shall not" is a command; therefore, I dare not want more out of life for fear that I will transgress this command. However, as a human, I do want and therefore am not only a transgressor but am faced with the dilemma of being good and not wanting, or being bad and wanting. "Shall not want" means being satisfied with one's status quo, but without wanting and, therefore, without change, status quo becomes stagnation and death. Living people need to live life while they are alive. I admit I want: I hope that through my want I will evoke changes for the betterment of life for many.

In what way is it true? It is not true. It tells humans to settle for what is and to reject what could be.

**He makes me lie down in green pastures.**
**He leads me beside still waters;**

AARON: In what way isn't this verse true?

Here's my first real dispute with the psalm. I also think God leads us to and through desert places, and through times when the water of our life is choppy and not still. There have been times when I haven't felt spiritually fed or rested, and times when my spiritual thirst has not been quenched.

MORDECHAI: Tortured by problems I have no control over, being worried about matters pertaining to livelihood, relentless pursuers, endless distractions, feelings of insecurities, the waters of chaos often drown me to senselessness and despair.

ANDREA: Historically, pastures and water implied means and methods of human sustenance. In the age of agribusinesses, pastures and still waters conjure images seen in pastoral watercolor paintings—a time past that can only exist in one's mind as quiet and serene. Utopia.

In what way is it true? It is not true. To each their own notion of utopia. Again, I must resist the idea of being led and dominated, it smothers me.

**He restores my soul.**

SONYA: We don't always make the time to meet God.

CHARLOTTE: We are not always "available" to God.

MORDECHAI: There have been countless times when I have not allowed myself to be renewed and restored—when I fail to forgive others for harming me, when I hold on to grudges and feelings of hatred. Too many times I have chosen misery over abundance. I have denied my soul opportunities for healing and growth. . . . By hardening my own heart I have allowed death to enter my relationships, and as a result I did not allow myself to be renewed.

**He leads me in paths of righteousness**
**for His name's sake.**

ANDREA: In what way is it true? It is not true.

I do not believe that such a perspective is healthy since it requires that those who submit do so entirely, while those who do not [submit] seize Godlike opportunities to dominate not only those who have submitted, but all the resources as well. The owners of the means of production and the manipulators of the natural resources are not those who are led in paths of righteousness for His name's sake. If there really is a God, and that God allowed for humans to have life on this earth, then it cannot be that we live for the lip service to and gratification of righteousness for His name's sake. Who decided that human happiness and fulfillment have to occur only in the context of gratifying God?

CHARLOTTE: See Mark Twain's *The Mysterious Stranger*, in which he shows that man is more sinful than Satan. In brief, man knows right from wrong but invariably chooses wrong. Satan has never been instructed in moral law.

AARON: Sometimes God leads and I consciously or unconsciously choose not to follow. I believe that is what sin is—not just missing or falling short of the mark, but choosing the wrong path.

MORDECHAI: I wish I could worship without any ulterior motives. So many people have warped the meaning of faith, while claiming to act in His holy name. In my own life I have often used religion as a way of oppressing people I didn't like.

**Even though I walk through**
**the valley of the shadow of death,**
**I fear no evil;**
**for You are with me;**

SONYA: In what way isn't this verse true?

I don't think that the "shadow of death" taken literally is evil. I believe that this evil is ignorance.

ANDREA: In what way is it true? It is not true.

Evil and death are the two concepts that humans most fear. It is my hope that death will come to me quietly, while I am busily engaged in living life; not the other way around.

CHARLOTTE: In what way isn't this verse true?

It is hard to have such a complete faith. Would it be possible to banish fear and hold tight to faith?

AARON: In what way isn't this verse true?

I think the biggest dilemma for biblical faith, Jewish, *and more so Christian*, in this century is the Holocaust. Here is where I struggle with the presence of God in the valley of the shadow of death. Here is where I most fear evil. Why did so many people who claimed to be people of God not reach out in compassion for other people of God in the death camps? Why did so many who claimed to follow God abandon their neighbor? Yet, the paradox is, I do not believe for a moment that God ever abandoned God's suffering people, nor did He lead them there to be slaughtered. I believe God cried there and suffered there and called in weakness on other people to act *for His name's sake* there. Having not been through such an experience, I cannot speak for whether or not I would have felt utterly abandoned by God in the death camps; but I very much suspect I would have.

MORDECHAI: In what way isn't this verse true?

Those people I have visited in the hospital over the years who have suffered from dreadful diseases such as cancer, AIDS, and so on, have often felt as if God has abandoned them. There is something to be said about the old Talmudic remark on the verse in Exodus 15:11: "Who among the Mighty (*Aleemim*) is liken unto You? Some read it [the biblical verse] with a different consonant, as "Who is like You, O Lord among the *dumb* (*Elim*)?" To my pious and learned grandfather as he walked with his family to the crematorium, he once remarked: "If we are supposed to be Your 'chosen people,' why don't You choose somebody else for a change?"

AARON: In what way isn't this verse true?

When I don't learn from consequences or live out with my life what I learn from the texts of Scripture; when I don't feel the rod and staff of God comforting me or others through the caring activity of the people of God; when I don't feel that I am kept safe from harm—it certainly doesn't seem true.

**You prepare a table before me
in the presence of my enemies;
You anoint my head with oil,
my cup overflows.**

AARON: In what way isn't this verse true?

1. *Table*. It can be difficult for me to feel this is true when I feel excluded or unwelcome at any table of God's people; or when I somehow don't feel nourished.

2. *Oil.* I don't always act as if I am set apart.

3. *Cup.* I don't always feel grateful.

MORDECHAI: When I have not shared my prosperity with others in need, when I have been tightfisted and zealous in protecting what I consider as "mine," I have been like one whose cup of blessing is almost empty. I know God doesn't want me to live in a world of scarcity. If I believe that the Lord is my Shepherd, then I must open my heart and door to share a blessing with somebody in need.

**Surely goodness and mercy shall follow me
all the days of my life;
and I shall dwell
in the house of the LORD
for ever.**

ANDREA: In what way isn't this verse true?

No matter how many good and merciful deeds one has done throughout life, people seem to most enjoy finding flaws to harp on. People love to bring even the most giving and helping people low so they can gossip about them behind their backs.

AARON: In what way isn't this verse true?

It seems less than true when anyone is not shown mercy or goodness by people who claim to act in God's name.

MORDECHAI: In what way isn't this verse true?

When I act as if I did not need or want God's guidance, I act as if I were a true Epicurean who eats, drinks, and parties, for tomorrow we all die. At times my desire for pleasure seems to blind me to my own soul's true vocation—dwelling in the Presence of the Lord.

The Hebrew word for "dwelling" also denotes "sitting." This verse would seem to warn me not to be in such a rush: rushing leads to restlessness, which is the opposite of dwelling in peace. This has been a tough lesson for me to learn, since I don't surrender to anybody—even God.

*In what way would you like this verse to be true?*

**The LORD is my shepherd,**

ANTON: How would you like to see this verse become true?

By having an experience of relatedness with the Lord. To have more knowledge and experiential awareness of my relationship with God. To have experienced what a shepherd does. I wish that those who are relating with the

Lord could articulate for me what that relationship is like, so that I would know what he [the psalmist] is talking about. I know that I am given the ability to chose, and I have been making choices that are OK, but to be vividly aware that the Lord has been "shepherding" me to chose what I have chosen—I am not aware of it.

SONYA: How would you like to see this verse become true?

To come to an understanding of what the inner voice and intuition really is. To become more aware of inner strength than external circumstances; to have faith that God is always there.

CHARLOTTE: How would you like to see this verse become true?

I would like to see a time when all people recognize and follow the paths indicated by God's laws—and become loving shepherds of each other.

AARON: How would you like to see this verse become true?

I'd like to see everyone in the whole world act as if God was their shepherd by caring for each other and otherwise following God's leading. I know that is a big wish.

ANDREA: How would you like to see this verse become true?

Evildoers need to see Lord as their shepherd: they need better, more elevated leadership.

**I shall not want;**

ANTON: How would I like this verse to be true?

I would like to be able to experience clearly how I am relating to God in a more articulated manner.

CHARLOTTE: How would I like this verse to be true?

If we helped and shared with each other—perhaps more could say "I shall not want."

AARON: How would you like to see this verse become true?

I'd like to see the community of God's people reaching out and helping everyone in need so that no one would lack what he or she needed.

MORDECHAI: How would you like to see this verse become true?

Were I to embrace my world with more love and compassion, more feeling and less intellect, more surrender with less manipulation, I would see God's own Presence as a Shepherd in my own life and in the lives of others.

MIRIAM: How would I like this verse to be true?

I would love to win a twelve-million-dollar sweepstakes!

ANDREA: How would you like to see this verse become true?

I would prefer that the verse be changed to align with consideration for what humans are actually capable of achieving. This demand goes above and beyond what is humanly possible.

**He makes me lie down in green pastures.**

MORDECHAI: How would you like to see this verse become true?

I pray that more people could find inner peacefulness and healing. Our spirit seems so torn at times, we live in fear of tomorrow in many places. The big cities like L.A. and N.Y. have lots of gray cement but very little green.

**He leads me beside still waters;**

SONYA: How would you like to see this verse become true?

I wish I had the strength and commitment to meditate daily and receive the wonderful blessings.

CHARLOTTE: How would you like to see it become true?

Firstly, I'd like to see respect for nature's blessings worldwide. Secondly, often in the turmoil and sadness of life, I lose sight of the peace God offers.

AARON: How would you like to see it become true?

I'd like for me and the rest of the world to feel more serene, rested, and spiritually nourished.

MORDECHAI: How would you like to see it become true?

Water is often a symbol of spiritual teaching. The Talmud says all who are thirsty, let them drink water. What we need are genuine spiritual teachings that will still the restless spirit that rages inside so many of us.

If I can keep my sight on my spiritual center, the waters of chaos would subside, and become still and peaceful in my little world.

ANDREA: How would you like to see this verse become true?

Only in death.

**He restores my soul.**

SONYA: How would you like to see this verse become true?

I would like to make the time to meet God all the time.

AARON: How would you like to see this verse become true?

Perhaps some day we might say, "He restores *our* soul."

ANDREA: How would you like to see this verse become true?

I would like it if those who take their happiness and fulfillment in life from causing despair and grief for others suddenly believed this verse.

**He leads me in paths of righteousness
for his name's sake.**

CHARLOTTE: How would you like to see this verse become true?

I'd like to see more people "righteous" for whatever the reason!

AARON: How would you like to see this verse become true?

I'd like to be more aware of God's leading and more ready to follow in the ways of righteousness. I'd like to see more people embrace the care of their neighbors.

MICHAEL ABRAHAM: Being led into paths of righteousness "for His name's sake" is that to which we revert—the instinct of natural goodness. Living in the world entices us to constant inquiry. Inquiry is the only path that leads us to a choice of righteousness for His Name's sake.

**Even though I walk through
the valley of the shadow of death,
I fear no evil;
for you are with me;**

ANDREA: How would you like to see this verse become true?

I would not. Those who inflict pain on others deserve to fear evil and death. Those who strive to be good and kind deserve life to come to an end like the close of a story in a book—when all mysteries are revealed and all pieces have fallen into place.

AARON: How would you like to see this verse become true?

I think the primary way God acts in the world is through God's people. I'd like to see more people acting in God's name on behalf of the dying, the grieving, those in mortal danger. I'd like to see more people be able to say, "God was with me," and be able to say it because Jews or Christians were there for them in their hour of need.

MORDECHAI: How would you like to see this verse become true?

I wish more of us (including myself) would show a disbelieving world that God is present with us as we become present to each other. God's revelation is always mirrored through our own personal revelation of God to one another.

**Your rod and your staff,
they comfort me.**

AARON: How would you like to see this verse become true?

I'd like to see more people take seriously their role as the people of God—reading the texts and following the guidance of Scripture; seeing themselves (with wisdom and caution) as people who might serve as the rod and staff of the shepherd—comforting, teaching, and keeping their neighbor safe from harm.

MORDECHAI: How would you like to see this verse become true?

For me, the rod and staff are a call to action. The staff symbolizes support—that is, providing support to those who need it most. The rod symbolizes protection, and it would indicate providing protection to those who need it most.

**You prepare a table before me**
**in the presence of my enemies;**
**You anoint my head with oil,**
**my cup overflows.**

AARON: How would you like to see this verse become true?

More hospitality, more nourishment, more sense of God's love, and more claiming of the mission God gives, more gratitude for what has been given—in me and in the rest of God's people.

**Surely goodness and mercy shall follow me**
**all the days of my life;**
**and I shall dwell**
**in the house of the LORD**
**for ever.**

SONYA: How would you like to see this verse become true?

To not let my "ego" get in the way.

ANDREA: How would you like to see this verse become true?

Goodness and mercy should be rewarded by being remembered and mentioned even after the fact.

AARON: How would you like to see this verse become true?

I'd like to see everyone take the reality of God's goodness and mercy and the demands that mercy and goodness place on us (to mirror them to the world) seriously. For everyone.


### *Postscript*

After I gleaned all these various responses, I came across an observation made long ago by the great American philosopher and psychologist William James, who once compared the dogmatic and systematic theologians to "closed naturalists" who study only stuffed birds but never trouble to observe them alive in the field. Schools of theology have flourished—but at the expense and spiritual well-being of their followers. James writes:

> One feels that in the theologians' hands they are a set of titles obtained by a mechanical manipulation of synonyms; verbality has stepped into the place of vision, professionalism into that of life. Instead of bread we have stone, instead of a fish, a serpent. Did such a conglomeration of abstract terms give really the gist of our knowledge of the deity, schools of theology might continue to flourish, but religion, vital religion would have taken its flight from this world. What keeps

religion going is something else than abstract definitions and systems of concat-
enated adjectives, and something different from faculties of theology and their
professors. All these things are aftereffects, secondary accretions upon those
phenomena of vital conversation with the unseen divine, of which I have shown you
so many instances, renewing themselves in *saecula saeculorum* in the lives of
humble private men.[11]

The responses I have gathered have been for me, a very humbling experience.
The spiritual voices articulated by (so-called) "common people" can teach many
professional rabbis and scholars alike. The great founder of the Hasidic
Movement, Israel ben Eliezer, better known as the famous Baal Shem Tov, taught
that within the heart of every simple Jew is a burning fire that yearns for God and
that transcends even the devotion of scholars. Unfortunately, the great majority
of these Jews found themselves in a wilderness of silence. Their spiritual voices
were muted because they listened to religious experts who no longer had any idea
what the language of faith meant.

For many of the people I have worked with in my community, the *lectio divina*
offered a way of articulating their spiritual journey. These Jews learned to see
their own life stories within a broader, more spiritual context; most important,
they learned to speak *to* God and not just *about* God. Their lives became a mirror
of David's own life—his struggles, his weaknesses, his tribulations, his moral
rehabilitation, and his redemption from the hands of those who sought him harm.
Once we started sharing our stories of personal redemption, the imagery of Psalm
23 took on a new meaning as a personal affirmation of our personal faith in a
personal God. Each person's participation offered a glimpse of how faith can be
witnessed in today's times.

As many of the selections indicated, the majority of individuals spoke of
different traumas they had experienced and survived. Several respondents
mentioned how they felt they were picked up and carried out of the pit they were
situated in. Others mentioned how God gave them the courage and strength
when they were convinced they had no more power to withstand pain and
suffering.

Some of the congregants felt that it was too hard for them to respond
personally in writing; therefore, some responses were recorded by me as they told
me their stories of exodus and shepherding. Holocaust survivors felt a special
affinity to the shepherd imagery, though many of their families were exterminated by the Nazis. Survivors and their children often feel an anxiety that they
could easily have perished with the others.

---

11. William James, *The Varieties of Religious Experience*, first pub. 1902 (New York: Modern
Library, 1936), p. 437.

Other respondents emphasized the importance of being available for others who needed them. This enabled them to express gratitude to God for rescuing and restoring their human dignity.

Those with a gnostic and metaphysical disposition saw Psalm 23 as a symbol of how God interacts with the universe. These individuals looked for the unitive vision provided by the psalm, and had perhaps the easiest time expressing what the psalm meant to them personally.

Of all the responses that were challenging, Andrea's responses were in many ways the most intriguing. Andrea was married to a very Orthodox man. Unknown to most people, her husband was a wife- and child-beater, and he often invoked religion as an excuse for his forceful and abusive behavior. Her husband lorded faith over her like a billy club, and she came to despise everything that he stood for. When the divorce eventually materialized, she soon discovered profound lack of support from the religious community. In many instances, she was blamed for allowing the marriage to crumble.

Though she was essentially abandoned as a single unemployed mother, she never gave up her devotion to helping the synagogue. Her commitment in all areas of lay ministry has been exceptional. In her responses, she made it a point to spell God as "G-d." Only the very Orthodox show this kind of reverence to God's name. In my conversations with her I discovered a deeply religious person who was trying to piece her faith back together again. I did my best to remind her that the diabolic is the dark manifestation of pathological religion, but that healthy faith is liberative and healing. Part of her spiritual odyssey was to recognize that despite the dark night of the soul, God was still with her.

A caring community provides the greatest medicine to those battered by their encounter with the diabolical. Suggestions were made to help her achieve a catharsis through the *lectio divina*. I am hopeful this exercise will help her faith develop into something far more personal and meaningful. Over a period of many weeks of daily conversations, she finally admitted freely that she was open to the possibility of genuine faith experience, and that the world does have a number of genuinely spiritual people.

Several weeks later, she had told me about a discussion she had with her Orthodox son concerning a theme in Jewish spirituality. I noticed that there was a light of enthusiasm in her eyes. I have introduced her to some books dealing with women's spirituality; I believe that this will help her considerably, for already she is learning to distinguish between healthy and unhealthy spirituality and religion.

It would be interesting to see whether the *lectio divina* takes root in my own community. I am, however, reasonably certain that the *lectio* has paved a way for people to articulate meaningfully their own journey toward God. The shepherd imagery of Psalm 23 has made some inroads in the life of my community. It would seem that out of the dark night of their soulful journey, the embers of dawn are finally surfacing; only God knows where the path will take them from here. All I can do is to continue gently to remind them that the Shepherd of Psalm 23 has not abandoned them.

# APPENDIX 1

# THE MAIMONIDES–IBN DAUD DEBATE ABOUT GOD-TALK

Maimonides' own philosophical position was consistent in how he determined *Halachah* (law). How critical is proper faith? In a famous passage in his *Hilchot Teschuvah* (Laws of Penitence), Maimondes argued that proper belief was a precondition to inheriting the heavenly Afterlife. This excluded "He who says there is one ruler, but He is a body and has form." Abraham Ibn Daud, an older contemporary and arch-critic of Maimonides' *Mishneh Torah*, comments in his notes on Maimonides:

> Why has he called such a person a heretic? There are many people greater than [he] and superior *to him (mimenu)*[1] who adhere to such a belief on the basis of what they have seen in sundry verses of Scriptures. How much more so does this apply to the words contained of those *aggadot* which corrupt right opinion about religious matters?

We must note that Ibn Daud did not disagree with Maimonides on the issue of Divine corporeality. In the beginning of *Hilchot Yesodei Hatorah* (1:8–9),

---

1. Many of the medieval scholars were shocked that Ibn Daud would say that those who believed in the divine corporeality would be considered *superior* to Maimonides. Therefore, some have interpreted the phrase *mimenu* to mean "better than us" (cf. Genesis 23:6, 26:16). *Sefer Avodat Hamelech.*

Maimonides already stated that *we do not subscribe to a belief that God is corporeal*—all such imagery is strictly metaphorical. I. Twersky, one of today's contemporary experts on Ibn Daud and Maimonides, points out that Ibn Daud did not disagree with Maimonides in principle, for he, too, opposed literal belief in anthropomorphism. Elsewhere Ibn Daud wrote, "It is not proper to speak of the Creator thusly."[2]

Why did Ibn Daud strongly disagree with Maimonides? For one thing, he disagreed with Maimonides' sweeping criticism of unsophisticated people who took these expressions literally on the basis of their understanding of the Scripture's *peshat* (simple meaning). Maimonides' sweeping condemnation excluded even observant Jews from the community on the basis of erroneous beliefs. To Ibn Daud, philosophical faith was not an *a priori* requirement of the Torah. Some of the people Maimonides unabashedly criticized were talmudic scholars whom Ibn Daud respected. In his essay on resurrection, the aged Maimonides complained about the many talmudic sages who either were ambivalent as to the issue of corporeality or maintained that anyone who did not believe so was to be considered a heretic and an *Apikorus* (a follower of Epicurean philosophy).[3] The issue of anthropomorphic imagery was not important enough to be a dogma, nor were all anthropomorphisms necessarily harmful to faith.

One such scholar, Rabbi Moshe Takku, a talmudist and contemporary of Maimonides, took issue with the philosophical faith espoused by Maimonides and Saadia Gaon. Takku argued that the simple meaning of the Torah was not to be twisted. According to Takku, God does somehow dwell in a place called heaven and occasionally "sits" on a throne.[4] The attempts of the philosophers not only contradicted the simply meaning of the Scriptures, but they also set arbitrary limitations on the scope of God's power.

Ibn Daud argued: why should the simple believer be considered a heretic? Many talmudists appear to have believed that God could be corporeal. These talmudic teachers were opposed to the integration of Greek wisdom and Torah. Moreover, the entire Bible is full of anthropomorphic expressions depicting various physical activities and organs of God (see Deuteronomy 26:8, Genesis 3:8, and so on). The Song of Songs was interpreted by the rabbis as containing attributes and descriptions of God Himself. According to Gershom Scholem, the debate between Maimonides and Ibn Daud focused in part on the use of the *Shiur Komeh*, a second-century work that describes the mystical body of God. In the

---

2. Isadore Twersky, *Rabad of Posquieres* (Philadelphia: Jewish Publication Society, 1980), p. 284.

3. David Hartman and Abraham Halkin, *Crisis and Leadership—Epistles of Maimonides* (Philadelphia: Jewish Publication Society, 1985), pp. 212–213.

4. Louis Jacobs, *Principles of the Jewish Faith*, first pub. 1964 (Northvale, NJ: Jason Aronson, 1988), pp. 122–123.

*Shiur Komeh*, the height of Creator is portrayed as being between 236,000 and 30 million parasangs long. Its brazen use of anthropomorphic imagery was theologically dangerous and could easily be misunderstood by the masses. Though this book was popular in French circles, Maimonides regarded the *Shiur Komeh* as a forgery that deserved to be destroyed.[5] This book was, in Maimonides' view, an embarrassment to Jewish rationalism. Ibn Daud maintained that the book was a mystical text and should not be treated as a pagan work.[6]

Some modern talmudic scholars view the Maimonides–Ibn Daud controversy differently. Ibn Daud asserted that *intention* is not the critical aspect of the act of worship; the critical aspect is what is represented in the act of worship. Linguistic representations of God taken at face value do not render a person an *Apikorus*. Maimonides maintained that intention *is* the critical aspect of worship.[7] Moreover, it is possible for even one who subscribes to the God of the Torah to still subscribe to idolatrous beliefs.

Did Maimonides know about Ibn Daud's criticism? It would appear that Maimonides was well aware of Ibn Daud's criticism of him.[8] Maimonides writes:

> Such a man [who believes in incorpeality] is indubitably more blameworthy *than a worshipper of idols* who regards the latter as intermediaries or as having the power to do *good or ill*. Know accordingly, you are that man, that when you believe in the doctrine of the corporeality of God or believe that one of the states of the body belongs to Him, *you provoke His jealousy and anger, kindle the fire of His wrath and are a hater, an enemy, and an adversary of God,*[9] much more so than an idolater. If, however, it should occur to you that who one believes in the corporeality of God should be excused because of his having been brought up in this doctrine or because of his ignorance and the shortcomings of his apprehension,

---

5. Cf. *Teshuvot HaRambam*, ed. J. Blau (Jerusalem: Jerusalem Press, 1957), chapter 117.

6. See Gershom Scholem, *On the Mystical Shape of the Godhead* (New York: Schocken, 1991), pp. 15–55.

7. Rabbi Hayim of Brisk states that, according to Maimonides, an *Apikorus* (a heretic) who errs accidentally (*b'shogag*) is still an *Apikorus*! Rabbi Moshe Sternbach, *Hderech LaTeshuavah* (Jerusalem, 1991).

8. This is evidenced by the way Maimonides uses the same phrase—*shivushim* (confusing)—that Ibn Daud uses—*Hamishuvash* [that *confuse* the mind]. (Kapach's commentary on *Sefer Hamada*.)

9. Note the anthropopathic terms Maimonides invokes: "His jealousy and anger," "kindle the fire of His wrath," and "are a hater, an enemy, and an adversary of God." This passage from Maimonides is probably one of the most anthropopathic passages in his works. It is ironic that Maimonides employed such colorful language against those people who would subscribe to an anthromorphic God. Why did Maimonides use such pathetic language? Was he being sarcastic? Perhaps the answer to this question may be found in the writings of the first-century Jewish philosopher, Philo of Alexandria, who remarked, "He hoped to be able to eradicate evil, namely by representing the Supreme Cause as dealing with threats and oftentimes showing indignation and implacable anger. . . . *For this is the only way in which a fool can be admonished.*" (*Cherubim* 24:77.)

you ought to hold a similar belief with regard to *an idolater;* for he only worships idols because of his ignorance or because of his upbringing: *They continue in the custom of their fathers.* If, however, you should say that the external sense of the biblical text causes men to fall into this doubt, you ought to know that *an idolater* is similarly impelled to his idolatry by imaginings and defective representations.[10]

In Maimonides' elaborate parable of the palace, he states that the men who know physics and metaphysics, together with the prophets (who are of course, by definition, philosophers) enter the castle, while those who study the Law (that is, the talmudists?) are looking futilely for a way in. There was no question in Maimonides' mind that the halachic scholar who was articulate and steeped in philosophy and science stood on a much higher level than the halachic scholar who just dabbled in the traditional talmudic wisdom. Moreover, *one could not truly worship God without it.*[11] Maimonides' parable created such an uproar in rabbinic circles that his books was burned in many communities. One commentator to Maimonides' *Guide* scathingly wrote:

> Many rabbinical scholars declare that the Master did not write this chapter, and if he did, it must be hidden, or, more fittingly—burned. How could he have placed those who know natural things in a higher rank than those who occupy themselves with religion, and especially, how could he dare place them in the "inner court of the king?" If this was so, then the philosophers who concern themselves with science and metaphysics rank above those who devote themselves to the Torah.[12]

Many of Maimonides' staunchest critics viewed the philosophical redefinition of faith with great suspicion and fear. They saw Maimonidean faith as a by-product of the mind, an intellectual assent that carried within it its own seeds of skepticism and doubt. These rabbis were not interested in merging Greek wisdom with Judiac faith. Philosophic faith could undermine people's devotion to God. Many of the rabbis of the medieval period viewed Maimonidean faith as a philosophical labyrinth that would keep a person in a perpetual state of doubt and ambivalence. By making the study of philosophy requisite to faith, the talmudists were afraid that faith would be better served if people did not engage in abstract philosophical speculations. The debate about anthropomorphisms did not end in the thirteenth century. The popular Jewish imagination (fueled by Jewish mysticism) refused to budge on the issue of anthropomorphisms. Liturgical poetry continued to employ colorful anthropomorphisms based on the imagery of Scriptures and the Kabbalah.

---

10. Maimonides, *Guide*, S. Pines' translation, I, end of chapter 36.
11. Maimonides, *Guide* III, 5.
12. See Shem Tov's commentary on the *Guide*, II, chapter 53.

### Hallahs in the Ark—A Folk Tale about the
### Maimonideans–Ibn Daud Controversy

Folktales are very important resources for spiritual reflection and inspiration. These stories tell us not only about the characters; they also tell us much about ourselves. Folktales provide us with an inside view of faith and its transformative power in the lives of individuals and society.

One of the most charming stories in the Middle Ages deals directly with how cognitive faith can weaken the faith of the common faithful Jew. At the heart of this story is the controversy between Maimonides and Ibn Daud. This is a sixteenth-century story about a Marrano Jew who had heard the rabbi give an inspiring sermon about the show-bread (see Exodus 25:30) and how it was presented in the Temple for the entire week. The rabbi at the end of the sermon lamented, "But nowadays, by reason of our manifold sins, we have nothing that is prepared and which should serve to bring a flow [of blessing] upon what is unprepared."

When the simple Jew heard this, he felt he had to do something about it; so he ordered his wife to bake twelve loaves of bread, which he placed in the holy Ark; he later found that the loaves had disappeared! He then said:

All praise and thanksgiving to His Blessed Name, for He has not despised the offering of the poor and has already accepted our bread and eaten it hot! . . . We have no way of honoring God, but we see that He finds these breads sweet and pleasant. It is therefore our duty to give Him pleasure through them! My Father in Heaven! May this bread I bring be sweet unto You!" And he went on doing this for some time.

One day the town rabbi came and saw the weekly ritual of the simple Jew; he scolded him for foolishly thinking that God had a physical body. He said:

You Fool! Do you suppose that God eats and drinks! The synagogue attendant must be the one who takes your loaves and eats them, while you believe and suppose that God accepts them! It is a great sin to attribute any kind of corporeality to the Blessed God, who has neither physical shape nor body.

When it became known that the caretaker had taken the loaves of bread, the poor man contritely repented his behavior. When the famous mystic of Safad, Rabbi Isaac Luria, heard about this incident, he cursed the rabbi for interfering in this man's worship and said:

Go home and prepare a will for your household, for tomorrow at the time you are due to give your sermon, you are going to die! This has been decreed from Heaven.

When the rabbi inquired as to what his sin was, the mystic told him:

"From the day the show-bread was discontinued because of the Temple's destruction, God had no greater joy than the gift of this man's simple sincere offering." The following day the rabbi died exactly as the mystic had foretold.

Would Maimonides have considered the simple Jew guilty of sin? Would he have considered the rabbi correct in what he told the simple Jew? What would he have thought of the mystic's curse?

Maimonides would have agreed that the rabbi's criticism was justified. Maimonides probably would have been dismayed at the mystic's cursing the rabbi, for the rabbi acted in accordance with Jewish law and Maimonides' own halachic/theological decisions. Ibn Daud would have argued differently; he might have agreed in principle that what the rabbi did was correct but that the manner in which he criticized the simple Jew could have been gentler and more understanding. The simple Jew was not an idolater; he was merely naive. The mystic was correct in being upset at how the simple Jew was being treated, for the rabbi diminished his faith in God. One cannot blame such a person because he happens to be ignorant.

This story is in many ways a precursor to a genre of hasidic stories that also extolled the virtues of simple faith over the stodgy cognitive faith of talmudic scholars, theologians, and philosophers nearly two centuries later. This story also dramatizes how scholars and academics are often oblivious to the religious personality of the common person, whose simple devotion to God is valued and held dear.

# APPENDIX 2

# A BRIEF LITURGICAL HISTORY OF PSALM 23

The modern Jewish liturgy uses Psalm 23 at funerals and memorial services. If we examine the traditional Orthodox liturgy, we would find a far broader use of the psalm than is commonly assumed.

According to the sixteenth-century Jewish mystic Isaac Luria (better known as the Ari—the Lion), there is a custom of reciting the Twenty-third Psalm before a meal, after washing the hands and before making a blessing on the bread. According to the Ari, the Twenty-third Psalm serves as prayer of thanksgiving and trust.

The Ari observed that the Twenty-third Psalm contains fifty-seven words, the numerical equivalent of the Hebrew word for nourishment (*zan*). It also contains 227 letters, the numerical equivalent of the Hebrew word *bracha*, "blessing." The Ari concludes by saying that those who recite the psalm and live by it will be blessed with plentiful provision.

This would suggest that Psalm 23 must be seen as a psalm of thanksgiving and trust that God will continue to provide as a loving Shepherd. This psalm alerts us to the image of God as a Shepherd even as we partake of our daily meal of bread. It is in this miracle of sustenance that we encounter God as a Shepherd. Through the act of eating, we discover the nurturing power of God's pastoral love and care. This idea is mentioned in many places in the traditional liturgy; here is one example:[1]

---

1. Morning Amidah liturgy.

It is You Lord God, Who nourishes,
  sustains and supports all creatures
  from the horns of the mighty oxen
  to the eggs of lice.

Provide me with my allotment of bread
  and bring forth for me
  and all the members of my family my food—
  before I have need for it;
  in contentment but not in pain;
  in a permissible but not in a forbidden manner;
  in honor and not in disgrace;

For life and for peace;
  from the flow of blessing and success,
  from the flow of the Heavenly Spring,
  so that I will be able to perform your Will
  and engage in Your Torah
  and fulfill Your precepts.

May I not need the gifts of human charity
  and may I fulfill the verses:
You open your hand,
  satisfying the desire of
  every living thing (Psalms 145:16).
Cast your burden on the LORD,
and he will sustain you (Psalms 55:22).

During the Sabbath, it is traditional to eat three festive meals in the course of the day. According to the *Encyclopedia of Jewish Prayer*, this tradition arose because of the threefold appearance of the word "blessing" in the Creation story, which mentions blessing in conjunction with the fifth day, when God created the fish; the sixth day, when God created Adam; and the seventh day, when God created the Sabbath. Thus, Psalm 23 is sung three times after eating fish, to invoke God for the threefold blessing.

The 57 words in Psalm 23 also correspond to the Hebrew word for fish, *Dagim*, which add up to the same number. Some see the Hebrew word *Deshe* (*He makes me lie down in green pastures*) as an acronym for *Dalet* = *Dagim* (fish), *Shin* = Shabbat (Sabbath) and *Aleph* = Adam (humanity).[2]

---

2. Macy Nulman, *Encyclopedia of Jewish Prayer* (Northvale, NJ: Jason Aronson, 1993), p. 248.

# APPENDIX 3

# PSALM 23 AND THE SABBATH

**Shabbat** and Psalm 23

Isaac Luria placed Psalm 23 as part of the Sabbath-meal liturgy; Psalm 23 is recited at the beginning of the Kiddush prayer, which is recited over a glass of wine as we bless the Shabbat day. From what I have gathered, no one has ever explained why Isaac Luria placed Psalm 23 in the liturgy in this way. Here is a possible suggestion. Luria suggested to us that one of the ways a Jew discovers the Shepherd is through the rest and nurturing of the Sabbath (*Shabbat*). A thematic comparison of Psalm 23 and the Sabbath reveals a striking family resemblance.

**The LORD is my shepherd, I shall not want;**

This teaches us that when Shabbat comes; we should feel that God provides for all our weekly needs. *Shabbat* is the time each of us comes to experience God as our own personal Shepherd who is ever leading us, never forsaking us to chance.

**He makes me lie down in green pastures.**
**He leads me beside the still waters (*Ma Menuchot*);**
**He restores my soul;**

*Shabbat* is a time for rest and renewal; *Shabbat* is when we pick ourselves up from the drudgery of weekday problems. *Shabbat* is more than a day devoted to physical rest, it is a day dedicated to spiritual rest as well. *Shabbat* does not recognize the Cartesian division of body and soul. On *Shabbat*, we recognize that it is God who is the Master of time. The Hebrew word *menuchot, menucha* (rest) denotes tranquility. Abraham Joshua Heschel elaborates:

> To the biblical mind *menucha* is the same as happiness and stillness, as peace and harmony. . . . It is the state in which there is no strife and no fighting, no fear and no distrust. The essence of good life is *menucha*. "The Lord is my shepherd, He maketh me lie down in green pastures; He leadeth me beside the still waters" (the waters of *menuchot*). In later times *menucha* becomes a synonym for the life in the world to come, for eternal life. Six evenings a week we pray: "Guard our going out and our coming in"; on the *Shabbat* evening we pray instead: "Embrace us with a tent of Your Peace."[1]

**He leads me in paths of righteousness**
**for His name's sake.**

*Shabbat* is a time when we renew our souls with the study of God's Torah, which teaches us how to act righteously and justly (*tsedek*) during the week.

**Even though I walk through**
**the valley of the shadow of death,**
**I fear no evil;**
**for you are with me;**
**your rod and your staff,**
**they comfort me.**

Thus, the *Shabbat* is a day on which we realize that, despite all our problems, it is God who is with us. Shabbat teaches us how to place our trust in God to help us get through problems of the week.

**You prepare a table before me**
**in the presence of my enemies;**
**You anoint my head with oil,**
**my cup overflows.**

On *Shabbat*, we feast ourselves on three traditional meals while extolling God for being the Source of our bounty and blessing. Shabbat teaches us that we are incapable of sustaining ourselves; it is only through the bounty of God that we have blessing and life. During the *Shabbat*, we sing songs reminding us how God helped a nation of refugees survive the pains of the wilderness life.

---

1. Abraham Heschel, *The Sabbath* (New York: Farrar, Straus, and Giroux, 1951), pp. 22–23.

**Surely goodness and mercy
shall follow me
all the days of my life;
and I shall dwell in the house
of the LORD forever.**

*Shabbat* speaks loudly about incorporating her values into the rest of the week. *Shabbat* hospitality serves as a model for shepherding people who are in need during the week. The spiritual restoration of oneself serves as a paradigm for restoring the impoverished and marginalized of society to a state of dignity and self-sufficiency. *Shabbat* is also a weekly reminder of the bliss and peacefulness that awaits us in the afterlife. *Shabbat* reminds each person that none of us is a creature of this world *per se*; each human being is a denizen of both worlds—the physical and the spiritual. *Shabbat* shows society and individuals how balance and centeredness can be achieved in both realms of existence.

In light of Isaac Luria's observation, Psalm 23 must be said not just when we come face to face with our mortality, as in a time of sickness and death; we also must incorporate the Shepherd image at our meals. God's shepherding Presence is also felt when we renew ourselves through the sanctification of the *Shabbat*.

# APPENDIX 4

# PSALM 23 AND PSALM 27

Many scholars have already observed the similarities between Psalm 23 and Psalm 27. Here are a number of comparisons worth perusing.

> The LORD is my shepherd, I shall not want.

In Psalms 27:1

> The LORD is my light and my salvation; whom shall I fear?
> The LORD is the stronghold of my life; of whom shall I be afraid?

Both psalms express a desire to be led in the straight path that will enable one to dwell in the house of the Lord. Another similarity found in these two psalms is the reference to the spiritual path and way. In Psalms 27:11 we find:

Teach me your way, O LORD, and lead me on a level path because of my enemies (*shorrai*).

Whereas Psalm 23 states:

> He leads me in right paths for his name's sake.

The ancient Aramaic translation to Psalm 27:3 renders the phrase *shorrai* not as "enemies," as most of the English translations do, but rather as "my songs."

This translation transforms the entire spirit of the passage. According to this reading, the Psalmist expresses the desire that God should grant him the opportunity to be led in the proper path so that he may compose more psalms and songs in the future. This translation of the Targum keeps the theme of the verse consistent with Psalms 23:3.

Psalms 27:3 states:

> Though an army encamp against me, my heart shall not fear; though war rise up against me, yet I will be confident.

This corresponds to Psalms 23:4

> Even though I walk through the darkest valley, I fear no evil; for you are with me; your rod and your staff, they comfort me.

Here is another similarity between the two psalms. Psalms 27:4 states:

> One thing I asked of the LORD, that will I seek after: to live in the house of the LORD all the days of my life, to behold the beauty of the LORD, and to inquire in his Temple.

Psalm 23 states:

> Surely goodness and mercy shall follow me all the days of my life, and I shall dwell in the house of the LORD forever.

In each case the psalmist wishes to dwell in the house of God for eternity. It is for this reason that he wishes to be pursued by goodness and mercy all the days of his life. The Twenty-third Psalm also fits well with Psalm 24, which states the preconditions for dwelling in the house of the Lord:

> Who shall ascend the hill of the Lord? And who shall stand in his holy place? Those who have clean hands and pure hearts, who do not lift up their souls to what is false, and do not swear deceitfully.
>
> Psalms 24:3–4

# BIBLIOGRAPHY

Anderson, Bernard. *Out of the Depths—The Psalms Speak For Us Today*. Philadelphia: Westminster Press, 1983.

Aquinas, Thomas. *Summa Theologica*. Great Books of the Western World. Vol. 19. Chicago: Encyclopedia Britannica, 1952.

Aristotle. *Nicomachean Ethics*. Great Books of the Western World. Vol. 19. Chicago: Encyclopedia Britannica, 1952.

———. *Poetics*. Great Books of the Western World. Vol. 19. Chicago: Encyclopedia Britannica, 1952.

Augustine. *On Christian Doctrine*, II, chapter 16:23. Great Books of the Western World. Vol. 18. Chicago: Encyclopedia Britannica, 1952.

Barbour, Ian. *Religion in an Age of Science*. San Francisco: HarperCollins, 1990.

Berger, Peter. *The Heretical Imperative*. New York: Anchor Press–Doubleday, 1979.

———. *The Rumor of Angels*. New York: Anchor Books, 1990.

Blumenthal, David. *Facing the Abusing God*. Louisville, KY: Westminster/John Knox, 1993.

Bockl, George. *God beyond Religion—Personal Journeyings from Religiosity to Spirituality*. Marina Del Rey, CA: Devorss, 1988.

Bohm, David. *Wholeness and the Implicate Order*. London: Routledge and Kegan Paul, 1980.

Bokser, Ben Zion. *Kook: Abraham Isaac Kook*. New York: Paulist Press, 1978.

Borowitz, Eugene. *Reform Judaism Today*. Book One: *Reform in the Process of Change*. New York: Behrman House, 1978.

Boslough, John. *Stephen Hawking's Universe*. New York: William Morrow, 1985.

Bromiley, Gerhard W. *The Theological Dictionary of the New Testament*. Abridged edition. Grand Rapids, MI: Eerdmans, 1985.

251

Brueggemann, Walter. *Finally Comes the Poet*. Minneapolis: Fortress, 1989.

―――. *The Hopeful Imagination*. Philadelphia: Fortress, 1986.

―――. *Praying the Psalms*. Winona, MN: Saint Mary's Press, 1993.

Buber, Martin. *Eclipse of God*. Atlantic Highlands, NJ: Humanities Press, 1952. Reprinted 1988.

―――. *I and Thou*. Trans. Walter Kaufmann. New York: Scribners, 1970.

―――. *On Judaism*. Ed. Nachum Glazer. New York: Shocken, 1967.

―――. *Meetings*. LaSalle, IL: Open Court, 1973.

Campbell, James. *Understanding Dewey*. LaSalle, IL: Open Court, 1995.

Capra, Fritjof. *The Tao of Physics: An Exploration of the Parallels between Modern Physics and Eastern Mysticism*. New York: Bantam, 1977.

Cohen, Noah. *Ts'ar Ba'ale Hayim—The Prevention of Cruelty to Animals*. New York: Feldheim, 1959.

Cohn, Norman. *Cosmos, Chaos, and the World to Come: The Ancient Roots of Apocalyptic Faith*. New Haven: Yale University Press, 1993.

Cox, Harvey. *The Secular City*. New York: Collier, 1968.

Da'Antonio, Michael. *Dispatches from America's Frontier, Heaven on Earth*. New York: Crown, 1992.

Davies, Paul. *God and the New Physics*. New York: Simon and Schuster, 1984.

―――. *Other Worlds*. New York: Touchstone, 1980.

Davis, Walter. *Shattered Dream: America's Search for Its Soul*. Valley Forge, PA: Trinity Press International, 1995.

Descartes, René. *Discourse on Method*. Part 2. Great Books of the Western World. Vol. 31. Chicago: Encyclopædia Britannica, 1952.

Dewey, John. *A Common Faith*. In *Later Works 1925–1953*. Ed. Jo Ann Boydston. Carbondale, IL: Southern Illinois University Press, 1981–1990.

Donovan, Mary Ellen, and Ryan, William. *Love Blocks*. New York: Viking, 1989.

Dorf, Elliot. *Knowing God*. Northvale, NJ: Jason Aronson, 1993.

Dossey, Larry. *Healing Words*. San Francisco: HarperSan Francisco, 1994.

Dresner, Samuel. *The World of a Hasidic Master: Levi Yitzchak of Berditchev*. Northvale, NJ: Jason Aronson, 1994.

Driver, G. R., and Miles, J. C. *The Babylonian Laws*. Vol. 1–2. Oxford: Oxford University Press, Clarendon Press, 1952–55.

Eliade, Mircea. *Images and Symbols: Studies in Religious Symbolism*. Princeton, NJ: Princeton University Press, 1952, 1991.

―――. *The Quest: History and Meaning in Religion*. Chicago: University of Chicago Press, 1969.

Farbridge, Maurice H. *Studies in Biblical and Semitic Symbolism*. Reprint. New York: Ktav, 1970.

Fein, Leonard. *Where Are We? The Inner Life of America's Jews*. New York: Harper and Row, 1988.

Fretheim, Terrance. *The Suffering of God*. Philadelphia: Fortress, 1984.

Freud, Sigmund. *Civilization and Its Discontents*. Great Books of the Western World. Vol. 54. Chicago: Encyclopædia Britannica, 1952.

———. *The Future of an Illusion*. London: Hogarth Press, 1934.

Friedman, David Noel. "The Twenty-Third Psalm." *Michigan Oriental Studies in Honor of George G. Cameron*. Ed. L. L. Orlin. Ann Arbor, MI: University of Michigan Press, 1976.

Geertz, Clifford. *The Interpretation of Cultures*. New York: Basic Books and Harper Torchbooks, 1973.

Glatzner, Nachum N. *Franz Rosenzweig: His Life and Thought*. Philadelphia: Jewish Publication Society, 1953.

Goswami, Amit. *The Self-Aware Universe*. New York: Tarcher/Putnam, 1993.

Greeley, Andrew. *Religion as Poetry*. New Brunswick, NJ: Transaction Publishers, 1995.

Green, Arthur. *Seek My Face, Speak My Name*. Northvale, NJ: Jason Aronson, 1992.

Greenberg, Sidney. *Lessons for Living*. Bridgeport, CT: Hartmore House, 1985.

Guthrie, Steward Elliot. *Faces in the Clouds: A New Theory of Religion*. Oxford and New York: Oxford University Press, 1993.

Hartman, David, and Halkin, Abraham. *Crisis and Leadership—Epistles of Maimonides*. Philadelphia: Jewish Publication Society, 1985.

Hartman, David. *Conflicting Visions*. New York: Schocken, 1990.

Hawking, Stephen W. *A Brief History of Time*. New York: Bantam Books, 1988.

Heller, David. *The Children's God*. Chicago: University of Chicago Press, 1986.

Heschel, Abraham Joshua. *God in Search of Man: A Philosophy of Judaism*. New York: Farrar, Straus and Giroux, 1986.

———. *Man Is Not Alone*. First published 1951. New York: Farrar, Straus and Giroux, 1990.

———. *Man's Quest for God*. New York: Scribners, 1954.

———. *The Sabbath*. New York: Farrar, Straus and Giroux, 1951.

Himmelfarb, Milton. *The Condition of Jewish Belief*. Northvale, NJ: Jason Aronson, 1988.

Hoberman, Joshua O. *The God I Believe In*. New York: Free Press, 1994.

Hopewell, James. *Congregation: Stories and Structures*. Philadelphia: Fortress, 1987.

Jacobs, Louis. *Jewish Theology*. New York: Behrman House, 1973.

———. *Principles of Jewish Belief*. First published 1964. Northvale, NJ: Jason Aronson, 1988.

James, William. *The Varieties of Religious Experience*. First published 1902. New York: Modern Library, 1936.

Jarvis, Debra. *The Journey through AIDS*. Batavia, IL: Lion Publishing, 1992.

Jastrow, Robert. *God and the Astronomers*. New York: Warner Books, 1978.

Jung, Carl. *Answer to Job*. Trans. R. F. C. Hull. Princeton: Princeton University Press, 1973.

———. *Man and His Symbols*. Garden City, NY: Doubleday, 1964.

———. *Memories, Dreams and Reflections*. Recorded and edited by Anelia Jaffe. Trans. by Richard and Clara Winston. London and New York: Vintage Books, 1963.

Kaplan, Aryeh *Meditation and the Kabbala*. York Beach, ME: Samuel Weiser, 1978.

Kaplan, Mordecai M. *The Meaning of God in Modern Jewish Religion*. New York: Jewish Reconstruction Press, 1962.

Katz, Steven. *Frontiers of Jewish Thought*. Washington, DC: Bnai Brith, 1992.

Keating, Thomas. *Intimacy with God*. New York: Crossroads, 1994.

Keen, Sam. *Hymns to an Unknown God*. New York: Bantam, 1994.

Keller, W. Philip. *A Shepherd Looks at Psalm 23*. New York: Harper & Row, 1970.

Kohn, Eugene. *Religion and Humanity*. Philadelphia: Reconstructionist Press, 1953.

Kranzler, David. *Thy Brother's Blood*. New York: Artscroll, 1987.

Lifton, Robert Jay. *The Protean Self*. New York: Basic Books, 1993.

Luzzatto, Moshe Hayim. *Derech Hashem*. Trans. Aryeh Kaplan. New York: Feldheim, 1977.

Maimonides, Moses. *Guide to the Perplexed*. Trans. Michael Friedlander. London: Pardes, 1904.

———. *Guide to the Perplexed*. Trans. Shlomo Pines. Chicago: University of Chicago Press, 1963.

Matt, Daniel. *Zohar—The Book of Enlightenment*. New York: Paulist Press, 1983.

Merton, Thomas. *Love and Living*. Orlando, FL: Harcourt, Brace, Jovanovich, 1979.

———. *New Seeds of Contemplation*. New York: New Directions, 1961.

Mitchell, Stephen. *The Book of Job*. London: Kyle Cathie, 1989.

Moghabghab, Faddoul. *Shepherd's Song*. New York: Hutton, 1901.

Moore, Thomas. *Care of the Soul*. New York: HarperCollins, 1992.

*Nachmanides' Commentary on the Torah*. Vol. 2: Exodus. Trans. Charles Chavel. New York: Shilo, 1973.

*Nachmanides' Writings and Discourses*. Trans. Charles Chavel. New York: Shilo, 1978.

Nasr, Seyyed Hossein. *Knowledge and the Sacred*. Albany, NY: SUNY Press, 1989.

Neusner, Jacob. *The Foundation of the Theology of Judaism*. Northvale, NJ: Jason Aronson, 1991.

New Standard Revised Version of the Bible. New York: Friendship Press, 1989.

Nulman, Macy. *Encyclopedia of Jewish Prayer*. Northvale, NJ: Jason Aronson, 1993.

Otto, Rudolf. *The Idea of the Holy*. First published 1923. Oxford: Oxford University Press, 1958.

———. *Mysticism East and West: A Comparative Analysis of the Nature of Mysticism*. New York: Macmillan, 1932.

Plaskow, Judith. *Standing Again at Sinai*. San Francisco: Harper and Row, 1990.

Plato. *Republic*. Trans. Benjamin Jowett. Great Books of the Western World. Vol. 7. Chicago: Encyclopædia Britannica, 1952.

Progoff, Ira. *The Dynamics of Hope*. New York: Dialogue House, 1985.

———. *Jung's Psychology and Its Social Meaning*. New York: Dialogue House Library, 1953, reprinted 1981.

Ricoeur, Paul. *Freud and Philosophy*. Trans. D. Savage. New Haven and London: Yale University Press, 1970.

———. *The Symbolism of Evil*, Boston: Beacon, 1967.

Rizzuto, Ana-Maria. *The Birth of the Living God*. Chicago: University of Chicago Press, 1979.

Rosen, Ruth. *Jesus for Jews*. New York: Inquirer's Edition, 1987.

Saadia Gaon. *Book of Doctrines and Beliefs*. Trans. Alexander Altmann. Reprinted in *Three Jewish Philosophers*. New York: Harper and Row, 1965.

Schindler, Pinchas. *Hasidic Responses to the Holocaust in the Light of Hasidic Thought*. Hoboken, NJ: Ktav, 1990.

Scholem, Gershom G., *On the Mystical Shape of the Godhead*. New York: Schocken, 1991.

———. *Major Trends in Jewish Mysticism*. New York: Schocken, 1946.

Sharansky, Natan. *Fear No Evil*. New York: Random House, 1988.

Shea, John. *Stories of God—An Unauthorized Biography*. Chicago, IL: Thomas More Press, 1978.

Shevack, Michael, and Bemporad, Jack. *Stupid Ways, Smart Ways to Think about God*. Liguori, MO: Triumph Books, 1993.

Smedes, Lewis. *Forgive and Forget*. New York: Harper and Row, 1984.

Smith, Jonathan. *Drudgery Divine*. Chicago: University of Chicago Press, 1990.

Stern, David. *Parables in Midrash: Narratives and Exegesis in Rabbinic Literature*. Cambridge, MA: Harvard University Press, 1991.

Strat, Colette. *Philosophy in the Middle Ages*. Cambridge and New York: Cambridge University Press, 1993.

Teilhard de Chardin, Pierre. *The Divine Milieu: An Essay on the Interior Life*. New York: Harper and Row, 1968.

Terrien, Samuel. *The Psalms and Their Meaning for Today*. New York: Bobbs-Merrill, 1952.

Tillich, Paul. *Theology and Culture*. New York and Oxford: Oxford University Press, 1964.

Twersky, Isadore. *Rabad of Posquieres*. Edited by Robert C. Kimball. Philadelphia: Jewish Publication Society, 1980.

Wein, Sherwin. *"Judaism beyond God" a Radical New Way to Be Jewish*. Buffalo, NY: Prometheus Books, 1985.

Wittgenstein, Ludwig. *Philosophical Investigations*. Trans. G. E. M. Anscombe. Oxford: Oxford University Press, 1968.

Wolfson, Harry. *Repercussions of the Kalam in Jewish Philosophy*. Cambridge, MA: Harvard University Press, 1979.

Wolfson, Harry Austryn. *Philo*. Cambridge, MA: Harvard University Press, 1947.

Wolpin, Nisson. *A Path through the Ashes*. Brooklyn, NY: Messorah, 1986.

Wyschogrod, Michael. *The Body of Faith*. San Francisco: Harper and Row, 1983.

Yonge, C. D. *The Works of Philo*. Peabody, MA: Hendrikson, 1993.

Zeigler, Mel. *Amen—The Diary of Rabbi Martin Segal*. New York: World, 1971.


### Hebrew Sources

Bazak, Yaakov. *Mizmorei Tehillim Be' Tefillot Hashabbat*. Tel Aviv: Yavnah Press, 1991.

Feinstein, Moshe. *Igeret Moshe, Helek I of Yoreh Deah*. Brooklyn, NY: Moriah, 1959.

HaCohen, Eliyahu. *Mi'eel Tsedakka*. Ed. Hillel Kooperman. Reprint: Jerusalem: Jerusalem Press, 5752 [1992].

Heschel, Abraham Joshua. *Torah Min HaShmayim B'Asplakalaria Shel HaDorot*. London and New York: Soncino, 1963.

Malbim (Rabbi Meir Leibush). *Commentary to 2 Samuel, Mikraot Gedolot*. Reprint: New York: M. Press, 1974.

*Midrash Tehillim Hamachunah Shachar Tov*. Introduction by Sholomo Buber. Vilna: 1891. Reprint: Jerusalem: Vagshal, 1977.

*Da'at Mikrah*. Musad HaRav Kook. Amos Hacham's Commentary to Job.

Kasher, Menachem. *Torah Shelemah*. Vol. 8. Reprint: New York: Beit HTorah Shleimah, 1992.

Kimchi, David. *Rabbi David Kimchi's (Radak) Commentary to the Psalms*. New York: Mikraot Gedolot. Reprint: New York: M. Press, 1974.

———. *Sefer Hashorasheem—Radicum Liber Hebraeum Bibliorum Lexicon*. Ed. Jo. H. R. Biesenthal and F. Lebrecht. Reprint: Jerusalem: 1967.

Maimonides, Moses. *Commentary to Mishnah*. 3 volumes. With commentary by Yosef David Kapach. Jerusalem: Hotzaat Mosad HaRav Kook, 1963.

———. *Mishneh Torah*. 5 volumes. Reprint: New York: S. Goldman-Otzar Haseforiem, 1968.

*Midrash Rabbah on the Torah*. Vilna: 1896.

*Musafe Rashi* (Addendum to Rashi's Commentary). Reprinted in the *Mikraot Gedolot HaMaor*. Reprinted by Aharon Samet and Rabbi Daniel Bitton. Jerusalem: 1990.

Schneersohn, Menachem Mendel. *Derech Mitzvotecha. Ma'mar Shoresh Mitzva Tefila*. Reprint: Brooklyn, NY: Kehot, 1992.

Schneersohn, Sholom Dov Baer. *Sefer Mamamreem 5666*. Reprint: Brooklyn, NY: Kehot, 1976.

———. *Sefer Mamamreem 5670*. Reprint: Brooklyn, NY: Kehot, 1976.

Sternbach, Moshe. *Hderech LaTeshuavah*. Jerusalem: 1991.

*Talmud Bavli (The Babylonian Talmud)*. Reprint: Gateshead, Great Britain: S. Goldman-Otzar Haseforiem, 1973.

Zalman, Shneur. *Torah Or*. Reprint: Brooklyn, NY: Kehot, 1985.

# ACKNOWLEDGMENTS

The author gratefully acknowledges permission to reprint from the following sources:

*Abraham Isaac Kook,* translated by Ben Zion Bokser. Copyright © 1978 by Paulist Press. Used by permission of publisher.

*A Shepherd Looks at Psalm 23,* by W. Philip Keller. Copyright © 1970 by W. Philip Keller. Used by permission of Zondervan Publishing House.

*Hymns to an Unknown God,* by Sam Keene. Copyright © 1994 by Bantam Books. Used by permission of publisher.

*Renewing the Covenant,* by Eugene Borowitz. Copyright © 1991 by Eugene Borowitz. Used by permission of the Jewish Publication Society.

*Rumor of Angels,* by Peter Berger. Copyright © 1990 by Doubleday. Used by permission of publisher.

Scripture quotations from the New Revised Standard Version of the Bible. Copyright © 1989 by the Division of Christian Education of the National Council of Churches of Christ in the U.S.A. Used by permission of publisher.

Selected illustrations from *Bible Illustrator.* Copyright © 1990–1992 by Parsons Technology.

"How Basic Is Basic Judaism: A Critical Review of Milton Steinberg's *Basic Judaism,*" by Irving Kristol. Copyright © 1948 by *Commentary* Magazine. Used by permission of publisher.

*The Body of Faith*, by Michael Wyschogrod. Copyright © 1996 by Michael Wyschogrod. Used by permission of Jason Aronson Inc.

*The World of a Hasidic Master: Levi Yitzhak of Berditchev*, by Samuel H. Dresner. Copyright © 1994 by Samuel H. Dresner. Used by permission of Jason Aronson Inc.

# INDEX

## ABOUT THE AUTHOR

Rabbi Michael Samuel was ordained as a Lubavitch-trained rabbi and *dayyan* (judge) of Jewish Law, and has been involved in Jewish education for over twenty years. He received his Doctorate of Ministry from the San Francisco Theological Seminary in 1995, and is also a licensed pastoral therapist. Currently the spiritual leader of Congregation Shaaray Tefila in Glens Falls, New York, he has served as a pulpit rabbi for the last twelve years. Rabbi Samuel has written numerous articles on contemporary ethical and political problems and their relevance to Jewish tradition. He gives lectures and conducts workshops around the country on ethical themes drawn from the Talmud, Responsa, Jewish theology and Mysticism, biblical imagery, and spiritual formation in Jewish tradition. Rabbi Samuel lives in Glens Falls, New York, with his wife and children.